Course	Intro to Engineering Design (IED)
Course Number	**ENGR-2050**
	RENSSELAER POLYTECHNIC INSTITUTE

http://create.mheducation.com

ISBN-10: 1307090974   ISBN-13: 9781307090970

Contents

Credits

Preface

This book contains material developed for use in the interdisciplinary courses on product development that we teach. Participants in these courses include graduate students in engineering, industrial design students, and MBA students. While we aimed the book at interdisciplinary graduate-level audiences such as this, many faculty teaching graduate and undergraduate courses in engineering design have also found the material useful. *Product Design and Development* is also for practicing professionals. Indeed, we could not avoid writing for a professional audience, because most of our students are themselves professionals who have worked either in product development or in closely related functions.

This book blends the perspectives of marketing, design, and manufacturing into a single approach to product development. As a result, we provide students of all kinds with an appreciation for the realities of industrial practice and for the complex and essential roles played by the various members of product development teams. For industrial practitioners, in particular, we provide a set of product development methods that can be put into immediate practice on development projects.

A debate often heard in the academic community relates to whether design should be taught primarily by establishing a foundation of theory or by engaging students in loosely supervised practice. For the broader activity of product design and development, we reject both approaches when taken to their extremes. Theory without practice is ineffective because there are many nuances, exceptions, and subtleties to be learned in practical settings and because some necessary tasks simply lack sufficient theoretical underpinnings. Practice without guidance can too easily result in frustration and fails to exploit the knowledge that successful product development professionals and researchers have accumulated over time. Product development, in this respect, is like sailing: proficiency is gained through practice, but some theory of how sails work and some instruction in the mechanics (and even tricks) of operating the boat help tremendously.

We attempt to strike a balance between theory and practice through our emphasis on methods. The methods we present are typically step-by-step procedures for completing tasks, but rarely embody a clean and concise theory. In some cases, the methods are supported in part by a long tradition of research and practice, as in the chapter on product development economics. In other cases, the methods are a distillation of relatively recent and *ad hoc* techniques, as in the chapter on design for environment. In all cases, the methods provide a concrete approach to solving a product development problem. In our experience, product development is best learned by applying structured methods to ongoing project work in either industrial or academic settings. Therefore, we intend this book to be used as a guide to completing development tasks either in the context of a course project or in industrial practice.

An industrial example or case study illustrates every method in the book. We chose to use different products as the examples for each chapter rather than carrying the same example through the entire book. We provide this variety because we think it makes the book more interesting and because we hope to illustrate that the methods can be applied to a wide range of products, from industrial equipment to consumer products.

We designed the book to be extremely modular—it consists of 19 independent chapters. Each chapter presents a development method for a specific portion of the product development process. The primary benefit of the modular approach is that each chapter can be used independently of the rest of the book. This way, faculty, students, and practitioners can easily access the material they find most useful.

This sixth edition of the book includes a new chapter on design of services, as well as updated examples and data. We have also revised the book throughout with insights from recent research and innovations in practice.

To supplement this textbook, we have developed a Web site on the Internet. This is intended to be a resource for instructors, students, and practitioners. We will keep the site current with additional references, examples, and links to available resources related to the product development topics in each chapter. Please make use of this information via the Internet at www.ulrich-eppinger.net.

The application of structured methods to product development also facilitates the study and improvement of development processes. We hope, in fact, that readers will use the ideas in this book as seeds for the creation of their own development methods, uniquely suited to their personalities, talents, and company environments. We encourage readers to share their experiences with us and to provide suggestions for improving this material. Please write to us with your ideas and comments at ulrich@wharton.upenn.edu and eppinger@mit.edu.

CHAPTER ONE

Introduction

EXHIBIT 1-1

Examples of engineered, discrete, physical products (clockwise from top left): Belle-V Ice Cream Scoop, AvaTech Avalanche Probe, iRobot Roomba Vacuum Cleaner, Tesla Model S Automobile, Boeing 787 Aircraft.

The economic success of most firms depends on their ability to identify the needs of customers and to quickly create products that meet these needs and can be produced at low cost. Achieving these goals is not solely a marketing problem, nor is it solely a design problem or a manufacturing problem; it is a product development problem involving all of these functions. This book provides a collection of methods intended to enhance the abilities of cross-functional teams to work together to develop products.

A *product* is something sold by an enterprise to its customers. *Product development* is the set of activities beginning with the perception of a market opportunity and ending in the production, sale, and delivery of a product. Although much of the material in this book is useful in the development of any product, we explicitly focus on products that are engineered, discrete, and physical. Exhibit 1-1 displays several examples of products from this category. Because we focus on engineered products, the book applies better to the development of power tools and computer peripherals than to magazines or sweaters. Our focus on discrete goods makes the book less applicable to the development of products such as gasoline, nylon, and paper. Because of the focus on physical products, we do not emphasize the specific issues involved in developing services or software. Even with these restrictions, the methods presented apply well to a broad range of products, including, for example, consumer electronics, sports equipment, scientific instruments, machine tools, and medical devices.

The goal of this book is to present in a clear and detailed way a set of product development methods aimed at bringing together the marketing, design, and manufacturing functions of the enterprise. In this introductory chapter, we describe some aspects of the industrial practice of product development and provide a roadmap of the book.

Characteristics of Successful Product Development

From the perspective of the investors in a for-profit enterprise, successful product development results in products that can be produced and sold profitably, yet profitability is often difficult to assess quickly and directly. Five more specific dimensions, all of which ultimately relate to profit, are commonly used to assess the performance of a product development effort:

- *Product quality:* How good is the product resulting from the development effort? Does it satisfy customer needs? Is it robust and reliable? Product quality is ultimately reflected in market share and the price that customers are willing to pay.

- *Product cost:* What is the manufacturing cost of the product? This cost includes spending on capital equipment and tooling as well as the incremental cost of producing each unit of the product. Product cost determines how much profit accrues to the firm for a particular sales volume and a particular sales price.

- *Development time:* How quickly did the team complete the product development effort? Development time determines how responsive the firm can be to competitive forces and to technological developments, as well as how quickly the firm receives the economic returns from the team's efforts.

- *Development cost:* How much did the firm have to spend to develop the product? Development cost is usually a significant fraction of the investment required to achieve the profits.

- *Development capability:* Are the team and the firm better able to develop future products as a result of their experience with a product development project? Development capability is an asset the firm can use to develop products more effectively and economically in the future.

High performance, along these five dimensions, should ultimately lead to economic success; however, other performance criteria are also important. These criteria arise from interests of other stakeholders in the enterprise, including the members of the development team, other employees, and the community in which the product is manufactured. Members of the development team may be interested in creating an inherently exciting product. Members of the community in which the product is manufactured may be concerned about the degree to which the product creates jobs. Both production workers and users of the product hold the development team accountable to high safety standards, whether or not these standards can be justified on the strict basis of profitability. Other individuals, who may have no direct connection to the firm or the product, may demand that the product make ecologically sound use of resources and create minimal dangerous waste products.

Who Designs and Develops Products?

Product development is an interdisciplinary activity requiring contributions from nearly all the functions of a firm; however, three functions are almost always central to a product development project:

- *Marketing:* The marketing function mediates the interactions between the firm and its customers. Marketing often facilitates the identification of product opportunities, the definition of market segments, and the identification of customer needs. Marketing also typically arranges for communication between the firm and its customers, sets target prices, and oversees the launch and promotion of the product.
- *Design:* The design function plays the lead role in defining the physical form of the product to best meet customer needs. In this context, the design function includes engineering design (mechanical, electrical, software, etc.) and industrial design (aesthetics, ergonomics, user interfaces).
- *Manufacturing:* The manufacturing function is primarily responsible for designing, operating, and/or coordinating the production system in order to produce the product. Broadly defined, the manufacturing function also often includes purchasing, distribution, and installation. This collection of activities is sometimes called the *supply chain*.

Different individuals within these functions often have specific disciplinary training in areas such as market research, mechanical engineering, electrical engineering, materials science, or manufacturing operations. Several other functions, including finance and sales, are frequently involved on a part-time basis in the development of a new product. Beyond these broad functional categories, the specific composition of a development team depends on the particular characteristics of the product.

Rarely are products developed by a single individual. The collection of individuals developing a product forms the *project team*. This team usually has a single team leader, who could be drawn from any of the functions of the firm. The team can be thought of as

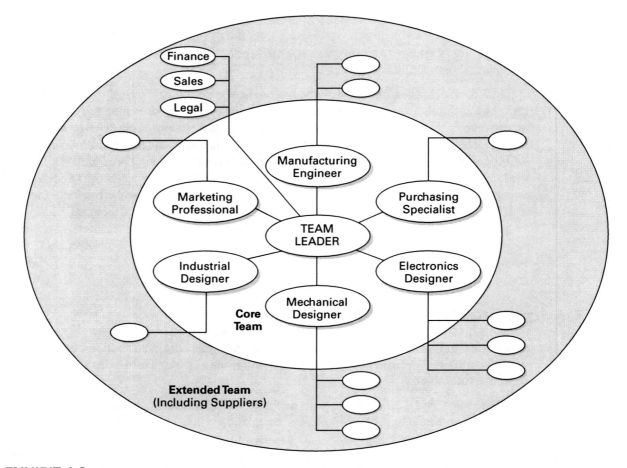

EXHIBIT 1-2   The composition of a product development team for an electromechanical product of modest complexity.

consisting of a *core team* and an *extended team*. In order to work together effectively, the core team usually remains small enough to meet in a conference room, while the extended team may consist of dozens, hundreds, or even thousands of other members. (Even though the term *team* is inappropriate for a group of thousands, the word is often used in this context to emphasize that the group must work toward a common goal.) In most cases, a team within the firm will be supported by individuals or teams at partner companies, suppliers, and consulting firms. Sometimes, as is the case for the development of a new airplane, the number of external team members may be even greater than that of the team within the company whose name will appear on the final product. The composition of a team for the development of an electromechanical product of modest complexity is shown in Exhibit 1-2.

Throughout this book we assume that the team is situated within a firm. In fact, a for-profit manufacturing company is the most common institutional setting for product development, but other settings are possible. Product development teams sometimes work within consulting firms, universities, government agencies, and nonprofit organizations.

	Belle-V Ice Cream Scoop	AvaTech Avalanche Probe	iRobot Roomba Vacuum Cleaner	Tesla Model S Automobile	Boeing 787 Aircraft
Annual production volume	10,000 units/year	1,000 units/year	2,000,000 units/year	50,000 units/year	120 units/year
Sales lifetime	10 years	3 years	2 years	5 years	40 years
Sales price	$40	$2,250	$500	$80,000	$250 million
Number of unique parts (part numbers)	2 parts	175 parts	1,000 parts	10,000 parts	130,000 parts
Development time	1 year	2 years	2 years	4 years	7 years
Internal development team (peak size)	4 people	6 people	100 people	1000 people	7,000 people
External development team (peak size)	2 people	12 people	100 people	1000 people	10,000 people
Development cost	$100,000	$1 million	$50 million	$500 million	$15 billion
Production investment	$20,000	$250,000	$10 million	$500 million	$15 billion

EXHIBIT 1-3   Attributes of five products and their associated development efforts. All figures are approximate, based on publicly available information, estimates, and company sources.

Duration and Cost of Product Development

Most people without experience in product development are astounded by how much time and money are required to develop a new product. The reality is that very few products can be developed in less than 1 year, many require 3 to 5 years, and some take as long as 10 years. Exhibit 1-1 shows five engineered, discrete products. Exhibit 1-3 is a table showing the approximate scale of the associated product development efforts along with some distinguishing characteristics of the products.

The cost of product development is roughly proportional to the number of people on the project team and to the duration of the project. In addition to expenses for development effort, a firm will almost always have to make some investment in the tooling and equipment required for production. This expense is often as large as the rest of the product development budget; however, it is sometimes useful to think of these expenditures as part of the *fixed costs* of production. For reference purposes, this production investment is listed in Exhibit 1-3 along with the development expenditures.

The Challenges of Product Development

Developing great products is hard. Few companies are highly successful more than half the time. These odds present a significant challenge for a product development team. Some of the characteristics that make product development challenging are:

- *Trade-offs:* An airplane can be made lighter, but this action will probably increase manufacturing cost. One of the most difficult aspects of product development is recognizing, understanding, and managing such trade-offs in a way that maximizes the success of the product.
- *Dynamics:* Technologies improve, customer preferences evolve, competitors introduce new products, and the macroeconomic environment shifts. Decision making in an environment of constant change is a formidable task.
- *Details:* The choice between using screws or snap-fits on the enclosure of a computer can have economic implications of millions of dollars. Developing a product of even modest complexity may require thousands of such decisions.
- *Time pressure:* Any one of these difficulties would be easily manageable by itself given plenty of time, but product development decisions must usually be made quickly and without complete information.
- *Economics:* Developing, producing, and marketing a new product requires a large investment. To earn a reasonable return on this investment, the resulting product must be both appealing to customers and relatively inexpensive to produce.

For many people, product development is interesting precisely because it is challenging. For others, several intrinsic attributes also contribute to its appeal:

- *Creation:* The product development process begins with an idea and ends with the production of a physical artifact. When viewed both in its entirety and at the level of individual activities, the product development process is intensely creative.
- *Satisfaction of societal and individual needs:* All products are aimed at satisfying needs of some kind. Individuals interested in developing new products can almost always find institutional settings in which they can develop products satisfying what they consider to be important needs.
- *Team diversity:* Successful development requires many different skills and talents. As a result, development teams involve people with a wide range of different training, experience, perspectives, and personalities.
- *Team spirit:* Product development teams are often highly motivated, cooperative groups. The team members may be colocated so they can focus their collective energy on creating the product. This situation can result in lasting camaraderie among team members.

Approach of This Book

We focus on product development activities that benefit from the participation of all the core functions of the firm. For our purposes, we define the core functions as marketing, design, and manufacturing. We expect that team members have competence in one or more specific disciplines such as mechanical engineering, electrical engineering, industrial design, market research, or manufacturing operations. For this reason, we do not discuss, for example, how to perform a stress analysis or to create a conjoint survey. These are disciplinary skills we expect someone on the development team to possess. The integrative methods in this book are intended to facilitate problem solving and decision making among people with different disciplinary perspectives.

Structured Methods

The book consists of methods for completing development activities. The methods are structured, which means we generally provide a step-by-step approach and often provide templates for the key information systems used by the team. We believe structured methods are valuable for three reasons: First, they make the decision process explicit, allowing everyone on the team to understand the decision rationale and reducing the possibility of moving forward with unsupported decisions. Second, by acting as "checklists" of the key steps in a development activity they ensure that important issues are not forgotten. Third, structured methods are largely self-documenting; in the process of executing the method, the team creates a record of the decision-making process for future reference and for educating newcomers.

Although the methods are structured, they are not intended to be applied blindly. The methods are a starting point for continuous improvement. Teams should adapt and modify the approaches to meet their own needs and to reflect the unique character of their institutional environment.

Industrial Examples

Each remaining chapter is built around an example drawn from industrial practice. The major examples include the following: a wireless security system, a laser-based cat toy, a digital copier, a thermostat, a mountain bike suspension fork, a power nailer, a dose-metering syringe, an electric scooter, a computer printer, a mobile telephone, office seating products, an automobile engine, a mobile robot, a seat belt system, a coffee-cup insulator, a coffee maker, and a microfilm cartridge. In most cases we use as examples the simplest products we have access to that illustrate the important aspects of the methods. When a syringe illustrates an idea as well as a jet engine, we use the syringe. However, every method in this book has been used successfully in industrial practice by hundreds of people on both large and small projects.

Although built around examples, the chapters are not intended to be historically accurate case studies. We use the examples as a way to illustrate development methods, and in doing so we recast some historical details in a way that improves the presentation of the material. We also disguise much of the quantitative information in the examples, especially financial data.

Organizational Realities

We deliberately chose to present the methods with the assumption that the development team operates in an organizational environment conducive to success. In reality, some organizations exhibit characteristics that lead to dysfunctional product development teams. These characteristics include:

- *Lack of empowerment of the team:* General managers or functional managers may engage in continual intervention in the details of a development project without a full understanding of the basis for the team's decisions.

- *Functional allegiances transcending project goals:* Representatives of marketing, design, or manufacturing may influence decisions in order to increase the political standing of themselves or their functions without regard for the overall success of the product.
- *Inadequate resources:* A team may be unable to complete development tasks effectively because of a lack of staff, a mismatch of skills, or a lack of money, equipment, or tools.
- *Lack of cross-functional representation on the project team:* Key development decisions may be made without involvement of marketing, design, manufacturing, or other critical functions.

While most organizations exhibit one or more of these characteristics to some degree, the significant presence of these problems can be so stifling that sound development methods are rendered ineffective. While recognizing the importance of basic organizational issues, we assume, for clarity of explanation, that the development team operates in an environment in which the most restrictive organizational barriers have been removed.

Roadmap of the Book

We divide the product development process into six phases, as shown in Exhibit 1-4. (These phases are described in more detail in Chapter 2, Development Processes and Organizations.) This book describes the concept development phase in its entirety and the remaining phases less completely, because we do not provide methods for the more focused development activities that occur later in the process. Each of the remaining chapters in this book can be read, understood, and applied independently.

- Chapter 2, Development Processes and Organizations, presents a generic product development process and shows how variants of this process are used in different industrial situations. The chapter also discusses the way individuals are organized into groups in order to undertake product development projects.
- Chapter 3, Opportunity Identification, describes a process for creating, identifying, and screening ideas for new products.
- Chapter 4, Product Planning, presents a method for deciding which products to develop. The output of this method is a mission statement for a particular project.
- Chapters 5 through 9, Identifying Customer Needs, Product Specifications, Concept Generation, Concept Selection, and Concept Testing, present the key activities of the concept development phase. These methods guide a team from a mission statement through a selected product concept.
- Chapter 10, Product Architecture, discusses the implications of product architecture on product change, product variety, component standardization, product performance, manufacturing cost, and project management; it then presents a method for establishing the architecture of a product.
- Chapter 11, Industrial Design, discusses the role of the industrial designer and how human interaction issues, including aesthetics and ergonomics, are treated in product development.
- Chapter 12, Design for Environment, considers the environmental impacts associated with products and presents a method for reducing these impacts through better design decisions.
- Chapter 13, Design for Manufacturing, discusses techniques used to reduce manufacturing cost. These techniques are primarily applied during the system-level and detail-design phases of the process.

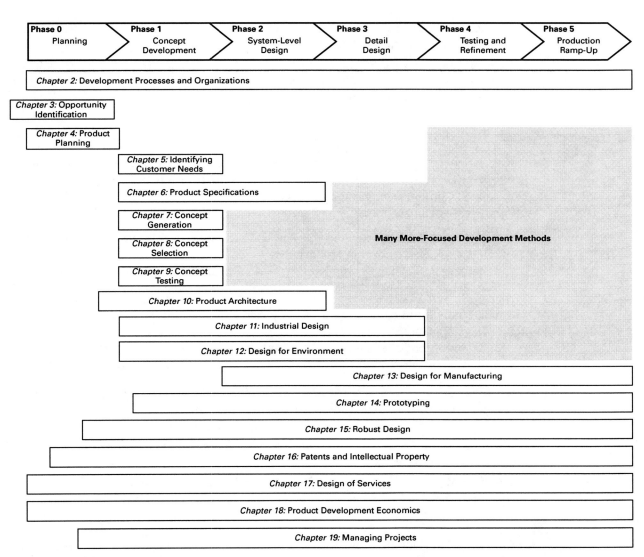

EXHIBIT 1-4 The product development process. The diagram shows where each of the integrative methods presented in the remaining chapters is most applicable.

- Chapter 14, Prototyping, presents a method to ensure that prototyping efforts, which occur throughout the process, are applied effectively.
- Chapter 15, Robust Design, explains methods for choosing values of design variables to ensure reliable and consistent performance.
- Chapter 16, Patents and Intellectual Property, presents an approach to creating a patent application and discusses the role of intellectual property in product development.
- Chapter 17, Design of Services, shows how the methods in this book can be applied to the development of intangible products, and introduces a method for representing those products, the service process flow diagram.

- Chapter 18, Product Development Economics, describes a method for understanding the influence of internal and external factors on the economic value of a project.
- Chapter 19, Managing Projects, presents some fundamental concepts for understanding and representing interacting project tasks, along with a method for planning and executing a development project.

References and Bibliography

A wide variety of resources for this chapter and for the rest of the book are available on the Internet. These resources include data, templates, links to suppliers, and lists of publications. Current resources may be accessed via
www.ulrich-eppinger.net

Wheelwright and Clark devote much of their book to the very early stages of product development, which we cover in less detail.

Wheelwright, Stephen C., and Kim B. Clark, *Revolutionizing Product Development: Quantum Leaps in Speed, Efficiency, and Quality*, The Free Press, New York, 1992.

Katzenbach and Smith write about teams in general, but most of their insights apply to product development teams as well.

Katzenbach, Jon R., and Douglas K. Smith, *The Wisdom of Teams: Creating the High-Performance Organization,* Harvard Business School Press, Boston, 1993.

These three books provide rich narratives of development projects, including fascinating descriptions of the intertwined social and technical processes.

Kidder, Tracy, *The Soul of a New Machine,* Avon Books, New York, 1981.

Sabbagh, Karl, *Twenty-First-Century Jet: The Making and Marketing of the Boeing 777,* Scribner, New York, 1996.

Walton, Mary, *Car: A Drama of the American Workplace,* Norton, New York, 1997.

Exercises

1. Estimate what fraction of the price of a pocket calculator is required to cover the cost of developing the product. To do this you might start by estimating the information needed to fill out Exhibit 1-3 for the pocket calculator.
2. Create a set of scatter charts by plotting each of the rows in Exhibit 1-3 against the development cost row. For each one, explain why there is or is not any correlation. (For example, you would first plot "annual production volume" versus "development cost" and explain why there seems to be no correlation. Then repeat for each of the remaining rows.)

Thought Question

1. Each of the chapters listed in Exhibit 1-4 presents a method for a portion of the product development process. For each one, consider what types of skills and expertise might be required. Can you make an argument for staffing the development team from start to finish with individuals possessing all of these skills and areas of expertise?

CHAPTER TWO

Development Processes and Organizations

EXHIBIT 2-1
A wireless security alarm system control panel, one of Tyco's products.

Tyco International is a leading manufacturer of sensors and controls, including home and industrial security systems. One of Tyco's products is the wireless security alarm system control panel shown in Exhibit 2-1. Senior managers at Tyco wanted to establish a common product development process structure that would be appropriate for all of the many different operating divisions across the company. They also needed to create a product development organization that would allow Tyco to compete effectively in a variety of competitive business markets. Some of the questions Tyco faced were:

- What are the key product development activities that must be included in every project?
- What project milestones and review gates can be used to manage the overall development process by phases?
- Is there a standard development process that will work for every operating division?
- What role do experts from different functional areas play in the development process?
- Should the development organization be divided into groups corresponding to projects or to technical and business functions?

This chapter helps answer these and related questions by presenting a generic development process and showing how this process can be adapted to meet the needs of particular industrial situations. We highlight the activities and contributions of different functions of the company during each phase of the development process. The chapter also explains what constitutes a product development organization and discusses why different types of organizations are appropriate for different settings.

The Product Development Process

A process is a sequence of steps that transforms a set of inputs into a set of outputs. Most people are familiar with the idea of physical processes, such as those used to bake a cake or to assemble an automobile. A *product development process* is the sequence of steps or activities that an enterprise employs to conceive, design, and commercialize a product. Many of these steps and activities are intellectual and organizational rather than physical. Some organizations define and follow a precise and detailed development process, while others may not even be able to describe their process. Furthermore, every organization employs a process at least slightly different from that of every other organization. In fact, the same enterprise may follow different processes for each of several different types of development projects.

A well-defined development process is useful for the following reasons:

- *Quality assurance:* A development process specifies the phases a development project will pass through and the checkpoints along the way. When these phases and checkpoints are chosen wisely, following the development process is one way of assuring the quality of the resulting product.
- *Coordination:* A clearly articulated development process acts as a master plan that defines the roles of each of the players on the development team. This plan informs the members of the team when their contributions will be needed and with whom they will need to exchange information and materials.

- *Planning:* A development process includes milestones corresponding to the completion of each phase. The timing of these milestones anchors the schedule of the overall development project.
- *Management:* A development process is a benchmark for assessing the performance of an ongoing development effort. By comparing the actual events to the established process, a manager can identify possible problem areas.
- *Improvement:* The careful documentation and ongoing review of an organization's development process and its results may help to identify opportunities for improvement.

The generic product development process consists of six phases, as illustrated in Exhibit 2-2. The process begins with a planning phase, which is the link to advanced research and technology development activities. The output of the planning phase is the project's mission statement, which is the input required to begin the concept development phase and which serves as a guide to the development team. The conclusion of the product development process is the product launch, at which time the product becomes available for purchase in the marketplace.

One way to think about the development process is as the initial creation of a wide set of alternative product concepts and then the subsequent narrowing of alternatives and increasing specification of the product until the product can be reliably and repeatably produced by the production system. Note that most of the phases of development are defined in terms of the state of the product, although the production process and marketing plans, among other tangible outputs, are also evolving as development progresses.

Another way to think about the development process is as an information-processing system. The process begins with inputs such as the corporate objectives, strategic opportunities, available technologies, product platforms, and production systems. Various activities process the development information, formulating specifications, concepts, and design details. The process concludes when all the information required to support production and sales has been created and communicated.

A third way to think about the development process is as a risk management system. In the early phases of product development, various risks are identified and prioritized. As the process progresses, risks are reduced as the key uncertainties are eliminated and the functions of the product are validated. When the process is completed, the team should have substantial confidence that the product will work correctly and be well received by the market.

Exhibit 2-2 also identifies the key activities and responsibilities of the different functions of the organization during each development phase. Because of their continuous involvement in the process, we choose to articulate the roles of marketing, design, and manufacturing. Representatives from other functions, such as research, finance, project management, field service, and sales, also play key roles at particular points in the process.

The six phases of the generic development process are:

0. Planning: The planning activity is often referred to as "phase zero" because it precedes the project approval and launch of the actual product development process. This phase begins with opportunity identification guided by corporate strategy and includes assessment of technology developments and market objectives. The output of the planning phase is the project mission statement, which specifies the target market for the product, business goals, key assumptions, and constraints. Chapter 3, Opportunity

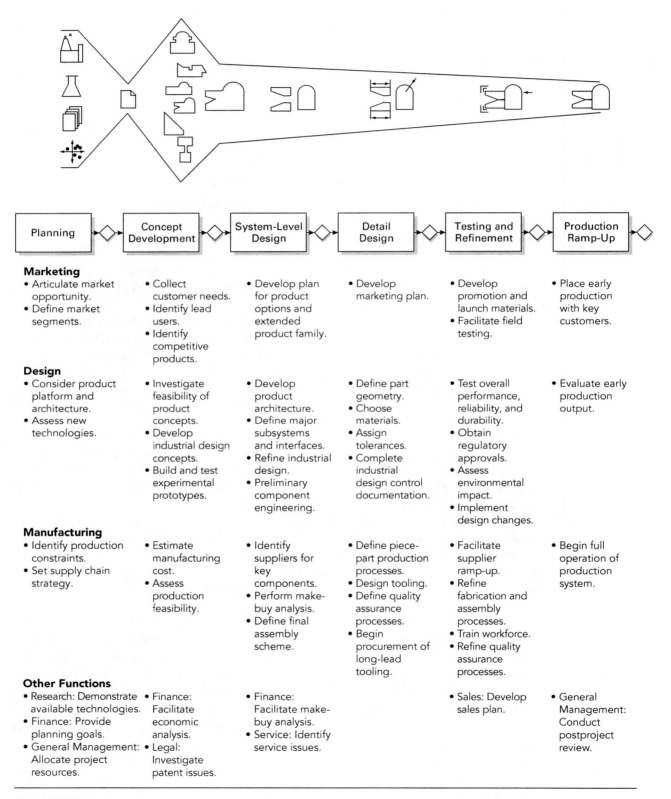

Planning		Concept Development		System-Level Design		Detail Design		Testing and Refinement		Production Ramp-Up	

Marketing

• Articulate market opportunity. • Define market segments.	• Collect customer needs. • Identify lead users. • Identify competitive products.	• Develop plan for product options and extended product family.	• Develop marketing plan.	• Develop promotion and launch materials. • Facilitate field testing.	• Place early production with key customers.

Design

• Consider product platform and architecture. • Assess new technologies.	• Investigate feasibility of product concepts. • Develop industrial design concepts. • Build and test experimental prototypes.	• Develop product architecture. • Define major subsystems and interfaces. • Refine industrial design. • Preliminary component engineering.	• Define part geometry. • Choose materials. • Assign tolerances. • Complete industrial design control documentation.	• Test overall performance, reliability, and durability. • Obtain regulatory approvals. • Assess environmental impact. • Implement design changes.	• Evaluate early production output.

Manufacturing

• Identify production constraints. • Set supply chain strategy.	• Estimate manufacturing cost. • Assess production feasibility.	• Identify suppliers for key components. • Perform make-buy analysis. • Define final assembly scheme.	• Define piece-part production processes. • Design tooling. • Define quality assurance processes. • Begin procurement of long-lead tooling.	• Facilitate supplier ramp-up. • Refine fabrication and assembly processes. • Train workforce. • Refine quality assurance processes.	• Begin full operation of production system.

Other Functions

• Research: Demonstrate available technologies. • Finance: Provide planning goals. • General Management: Allocate project resources.	• Finance: Facilitate economic analysis. • Legal: Investigate patent issues.	• Finance: Facilitate make-buy analysis. • Service: Identify service issues.		• Sales: Develop sales plan.	• General Management: Conduct postproject review.

EXHIBIT 2-2   The generic product development process. Six phases are shown, including some of the typical tasks and responsibilities of the key business functions for each phase.

Identification, explains a process for gathering, evaluating, and choosing from a broad range of product opportunities. Chapter 4, Product Planning, presents a discussion of the subsequent product planning process.

1. *Concept development:* In the concept development phase, the needs of the target market are identified, alternative product concepts are generated and evaluated, and one or more concepts are selected for further development and testing. A concept is a description of the form, function, and features of a product and is usually accompanied by a set of specifications, an analysis of competitive products, and an economic justification of the project. This book presents several detailed methods for the concept development phase (Chapters 5–9). We expand this phase into each of its constitutive activities in the next section.

2. *System-level design:* The system-level design phase includes the definition of the product architecture, decomposition of the product into subsystems and components, preliminary design of key components, and allocation of detail design responsibility to both internal and external resources. Initial plans for the production system and final assembly are usually defined during this phase as well. The output of this phase usually includes a geometric layout of the product, a functional specification of each of the product's subsystems, and a preliminary process flow diagram for the final assembly process. Chapter 10, Product Architecture, discusses some of the important activities of system-level design.

3. *Detail design:* The detail design phase includes the complete specification of the geometry, materials, and tolerances of all of the unique parts in the product and the identification of all of the standard parts to be purchased from suppliers. A process plan is established and tooling is designed for each part to be fabricated within the production system. The output of this phase is the *control documentation* for the product—the drawings or computer files describing the geometry of each part and its production tooling, the specifications of the purchased parts, and the process plans for the fabrication and assembly of the product. Three critical issues that are best considered throughout the product development process, but are finalized in the detail design phase, are materials selection, production cost, and robust performance. These issues are discussed respectively in Chapter 12, Design for Environment, Chapter 13, Design for Manufacturing, and Chapter 15, Robust Design.

4. *Testing and refinement:* The testing and refinement phase involves the construction and evaluation of multiple preproduction versions of the product. Early *(alpha)* prototypes are usually built with *production-intent* parts—parts with the same geometry and material properties as intended for the production version of the product but not necessarily fabricated with the actual processes to be used in production. Alpha prototypes are tested to determine whether the product will work as designed and whether the product satisfies the key customer needs. Later *(beta)* prototypes are usually built with parts supplied by the intended production processes but may not be assembled using the intended final assembly process. Beta prototypes are extensively evaluated internally and are also typically tested by customers in their own use environment. The goal for the beta prototypes is usually to answer questions about performance and reliability to identify necessary engineering changes for the final product. Chapter 14, Prototyping, presents a thorough discussion of the nature and use of prototypes.

5. *Production ramp-up:* In the production ramp-up phase, the product is made using the intended production system. The purpose of the ramp-up is to train the workforce and to work out any remaining problems in the production processes. Products produced during production ramp-up are sometimes supplied to preferred customers and are carefully evaluated to identify any remaining flaws. The transition from production ramp-up to ongoing production is usually gradual. At some point in this transition, the product is *launched* and becomes available for widespread distribution. A *postlaunch project review* may occur shortly after the launch. This review includes an assessment of the project from both commercial and technical perspectives and is intended to identify ways to improve the development process for future projects.

Concept Development: The Front-End Process

Because the concept development phase of the development process demands perhaps more coordination among functions than any other, many of the integrative development methods presented in this book are concentrated here. In this section we expand the concept development phase into what we call the *front-end process*. The front-end process generally contains many interrelated activities, ordered roughly as shown in Exhibit 2-3.

Rarely does the entire process proceed in purely sequential fashion, completing each activity before beginning the next. In practice, the front-end activities may be overlapped in time and iteration is often necessary. The dashed arrows in Exhibit 2-3 reflect the uncertain nature of progress in product development. At almost any stage, new information may become available or results learned that can cause the team to step back to repeat an earlier activity before proceeding. This repetition of nominally complete activities is known as development *iteration*.

The concept development process includes the following activities:

- *Identifying customer needs:* The goal of this activity is to understand customers' needs and to effectively communicate them to the development team. The output of this step is a set of carefully constructed customer need statements, organized in a hierarchical list, with importance weightings for many or all of the needs. Special attention is paid to the identification of *latent needs*, which are difficult for customers to articulate and unaddressed by existing products. A method for this activity is presented in Chapter 5, Identifying Customer Needs.

- *Establishing target specifications:* Specifications provide a precise description of what a product has to do. They are the translation of the customer needs into technical terms.

EXHIBIT 2-3   The many front-end activities comprising the concept development phase.

Targets for the specifications are set early in the process and represent the hopes of the development team. Later these specifications are refined to be consistent with the constraints imposed by the team's choice of a product concept. The output of this stage is a list of target specifications. Each specification consists of a metric, and marginal and ideal values for that metric. A method for the specification activity is given in Chapter 6, Product Specifications.

- *Concept generation:* The goal of concept generation is to thoroughly explore the space of product concepts that may address the customer needs. Concept generation includes a mix of external search, creative problem solving within the team, and systematic exploration of the various solution fragments the team generates. The result of this activity is usually a set of 10 to 20 concepts, each typically represented by a sketch and brief descriptive text. Chapter 7, Concept Generation, describes this activity in detail.

- *Concept selection:* Concept selection is the activity in which various product concepts are analyzed and sequentially eliminated to identify the most promising concept(s). The process usually requires several iterations and may initiate additional concept generation and refinement. A method for this activity is described in Chapter 8, Concept Selection.

- *Concept testing:* One or more concepts are then tested to verify that the customer needs have been met, assess the market potential of the product, and identify any shortcomings that must be remedied during further development. If the customer response is poor, the development project may be terminated or some earlier activities may be repeated as necessary. Chapter 9, Concept Testing, explains a method for this activity.

- *Setting final specifications:* The target specifications set earlier in the process are revisited after a concept has been selected and tested. At this point, the team must commit to specific values of the metrics reflecting the constraints inherent in the product concept, limitations identified through technical modeling, and trade-offs between cost and performance. Chapter 6, Product Specifications, explains the details of this activity.

- *Project planning:* In this final activity of concept development, the team creates a detailed development schedule, devises a strategy to minimize development time, and identifies the resources required to complete the project. The major results of the front-end activities can be usefully captured in a *contract book*, which contains the mission statement, the customer needs, the details of the selected concept, the product specifications, the economic analysis of the product, the development schedule, the project staffing, and the budget. The contract book serves to document the agreement (contract) between the team and the senior management of the enterprise. A project planning method is presented in Chapter 19, Managing Projects.

- *Economic analysis:* The team, often with the support of a financial analyst, builds an economic model for the new product. This model is used to justify continuation of the overall development program and to resolve specific trade-offs between, for example, development costs and manufacturing costs. Economic analysis is shown as one of the ongoing activities in the concept development phase. An early economic analysis will almost always be performed before the project even begins, and this analysis is updated as more information becomes available. A method for this activity is presented in Chapter 18, Product Development Economics.

- *Benchmarking of competitive products:* An understanding of competitive products is critical to successful positioning of a new product and can provide a rich source of ideas for the product and production process design. Competitive *benchmarking* is performed in support of many of the front-end activities. Various aspects of competitive benchmarking are presented in Chapters 5–9.

- *Modeling and prototyping:* Every stage of the concept development process involves various forms of models and prototypes. These may include, among others: early "proof-of-concept" models, which help the development team to demonstrate feasibility; "form-only" models, which can be shown to customers to evaluate ergonomics and style; spreadsheet models of technical trade-offs; and experimental test models, which can be used to set design parameters for robust performance. Methods for modeling, prototyping, and testing are discussed throughout the book, including in Chapters 5–7, 9, 11, 14, 15 and 17.

Adapting the Generic Product Development Process

The development process described by Exhibits 2-2 and 2-3 is generic, and particular processes will differ in accordance with the unique context of the firm and the challenges of any specific project. The generic process is most like the process used in a *market-pull* situation: a firm begins product development with a market opportunity and then uses whatever available technologies are required to satisfy the market need (i.e., the market "pulls" the development decisions). In addition to the market-pull process outlined in Exhibits 2-2 and 2-3, several variants are common and correspond to the following: *technology-push* products, *platform* products, *process-intensive* products, *customized* products, *high-risk* products, *quick-build* products, *product-service* systems, and *complex* systems. Each of these situations is described below. The characteristics of these situations and the resulting deviations from the generic process are summarized in Exhibit 2-4.

Technology-Push Products

In developing technology-push products, the firm begins with a new proprietary technology and looks for an appropriate market in which to apply this technology (that is, the technology "pushes" development). Gore-Tex, an expanded Teflon sheet manufactured by W. L. Gore Associates, is a striking example of technology push. The company has developed dozens of products incorporating Gore-Tex, including artificial veins for vascular surgery, insulation for high-performance electric cables, fabric for outerwear, dental floss, and liners for bagpipe bags.

Many successful technology-push products involve basic materials or basic process technologies. This may be because basic materials and processes are deployed in thousands of applications, and there is therefore a high likelihood that new and unusual characteristics of materials and processes can be matched with an appropriate application.

The generic product development process can be used with minor modifications for technology-push products. The technology-push process begins with the planning phase, in which the given technology is matched with a market opportunity. Once this matching has occurred, the remainder of the generic development process can be followed. The team includes an assumption in the mission statement that the particular technology will be embodied in the product concepts considered by the team. Although many extremely successful products have arisen from technology-push development, this approach can be perilous. The product is unlikely to succeed unless (1) the assumed technology offers a clear competitive advantage in meeting customer needs, and (2) suitable alternative technologies

Process Type	Description	Distinct Features	Examples
Generic (Market-Pull) Products	The team begins with a market opportunity and selects appropriate technologies to meet customer needs.	Process generally includes distinct planning, concept development, system-level design, detail design, testing and refinement, and production ramp-up phases.	Sporting goods, furniture, tools.
Technology-Push Products	The team begins with a new technology, then finds an appropriate market.	Planning phase involves matching technology and market. Concept development assumes a given technology.	Gore-Tex rainwear, Tyvek envelopes.
Platform Products	The team assumes that the new product will be built around an established technological subsystem.	Concept development assumes a proven technology platform.	Consumer electronics, computers, printers.
Process-Intensive Products	Characteristics of the product are highly constrained by the production process.	Either an existing production process must be specified from the start, or both product and process must be developed together from the start.	Snack foods, breakfast cereals, chemicals, semiconductors.
Customized Products	New products are slight variations of existing configurations.	Similarity of projects allows for a streamlined and highly structured development process.	Motors, switches, batteries, containers.
High-Risk Products	Technical or market uncertainties create high risks of failure.	Risks are identified early and tracked throughout the process. Analysis and testing activities take place as early as possible.	Pharmaceuticals, space systems.
Quick-Build Products	Rapid modeling and prototyping enables many design-build-test cycles.	Detail design and testing phases are repeated a number of times until the product is completed or time/budget runs out.	Software, cellular phones.
Product-Service Systems	Products and their associated service elements are developed simultaneously.	Both physical and operational elements are developed, with particular attention to design of the customer experience and the process flow.	Restaurants, software applications, financial services.
Complex Systems	System must be decomposed into several subsystems and many components.	Subsystems and components are developed by many teams working in parallel, followed by system integration and validation.	Airplanes, jet engines, automobiles.

EXHIBIT 2-4   Summary of variants of generic product development process.

are unavailable or very difficult for competitors to utilize. Project risk can possibly be minimized by simultaneously considering the merit of a broader set of concepts that do not necessarily incorporate the new technology. In this way, the team verifies that the product concept embodying the new technology is superior to the alternatives.

Platform Products

A platform product is built around a preexisting technological subsystem (a technology *platform*). Examples of such platforms include the Intel chipset in a personal computer, the Apple iPhone operating system, and the blade design in a Gillette razor. Huge investments are made in developing such platforms, and therefore every attempt is made to incorporate them into several different products. In some sense, platform products are very similar to technology-push products in that the team begins the development effort with an assumption that the product concept will embody a particular technology. One difference is that a technology platform has already demonstrated its usefulness in the marketplace in meeting customer needs. The firm can in many cases assume that the technology will also be useful in related markets. Products built on technology platforms are much simpler to develop than if the technology were developed from scratch. For this reason, and because of the possible sharing of costs across several products, a firm may be able to offer a platform product in markets that could not justify the development of a unique technology.

Process-Intensive Products

Examples of process-intensive products include semiconductors, foods, chemicals, and paper. For these products, the production process places strict constraints on the properties of the product, so that the product design cannot be separated, even at the concept phase, from the production process design. In many cases, process-intensive products are produced in very high volumes and are bulk, as opposed to discrete, goods.

In some situations, a new product and new process are developed simultaneously. For example, creating a new shape of breakfast cereal or snack food will require both product and process development activities. In other cases, a specific existing process for making the product is chosen in advance, and the product design is constrained by the capabilities of this process. This might be true of a new paper product to be made in a particular paper mill or a new semiconductor device to be made in an existing wafer fabrication facility.

Customized Products

Examples of customized products include switches, motors, batteries, and containers. Customized products are slight variations of standard configurations and are typically developed in response to a specific order by a customer. Development of customized products consists primarily of setting values of design variables such as physical dimensions and materials. Templates for specifying customized products may be provided with online design tools. When a customer orders a new product, the firm executes a structured design and development process to create the product to meet the customer's needs. Such firms typically have created a highly detailed development process involving a well-defined sequence of steps with a structured flow of information (analogous to a production process). For customized products, the generic process is augmented with a detailed description of the specific information-processing activities required within each of the phases. Such development processes may consist of hundreds of carefully defined activities and may be highly automated.

High-Risk Products

The product development process addresses many types of risk. These include technical risk (Will the product function properly?), market risk (Will customers like what the team develops?), and budget and schedule risk (Can the team complete the project on time and within budget?). High-risk products are those that entail unusually large uncertainties related to the technology or market so that there is substantial technical or market risk. The generic product development process is modified in high-risk situations by taking steps to address the largest risks in the early stages of product development. This usually requires completing some design and test activities earlier in the process. For example, when there is great uncertainty regarding customer acceptance of a new product, concept testing using renderings or user-interface prototypes may be done very early in the process in order to reduce the market uncertainty and risk. If there is high uncertainty related to technical performance of the product, it makes sense to build working models of the key features and to test these earlier in the process. Multiple solution paths may be explored in parallel to ensure that one of the solutions succeeds. Design reviews must assess levels of risk on a regular basis, with the expectation that risks are being reduced over time and not being postponed.

Quick-Build Products

For the development of some products, such as software and many electronics products, building and testing prototype models is such a rapid process that the design-build-test cycle can be repeated many times. In fact, teams can take advantage of rapid iteration to achieve a more flexible and responsive product development process, sometimes called a *spiral product development process.* Following concept development in this process, the system-level design phase entails decomposition of the product into high-, medium-, and low-priority features. This is followed by several cycles of design, build, integrate, and test activities, beginning with the highest-priority items. This process takes advantage of the fast prototyping cycle by using the result of each cycle to learn how to modify the priorities for the next cycle. Customers may even be involved in the testing process after one or more cycles. When time or budget runs out, usually all of the high- and medium-priority features have been incorporated into the evolving product, and the low-priority features may be omitted until the next product generation.

Product-Service Systems

Services are largely intangible product offerings and are often provided in conjunction with tangible products. Examples of *product-service systems* are automobile rentals, restaurants, and mobile communications. Services are largely developed using the standard product development methods described throughout this book; however, because customers are so intimately involved in the service delivery process, service design teams pay careful attention to the range of customer needs and the timing of key touch points in creating the service experience. Many services are produced and consumed at the same time and therefore matching supply with demand is critical. Design of the service process flow may take advantage of a modular architecture in order to deliver customized services to every customer. Chapter 17, Design of Services, discusses these and other distinctions in the process for developing product-service systems.

Complex Systems

Larger-scale products such as automobiles and airplanes are complex systems comprising many interacting subsystems and components. When developing complex systems, modifications to the generic product development process address a number of system-level issues. The concept development phase considers the architecture of the entire system, and multiple architectures may be considered as competing concepts for the overall system. The system-level design phase becomes critical. During this phase, the system is decomposed into subsystems and these further into many components. Teams are assigned to develop each component. Additional teams are assigned the special challenge of integrating components into the subsystems and these into the overall system.

Detail design of the components is a highly parallel process in which the many development teams work at once, usually separately. Managing the network of interactions across the components and subsystems is the task of systems engineering specialists of many kinds. The testing and refinement phase includes not only component and system integration, but also extensive testing and validation at all levels.

Product Development Process Flows

The product development process generally follows a structured flow of activity and information flow. This allows us to draw *process flow diagrams* illustrating the process, as shown in Exhibit 2-5. The generic process flow diagram (a) depicts the process used to develop market-pull, technology-push, platform, process-intensive, customized, and

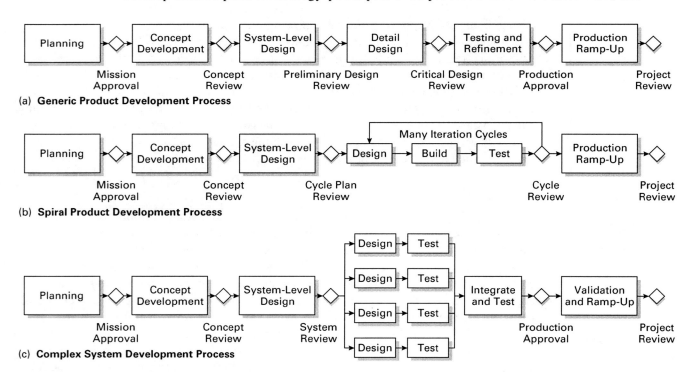

EXHIBIT 2-5   Process flow diagrams for three product development processes.

high-risk products. Each product development phase (or stage) is followed by a review (or gate) to confirm that the phase is completed and to determine whether the project proceeds. Quick-build products enable a spiral product development process (b) whereby detail design, prototyping, and test activities are repeated a number of times. The process flow diagram for development of complex systems (c) shows the decomposition into parallel stages of work on the many subsystems and components. Once the product development process has been established within an organization, a process flow diagram is used to explain the process to everyone on the team.

The Tyco Product Development Process

Tyco is primarily a market-pull enterprise. This means that Tyco generally drives its development projects based on a perceived market need and utilizes new or established technologies to meet that need. Its competitive advantage arises from highly effective marketing channels worldwide, strong brand recognition, a large installed base of equipment, and an ability to integrate new technologies into its product lines. For this reason, the technology-push process would not be appropriate. Most Tyco products are assembled from components fabricated with relatively conventional processes such as molding, machining, and electronics assembly. Products are generally customized for a particular customer in the final sales and installation processes, so the development process at Tyco is primarily aimed at creation of new models of products, rather than at the customization of existing models.

Tyco therefore established a common product development process similar to the generic phased process. The resulting Tyco Rally Point process flow is illustrated in Exhibit 2-6. Note that there are nine phases in the Rally Point process, with six of the phases (from concept definition to process verification) comprising the fundamental product development process activities. Each phase is followed by a critical review (called a Rally Point), which is required to gain approval to proceed to the next phase. The primary goal and key activities of each phase as well as the business function responsible for each activity are shown in Exhibit 2-7.

Although Tyco established Rally Point as its standard process, Tyco managers realized that this process would not be perfectly suitable for all Tyco development projects across all business units; therefore, one key activity in the concept definition phase is to select a Rally Point process variant if necessary. For example, some of Tyco's new products are based on existing technology platforms. To develop such derivative products, the team assumes the use of the existing technology platform during concept development. Also, some products are designed for specific customers as private-label variants of standard

Courtesy of Tyco International

EXHIBIT 2-6   Tyco's Rally Point product development process includes nine distinct phases and review gates.

Rally Point Phase	0. Project Registration	1. Concept Definition	2. Feasibility and Planning	3. Preliminary Design	4. Final Design	5. Product Verification	6. Process Verification	7. Launch	8. Post-Launch Assessment
Primary Goal	Define project and business unit needs	Develop project concept and charter	Create product description	Create preliminary detailed design	Detail and optimize design	Demonstrate product performance	Demonstrate process performance	Launch product	Identify lessons learned
Marketing and Sales	Identify customers and market size Describe competitive features and benefits Identify target cost and price	Capture voice of the customer Analyze customer needs Document customer needs	Develop marketing and sales plans Create phase-in and phase-out plans	Review concepts with customers		Initialize field trials	Complete field trials Finalize training plans	Finalize pricing and sales forecasts Complete sales and service training	Solicit customer feedback and satisfaction ratings Measure sales vs. forecast Complete phase-in and phase-out
Engineering	Identify project risks	Identify critical-to-quality specs Develop and select concepts Update project risks	Create functional specification and performance metrics Review concept selection Define product architecture Assess technical failures modes	Conduct a preliminary design review Build and test alpha prototypes Assess product failure modes	Freeze hardware and software design Complete engineering documentation Draft technical documentation Secure beta prototypes	Finalize design documentation Complete beta prototype and field testing Apply for regulatory approvals	Obtain regulatory approvals	Finalize product metrics	
Quality Assurance			Create preliminary test plan		Test beta prototypes for robustness	Complete quality assurance testing	Conduct process verification testing		
Manufacturing				Begin manufacturing process development Conduct a preliminary manufacturing process review	Finalize bill of materials (BOM) Develop manufacturing control plans	Update manufacturing control plans	Run manufacturing pilots Finalize manufacturing control plans		Register obsolete and scrap products
Purchasing				Create a supplier participation matrix Assess suppliers for certification	Identify long lead-time items		Verify supply chain readiness		
Legal		Search patents	Identify trade compliance issues	Identify potential patents	Prepare patent applications	Assure trade compliance			
Financial	Prepare preliminary business case	Refine business case	Complete financial package						Monitor return on investment
Project Management	Identify project timing, resources, and capital Prepare RP0 checklist & submit for approval	Assess team capabilities/skills Identify development team members Select a Rally Point process variant Prepare RP1 checklist & submit for approval	Plan integrated product development schedule Assign a project manager Update RP1 deliverables Prepare RP2 checklist & submit for approval	Update RP1-2 deliverables Prepare RP3 checklist & submit for approval	Update RP1-3 deliverables Prepare RP4 checklist & submit for approval	Update RP1-4 deliverables Prepare RP5 checklist & submit for approval	Update RP1-5 deliverables Prepare RP6 checklist & submit for approval	Finalize all deliverables Finalize launch plans and documentation Update RP1-6 deliverables Prepare RP7 checklist & submit for approval	Document best practices Prepare RP8 checklist & submit for approval

Courtesy of Tyco International

EXHIBIT 2-7 Key activities and the responsible functions comprising the Tyco Rally Point product development process.

Tyco products. In these cases, a streamlined process known as Rally Point EZ is used. Nevertheless, the standard Rally Point product development process is the baseline from which a particular project plan begins.

Product Development Organizations

In addition to crafting an effective development process, successful firms must organize their product development staff to implement the process in an effective manner. In this section, we describe several types of organizations used for product development and offer guidelines for choosing among these options.

Organizations Are Formed by Establishing Links among Individuals

A product development organization is the scheme by which individual designers and developers are linked together into groups. The links among individuals may be formal or informal and include, among others, these types:

- *Reporting relationships:* Reporting relationships give rise to the classic notion of *supervisor* and *subordinate*. These are the formal links most frequently shown on an organization chart.
- *Financial arrangements:* Individuals are linked by being part of the same financial entity, such as a business unit or department within a firm.
- *Physical layout:* Links are created between individuals when they share the same office, floor, building, or site. These links are often informal, arising from spontaneous encounters while at work.

Any particular individual may be linked in several different ways to other individuals. For example, an engineer may be linked by a reporting relationship to another engineer in a different building, while being linked by physical layout to a marketing person sitting in the next office. The strongest organizational links are typically those involving performance evaluation, budgets, and other resource allocations.

Organizational Links May Be Aligned with Functions, Projects, or Both

Regardless of their organizational links, particular individuals can be classified in two different ways: according to their *function* and according to the *projects* they work on.

- A function (in organizational terms) is an area of responsibility usually involving specialized education, training, or experience. The classic functions in product development organizations are marketing, design, and manufacturing. Finer divisions than these are also possible and may include, for example, market research, market strategy, stress analysis, industrial design, human factors engineering, process development, and operations management.
- Regardless of their functions, individuals apply their expertise to specific projects. In product development, a project is the set of activities in the development process for a particular product and includes, for example, identifying customer needs and generating product concepts.

Note that these two classifications must overlap: individuals from several different functions will work on the same project. Also, while most individuals are associated with only one function, they may contribute to more than one project. Two classic organizational structures arise from aligning the organizational links according to function or according to projects. In *functional organizations,* the organizational links are primarily among those who perform similar functions. In *project organizations,* the organizational links are primarily among those who work on the same project.

For example, a strict functional organization might include a group of marketing professionals, all sharing similar training and expertise. These people would all report to the same manager, who would evaluate them and set their salaries. The group would have its own budget and the people may sit in the same part of a building. This marketing group would be involved in many different projects, but there would be no strong organizational links to the other members of each project team. There would be similarly arranged groups corresponding to design and to manufacturing.

A strict project organization would be made up of groups of people from several different functions, with each group focused on the development of a specific product (or product line). These groups would each report to an experienced project manager, who might be drawn from any of the functional areas. Performance evaluation would be handled by the project manager, and members of the team would typically be colocated as much as possible so that they all work in the same office or part of a building. New ventures, or "start-ups," are among the most extreme examples of project organizations: every individual, regardless of function, is linked together by a single project—the growth of the new company and the creation of its product(s). In these settings, the president or CEO can be viewed as the project manager. Established firms will sometimes form an autonomous "tiger team" with dedicated resources for a single project when special focus is required to complete an important development project.

The *matrix organization* was conceived as a hybrid of functional and project organizations. In the matrix organization, individuals are linked to others according to both the project they work on and their function. Typically each individual has two supervisors, one a project manager and one a functional manager. The practical reality is that either the project or the function tends to have stronger links. This is because, for example, both functional and project managers cannot independently assign their shared staff, they cannot independently evaluate and determine the salaries of their subordinates, and both functional and project organizations cannot easily be grouped together physically. As a result, either the functional or the project organization tends to dominate.

Two variants of the matrix organization are called the *heavyweight project organization* and *lightweight project organization* (Hayes et al., 1988). A heavyweight project organization contains strong project links. The heavyweight project manager has complete budget authority, is heavily involved in performance evaluation of the team members, and makes most of the major resource allocation decisions. Although each participant in a project also belongs to a functional organization, the functional managers have relatively little authority and control. A heavyweight project team in various industries may be called an *integrated product team* (IPT), a *design-build team* (DBT), or simply a *product development team* (PDT). Each of these terms emphasizes the cross-functional nature of these teams.

A lightweight project organization contains weaker project links and relatively stronger functional links. In this scheme, the project manager is more of a coordinator and administrator. The lightweight project manager updates schedules, arranges meetings, and

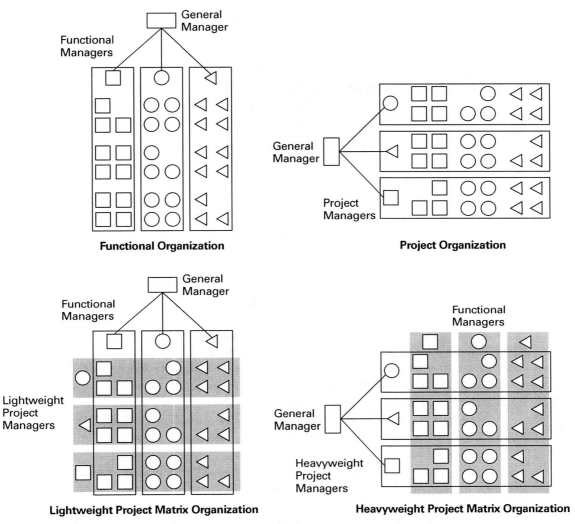

Functional Organization

Project Organization

Lightweight Project Matrix Organization

Heavyweight Project Matrix Organization

Adapted from Hayes, Robert H., Steven C. Wheelwright, and Kim B. Clark, Dynamic Manufacturing: Creating the Learning Organization, The Free Press, New York, 1988

EXHIBIT 2-8   Various product development organizations. For simplicity, three functions and three projects are shown.

facilitates coordination, but the manager has no real authority and control in the project organization. The functional managers are responsible for budgets, hiring and firing, and performance evaluation. Exhibit 2-8 illustrates the pure functional and project organizations, along with the heavyweight and lightweight variants of the matrix organization.

In this book, we refer to the *project team* as the primary organizational unit. In this context, the team is the set of all people involved in the project, regardless of the organizational structure of the product development staff. In a functional organization, the team consists of individuals distributed throughout the functional groups without any organizational linkages other than their common involvement in a project. In the other organizations, the team corresponds to a formal organizational entity, the project group, and has a formally appointed manager. For this reason, the notion of a team has much more meaning in matrix and project organizations than it does in functional organizations.

Choosing an Organizational Structure

The most appropriate choice of organizational structure depends on which organizational performance factors are most critical to success. Functional organizations tend to breed specialization and deep expertise in the functional areas. Project organizations tend to enable rapid and effective coordination among diverse functions. Matrix organizations, being hybrids, have the potential to exhibit some of each of these characteristics. The following questions help guide the choice of organizational structure:

- *How important is cross-functional integration?* Functional organizations may exhibit difficulty in coordinating project decisions that span the functional areas. Project organizations tend to enable strong cross-functional integration because of the organizational links of the team members across the functions.

- *How critical is cutting-edge functional expertise to business success?* When disciplinary expertise must be developed and retained over several product generations, then some functional links are necessary. For example, in some aerospace companies, computational fluid dynamics is so critical that the fluid dynamicists are organized functionally to ensure the firm will have the best possible capability in this area.

- *Can individuals from each function be fully utilized for most of the duration of a project?* For example, a project may require only a portion of an industrial designer's time for a fraction of the duration of a project. To use industrial design resources efficiently, the firm may choose to organize the industrial designers functionally, so that several projects can draw on the industrial design resource in exactly the amount needed for a particular project.

- *How important is product development speed?* Project organizations tend to allow for conflicts to be resolved quickly and for individuals from different functions to coordinate their activities efficiently. Relatively little time is spent transferring information, assigning responsibilities, and coordinating tasks. For this reason, project organizations are usually faster than functional organizations in developing innovative products. For example, consumer electronics manufacturers almost always organize their product development teams by project. This allows the teams to develop new products within the extremely short periods required by the fast-paced electronics market.

Dozens of other issues confound the choice between functional and project organizations. Exhibit 2-9 summarizes some of the strengths and weaknesses of each organizational type, examples of the types of firms pursuing each strategy, and the major issues associated with each approach.

Distributed Product Development Teams

It is well established that a highly effective way to organize a product development team includes colocation of the team members at a single site; however, the use of modern communication technology and digital development processes allows even globally distributed project teams to be effective. Reasons to utilize product development team members located at multiple sites may include the following:

- Access to information about regional markets.
- Availability of technical expertise.

| | Functional Organization | Matrix Organization | | Project Organization |
		Lightweight Project Organization	Heavyweight Project Organization	
Strengths	Fosters development of deep specialization and expertise.	Coordination and administration of projects is explicitly assigned to a single project manager. Maintains development of specialization and expertise.	Provides integration and speed benefits of the project organization. Some of the specialization of a functional organization is retained.	Resources can be optimally allocated within the project team. Technical and market trade-offs can be evaluated quickly.
Weaknesses	Coordination across different functional groups can be slow and bureaucratic.	Requires more managers and administrators than a nonmatrix organization.	Requires more managers and administrators than a nonmatrix organization.	Individuals may have difficulty maintaining cutting-edge functional capabilities.
Typical Examples	Customized products, where development involves slight variations to a standard design (e.g., motors, bearings, packaging).	Derivative products in many automobile, electronics, and aerospace companies.	New technology or platform projects in automobile, electronics, and aerospace companies.	Start-up companies. "Tiger teams" and "skunkworks" intended to achieve breakthroughs. Firms competing in highly dynamic markets.
Major Issues	How to integrate different functions (e.g., marketing and design) to achieve business goals.	How to balance functions and projects. How to simultaneously evaluate project and functional performance.		How to maintain functional expertise over time. How to share learning from one project to another.

EXHIBIT 2-9   Characteristics of different organizational structures.

- Location of manufacturing facilities and suppliers.
- Cost saving through lower wages.
- Outsourcing to increase product development capacity.

Notwithstanding the importance of using the right team members regardless of location, firms implementing globally distributed product development have experienced many challenges due to the weaker ties between team members separated by great distances. This may result in an increased number of design iterations and more difficult project coordination, particularly when such teams are newly formed. Fortunately, organizations having years of experience with global project teams report that distributed projects do work more smoothly over time.

The Tyco Product Development Organization

The primary functions involved in product development at Tyco are engineering, manufacturing, marketing, sales, purchasing, quality assurance, finance, legal, and project management (as listed in Exhibit 2-7). Each of these functions has a manager who reports to the general manager of the division; however, product development projects are led by project managers, with the resources for each project drawn from the functional areas.

In terms of the variants described in Exhibits 2-8 and 2-9, product development at Tyco primarily takes place in projects strongly reflecting a traditional functional organization structure. Project leaders are given only indirect control of the functional resources assigned to their teams. As explained above, a functional structure generally sacrifices some project efficiency in favor of greater ongoing development of the functional skills. To address this concern, Tyco has created a highly effective project management function, with project leaders who know the Rally Point process and how to coordinate the activities across the functions. This organizational choice has indeed led to very good product development performance for Tyco while maintaining very strong functional capabilities.

In recent years, Tyco has created new regional engineering centers at locations in high-growth markets such as China and India. Engineers at these centers are able to support product development projects across multiple Tyco business units around the world. This arrangement improves project performance by augmenting any project team with additional technical resources on an as-needed basis, which is particularly helpful in the later stages of the Rally Point process.

Summary

An enterprise must make two important decisions about the way it carries out product development. It must define both a product development process and a product development organization.

- A product development process is the sequence of steps an enterprise employs to conceive, design, and commercialize a product.
- A well-defined development process helps to ensure product quality, facilitate coordination among team members, plan the development project, and continuously improve the process.
- The generic process presented in this chapter includes six phases: planning, concept development, system-level design, detail design, testing and refinement, and production ramp-up.
- The concept development phase requires tremendous integration across the different functions on the development team. This front-end process includes identifying customer needs, analyzing competitive products, establishing target specifications, generating product concepts, selecting one or more final concepts, setting final specifications, testing the concept(s), performing an economic analysis, and planning the remaining project activities. The results of the concept development phase are documented in a contract book.
- The development process employed by a particular firm may differ somewhat from the generic process described here. The generic process is most appropriate for market-pull products. Other types of products, which may require variants of the generic process, include technology-push products, platform products, process-intensive products, customized products, high-risk products, quick-build products, product-service systems, and complex systems.

- Regardless of the development process, tasks are completed by individuals residing in organizations. Organizations are defined by linking individuals through reporting relationships, financial relationships, and/or physical layout.
- Functional organizations are those in which the organizational links correspond to the development functions. Project organizations are those in which the organizational links correspond to the development projects. Two types of hybrid, or matrix, organization are the heavyweight project organization and the lightweight project organization.
- The classic trade-off between functional organizations and project organizations is between deep functional expertise and coordination efficiency.
- Globally distributed product development teams allow access to specialized resources, market information, and/or technical expertise; however, global teams experience higher project coordination costs.

References and Bibliography

Many current resources are available on the Internet via
www.ulrich-eppinger.net

Staged product development processes have been dominant in manufacturing firms for the past 30 years. Cooper describes the stage-gate process and many of its enabling practices.

> Cooper, Robert G., *Winning at New Products: Creating Value through Innovation,* fourth edition, Basic Books, New York, 2011.

The spiral product development process has evolved primarily within the software industry; however, many aspects of spiral development can be applied in manufacturing and other industries. McConnell describes spiral software development, along with several other processes used to develop software products.

> McConnell, Steve, *Rapid Development: Taming Wild Software Schedules,* Microsoft Press, Redmond, WA, 1996.

The concept of heavyweight and lightweight project organizations is articulated by Hayes, Wheelwright, and Clark. Wheelwright and Clark also discuss product strategy, planning, and technology development activities, which generally precede the product development process.

> Hayes, Robert H., Steven C. Wheelwright, and Kim B. Clark, *Dynamic Manufacturing: Creating the Learning Organization,* The Free Press, New York, 1988.
>
> Wheelwright, Steven C., and Kim B. Clark, *Revolutionizing Product Development: Quantum Leaps in Speed, Efficiency, and Quality,* The Free Press, New York, 1992.

Sosa and Marle provide evidence that project teams whose members have prior positive creative experience working together perform better on innovative tasks.

> Sosa, Manuel E., and Franck Marle, "Assembling Creative Teams in New Product Development Using Creative Team Familiarity," *Journal of Mechanical Design,* Vol. 135, No. 8, 2013.

Andreasen and Hein provide some good ideas on how to integrate different functions in product development. They also show several conceptual models of product development organizations.

Andreasen, M. Myrup, and Lars Hein, *Integrated Product Development,* Springer-Verlag, New York, 1987.

Allen provides strong empirical evidence that physical layout can be used to create significant, although informal, organizational links. He also discusses the use of matrix organizations to mitigate the weaknesses of functional and project organizations.

Allen, Thomas J., *Managing the Flow of Technology: Technology Transfer and the Dissemination of Technological Information within the R&D Organization,* MIT Press, Cambridge, MA, 1977.

Galbraith's seminal book on organizational design contains much useful information that can be applied to product development. His 1994 book is an update of his earlier writing.

Galbraith, Jay R., *Designing Complex Organizations,* Addison-Wesley, Reading, MA, 1973.

Galbraith, Jay R., *Competing with Flexible Lateral Organizations,* second edition, Addison-Wesley, Reading, MA, 1994.

Exercises

1. Diagram a process for planning and cooking a family dinner. Does your process resemble the generic product development process? Is cooking dinner analogous to a market-pull, technology-push, platform, process-intensive, customization, high-risk, quick-build, product-service system, or complex system process?

2. Define a process for finding a job. For what types of endeavor does a well-defined process enhance performance?

3. What type of development process would you expect to find in an established company successful at developing residential air-conditioning units? How about for a small company that is trying to break into the market for racing wheelchairs?

4. Sketch the organization (in some appropriate graphical representation) of a consulting firm that develops new products for clients on a project-by-project basis. Assume that the individuals in the firm represent all of the different functions required to develop a new product. Would this organization most likely be aligned with functions, be aligned by projects, or be a hybrid?

Thought Questions

1. What role does basic technological research play in the product development process? How would you modify Exhibit 2-3 to better represent the research and technology development activities in product development?

2. Is there an analogy between a university and a product development organization? Is a university a functional or project organization?

3. What is the product development organization for students engaged in projects as part of a product development class?

4. Is it possible for some members of a product development organization to be organized functionally, while others are organized by project? If so, which members of the team would be the most likely candidates for the functional organization?

CHAPTER FOUR

Product Planning

Courtesy of Xerox

EXHIBIT 4-1
The Lakes project developed a new copier platform, including this new product, the Xerox Document Centre 265.

Xerox Corporation is a global enterprise offering a wide array of document-related products, services, and business solutions. Its mission is to be the leader in the global document market, providing document solutions that enhance business productivity. A key element of Xerox's competitive strategy is to exploit technological innovation in a rapidly changing market. Pursuing this strategy requires the ability to choose the right set of development projects and to define the scope of these projects in such a way that the projects are complementary. Exhibit 4-1 is a photo of the Xerox Document Centre 265, a product resulting from a Xerox project code-named Lakes.

The *product planning* process takes place before a product development project is formally approved, before substantial resources are applied, and before the larger development team is formed. Product planning is an activity that considers the portfolio of projects that an organization might pursue and determines what subset of these projects will be pursued over what time period. The product planning activity ensures that product development projects support the broader business strategy of the company and addresses these questions:

- What product development projects will be undertaken?
- What mix of fundamentally new products, platforms, and derivative products should be pursued?
- How do the various projects relate to each other as a portfolio?
- What will be the timing and sequence of the projects?

Each of the selected projects is then completed by a product development team. The team needs to know its mission before beginning development. The answers to these critical questions are included in a mission statement for the team:

- What market segments should be considered in designing the product and developing its features?
- What new technologies (if any) should be incorporated into the new product?
- What are the manufacturing and service goals and constraints?
- What are the financial targets for the project?
- What are the budget and time frame for the project?

This chapter explains how an organization can maximize the effectiveness of its product development efforts by first considering the set of potential projects it might pursue, deciding which projects are most desirable, and then launching each project with a focused mission. We present a five-step planning process beginning with the identification of opportunities and resulting in a mission statement for the project team.

The Product Planning Process

The *product plan* identifies the portfolio of products to be developed by the organization and the timing of their introduction to the market. The planning process considers product development opportunities identified by many sources, including suggestions from marketing, research, customers, current product development teams, and benchmarking of competitors. From among these opportunities, a portfolio of projects is

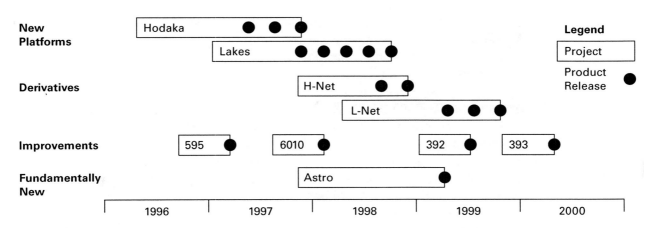

EXHIBIT 4-2   The product plan identifies the portfolio of projects to be pursued by the development organization. This plan divides projects into four categories: new platforms, derivatives of existing platforms, product improvements, and fundamentally new products.

chosen, timing of projects is outlined, and resources are allocated. Exhibit 4-2 is an example of a product plan listing products to be developed and indicating the time frame for each.

The product plan is regularly updated to reflect changes in the competitive environment, changes in technology, and information on the success of existing products. Product plans are developed with the company's goals, capabilities, constraints, and competitive environment in mind. Product planning decisions generally involve the senior management of the organization and may take place only annually or a few times each year. Some organizations have a director of planning who manages this process.

Organizations that do not carefully plan the portfolio of development projects to pursue are often plagued with inefficiencies such as:

- Inadequate coverage of target markets with competitive products.
- Poor timing of market introductions of products.
- Mismatches between aggregate development capacity and the number of projects pursued.
- Poor distribution of resources, with some projects overstaffed and others understaffed.
- Initiation and subsequent cancellation of ill-conceived projects.
- Frequent changes in the directions of projects.

Four Types of Product Development Projects

Product development projects can be classified as four types:

- *New product platforms:* This type of project involves a major development effort to create a new family of products based on a new, common platform. The new product family would address familiar markets and product categories. The Xerox Lakes project, aimed at the development of a new, digital copier platform, is an example of this type of project.

- *Derivatives of existing product platforms:* These projects extend an existing product platform to better address familiar markets with one or more new products. To develop a new copier based on an existing light-lens (not digital) product platform would be an example of this type of project.

- *Incremental improvements to existing products:* These projects may only involve adding or modifying some features of existing products to keep the product line current and competitive. A slight change to remedy minor flaws in an existing copier product would be an example of this type of project.

- *Fundamentally new products:* These projects involve radically different product or production technologies and may help to address new and unfamiliar markets. Such projects inherently involve more risk; however, the long-term success of the enterprise may depend on what is learned through these important projects. The first digital copier Xerox developed is an example of this type of project.

The Process

Exhibit 4-3 illustrates the steps in the product planning process. First, multiple opportunities are prioritized and a set of promising projects is selected. Resources are allocated to these projects and they are scheduled. These planning activities focus on a *portfolio* of opportunities and potential projects and are sometimes referred to as portfolio management, aggregate product planning, product line planning, or product management. Once projects have been selected and resources allocated, a mission statement is developed for each project. The formulation of a product plan and the development of a mission statement therefore precede the actual product development process.

Although we show the planning process as essentially linear, the activities of selecting promising projects and allocating resources are inherently iterative. The realities of schedules and budgets often force a reassessment of priorities and further refinement and culling of potential projects. The product plan is therefore reevaluated frequently and should be modified based on the latest information from development teams, research laboratories, production, marketing, and service organizations. People involved later in the process are often the first to realize that something about the overall plan or a project's mission is inconsistent, infeasible, or out of date. The ability to adjust the product plan over time is vital to the long-term success of the enterprise.

EXHIBIT 4-3   The product planning process. These activities address a portfolio of product development projects, resulting in a product plan and, for each selected project, a mission statement.

To develop a product plan and project mission statements, we suggest a five-step process:

1. Identify opportunities.
2. Evaluate and prioritize projects.
3. Allocate resources and plan timing.
4. Complete pre-project planning.
5. Reflect on the results and the process.

Step 1: Identify Opportunities

The planning process begins with the identification of product development opportunities. Such opportunities may involve any of the four types of projects defined above. This step can be thought of as the *opportunity funnel* because it brings together inputs from across the enterprise. Opportunities may be collected passively, but we also recommend that the firm explicitly attempt to generate opportunities. Chapter 3, Opportunity Identification, provides a process for generating, recognizing, and evaluating opportunities.

When employed actively, the opportunity funnel collects ideas continuously, and new product opportunities may arise at any time. As a way of tracking, sorting, and refining these opportunities, we recommend that each promising opportunity be described in a short, coherent statement and that this information be collected in a database. Several Web-based idea management systems are available for gathering and storing information on opportunities, although a simple list in a spreadsheet may be sufficient.

At Xerox, many opportunities had been gathered and discussed. Some were simple enhancements to existing products, and others were proposals for products based on entirely new technologies. Following are some examples of opportunity statements similar to those proposed at Xerox:

- Create a document distribution system in which a networked printing device resides on each office worker's desk and automatically delivers mail and other documents.
- Create document delivery software that allows the digital delivery and storage of most intraorganizational documents via a worker's personal computer.

This opportunity statement eventually became the Lakes project:

- Develop a new black and white (B&W), digital, networkable, document center platform for the office market, including scanning, storage, fax, distribution, and printing capabilities.

Step 2: Evaluate and Prioritize Projects

If managed actively, the opportunity funnel can collect hundreds or even thousands of opportunities during a year. Some of these opportunities do not make sense in the context of the firm's other activities, and in most cases, there are simply too many opportunities for the firm to pursue at once. The second step in the product planning process is therefore to select the most promising projects to pursue. Four basic perspectives are useful in evaluating and prioritizing opportunities for new products in existing product categories: competitive strategy, market segmentation, technological trajectories, and product platforms. After discussing these four perspectives, we then discuss evaluating opportunities for fundamentally new products, and how to balance the portfolio of projects.

Competitive Strategy

An organization's *competitive strategy* defines a basic approach to markets and products with respect to competitors. The choice of which opportunities to pursue can be guided by this strategy. Most firms devote much discussion at senior management levels to their strategic competencies and the ways in which they aim to compete. Several strategies are possible, such as:

- *Technology leadership:* To implement this strategy, the firm places great emphasis on basic research and development of new technologies and on the deployment of these technologies through product development.

- *Cost leadership:* This strategy requires the firm to compete on production efficiency, either through economies of scale, use of superior manufacturing methods, low-cost labor, or better management of the production system. Design for manufacturing methods (see Chapter 11) are therefore emphasized in the product (and process) development activities under this strategy.

- *Customer focus:* To follow this strategy, the firm works closely with new and existing customers to assess their changing needs and preferences. Carefully designed product platforms facilitate the rapid development of derivative products with new features or functions of interest to customers. This strategy may result in a broad product line featuring high product variety to address the needs of heterogeneous customer segments.

- *Imitative:* This strategy involves closely following trends in the market, allowing competitors to explore which new products are successful for each segment. When viable opportunities have been identified, the firm quickly launches new products to imitate the successful competitors. A fast development process is essential to effectively implement this strategy.

At Xerox, strategic discussions centered around how the company would participate in the digital revolution of the office associated with growth of the Internet. Xerox believed that the Internet would enable a paradigm shift in business practices from one of "print and then distribute" to one of "distribute and then print." The Lakes project would need to support this corporate vision.

Market Segmentation

Customers can be usefully thought of as belonging to distinct market segments. Dividing a market into segments allows the firm to consider the actions of competitors and the strength of the firm's existing products with respect to each well-defined group of customers. By mapping competitors' products and the firm's own

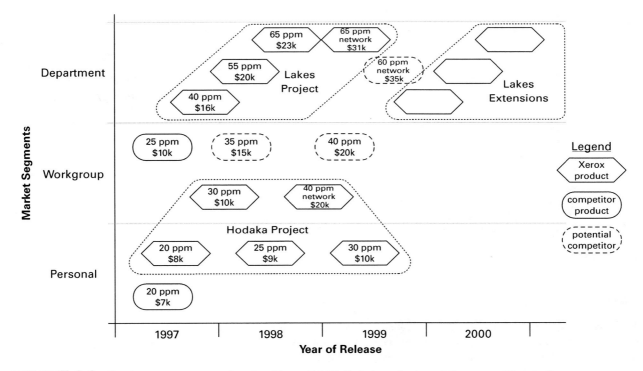

EXHIBIT 4-4 Product segment map showing Xerox B&W digital products and the competition in three market segments: personal, workgroup, and department machines. Key performance dimensions (pages per minute, networking capability) and price points are listed for each product in the map, along with the time of its market introduction.

products onto segments, the firm can assess which product opportunities best address weaknesses in its own product line and which exploit weaknesses in the offerings of competitors. Exhibit 4-4 shows a *product segment map* of this type for some Xerox products in which markets are segmented according to the number of users sharing office equipment.

Technological Trajectories

In technology-intensive businesses, a key product planning decision is when to adopt a new basic technology in a product line. For example, in the document business, the key technological issue at the turn of the century was the shift to digital image processing and printing. The product planning decision was when to develop digital products, as opposed to developing another product based on light-lens technology. *Technology S-curves* are a conceptual tool to help think about such decisions.

The technology S-curve displays the performance of the products in a product category over time, usually with respect to a single performance variable such as resolution, speed, or reliability. The S-curve illustrates a basic but important concept: Technologies evolve from initial emergence when performance is relatively low, through rapid growth in performance based on experience, and finally approach maturity where some natural

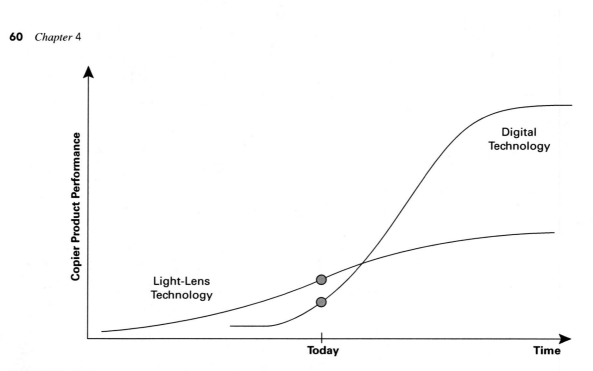

EXHIBIT 4-5   This technology S-curve illustrates that Xerox believed digital copier technologies were just emerging and would improve product performance in the coming years. Xerox believed that it could develop a full-featured digital copier in the near future with performance exceeding that of light-lens copiers.

technological limit is reached and the technology may become obsolete. The S-shaped trajectory captures this general dynamic, as shown in Exhibit 4-5. The horizontal axis may be cumulative research and development effort or time; the vertical axis may be a performance/cost ratio or any important performance dimension. While S-curves characterize technological change remarkably well in a wide variety of industries, it is often difficult to predict the future trajectory of the performance curve (how near or far is the ultimate performance limit).

Product Platform Planning

The product platform is the set of assets shared across a set of products. Components and subassemblies are often the most important of these assets. An effective platform can allow a variety of derivative products to be created more rapidly and easily, with each product providing the features and functions desired by a particular market segment. See Chapter 10, Product Architecture, for more discussion of the underlying architecture enabling the product platform and for a platform planning method.

Because platform development projects can take from 2 to 10 times as much time and money as derivative product development projects, a firm cannot afford to make every project a new platform. Exhibit 4-6 illustrates the leverage of an effective product platform. The critical strategic decision at this stage is whether a project will develop a derivative product from an existing platform or develop an entirely new platform. Decisions

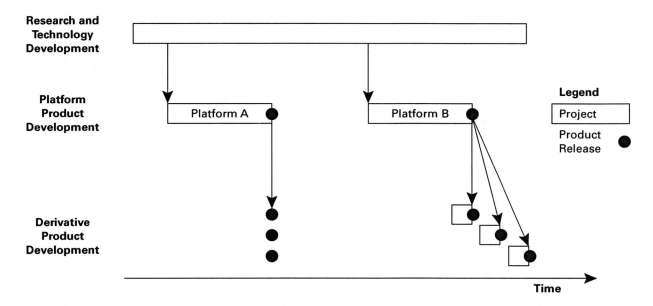

EXHIBIT 4-6   A platform development project creates the architecture of a family of products. Derivative products may be included in the initial platform development effort (Platform A) or derivative products may follow thereafter (Platform B).

about product platforms are very closely related to the technology development efforts of the firm and to decisions about which technologies to employ in new products.

One technique for coordinating technology development with product planning is the *technology roadmap.* A technology roadmap is a way to represent the expected availability and future use of various technologies relevant to the product being considered. This method has been used by Motorola, Philips, Xerox, and other leaders in fast-moving high-technology industries. The method is particularly useful for planning products in which the critical functional elements are well known in advance.

To create a technology roadmap, multiple generations of technologies are labeled and arranged along a time line, as shown in Exhibit 4-7. The technology roadmap can be augmented with the timing of projects and projects that would utilize these technological developments. (This is sometimes then called a *product–technology roadmap.*) The result is a diagram showing a product's key functional elements and the sequence of technologies expected to implement these elements over a given period of time. Technology roadmapping can serve as a planning tool to create a joint strategy between technology development and product development.

Evaluating Fundamentally New Product Opportunities

In addition to new versions of products in existing product categories, the firm faces many opportunities in either new markets or fundamentally new technologies. While investing scarce resources in the development of products using new technologies or for new markets is quite risky, some such investments are necessary to periodically

62   *Chapter* 4

EXHIBIT 4-7   This technology roadmap shows the life cycles of several digital photocopying technologies and identifies which technologies would be used in each product. For the Lakes platform, Xerox selected technologies for critical functions that could be extended to the higher speeds and color capability required of its derivative products.

rejuvenate the product portfolio (Christensen, 1997). Some criteria for evaluating fundamentally new product opportunities include:

- Market size (units/year × average price).
- Market growth rate (percent per year).
- Competitive intensity (number of competitors and their strengths).
- Depth of the firm's existing knowledge of the market.
- Depth of the firm's existing knowledge of the technology.
- Fit with the firm's other products.
- Fit with the firm's capabilities.

- Potential for patents, trade secrets, or other barriers to competition.
- Existence of a product champion within the firm.

While these criteria are particularly useful in evaluating fundamentally new product opportunities, they also apply generally to evaluating any product opportunity. These criteria can be used in a simple screening matrix to evaluate the overall attractiveness and types of risk for any given opportunity. Chapter 3, Opportunity Identification, includes the Real-Win-Worth-it analysis for opportunities, an example of criteria-based evaluation. Chapter 8, Concept Selection, describes screening matrices for selecting product concepts, but this method is directly applicable to selecting product opportunities as well.

Balancing the Portfolio

There are many methods to help managers manage an organization's portfolio of development projects. Several of these methods involve mapping the portfolio along useful dimensions so that managers may consider the strategic implications of their planning decisions. Cooper et al. (2001) describe numerous mapping approaches involving dimensions such as technical risk, financial return, market attractiveness, and the like. One particularly useful mapping, suggested by Wheelwright and Clark (1992), plots the portfolio of projects along two specific dimensions: the extent to which the project involves a change in the product line and the extent to which the project involves a change in production processes. Exhibit 4-8

Steven C. Wheelwright and Kim B. Clark, "Creating Plans to Focus Product Development," *Harvard Business Review*, March–April 1992, pp. 70–82

EXHIBIT 4-8   Product–process change matrix. The size of the circles indicates the relative cost of the development projects.

illustrates this mapping, called a *product–process change matrix*. This perspective can be useful to illuminate imbalances in the portfolio of projects under consideration and in assessing the consistency between a portfolio of projects and the competitive strategy. For example, a firm may discover that it has identified essentially no breakthrough opportunities or that it has no projects aimed at incremental improvements to existing products.

There are no general procedures for deciding exactly what the portfolio should look like; however, the firm's choice of competitive strategy should affect the shape of the product development portfolio. For example, a firm pursuing a low-cost strategy would expect the portfolio to contain more production process improvement projects. Firms following a strategy requiring high product variety would need to develop many derivative products based upon existing platforms. Firms implementing a strategy based on technological superiority may need to have a portfolio including more technology development and breakthrough projects in anticipation that not all of these risky projects will result in marketable new products. Note that planning research and technology development activities is closely coupled to, but generally outside the purview of, the product planning process.

Step 3: Allocate Resources and Plan Timing

It is likely that the firm cannot afford to invest in every product development opportunity in its desired balanced portfolio of projects. As timing and resource allocation are determined for the most promising projects, too many projects will invariably compete for too few resources. As a result, the attempt to assign resources and plan timing almost always results in a return to the prior evaluation and prioritization step to prune the set of projects to be pursued.

Resource Allocation

Many organizations take on too many projects without regard for the limited availability of development resources. As a result, skilled engineers and managers are assigned to more and more projects, productivity drops off dramatically, projects take longer to complete, products become late to the market, and profits are lower. *Aggregate planning* helps an organization make efficient use of its resources by pursuing only those projects that can reasonably be completed with the budgeted resources.

The Lakes project was only one of many projects proposed at Xerox; however, because Lakes involved the development of an entirely new platform, this project was substantially larger than the other projects being considered at the time. Any feasible portfolio of projects would be dominated by the resource demands of the Lakes platform development effort. In fact, for the managers at Xerox to find the resources necessary to execute Lakes, many other projects had to be eliminated or postponed until engineers were finished working on Lakes.

Estimating the resources required for each of the projects in the plan by month, quarter, or year forces the organization to face the realities of finite resources. In most cases, the primary resource to be managed is the effort of the development staff, usually expressed in person-hours or person-months. Other critical resources may also require careful planning, such as model shop facilities, rapid prototyping equipment, pilot production lines, testing facilities, and so on. Estimates of required resources in each period can be compared with available resources to compute an overall capacity utilization ratio (demand/capacity) as well as utilizations by resource types, as shown in Exhibit 4-9.

	Year 1					Year 2					Year 3				
	Mechanical Design	Electrical Engineering	Manufacturing Engineering	Software/Firmware	Industrial Design	Mechanical Design	Electrical Engineering	Manufacturing Engineering	Software/Firmware	Industrial Design	Mechanical Design	Electrical Engineering	Manufacturing Engineering	Software/Firmware	Industrial Design
Lakes Project	155	160	105	75	7	210	160	140	80	4	125	140	160	90	2
6010 Project	30	25	10	5	1	25	20	5	6	2			5		
595 Project	60	24	25			20	15	15							
Astro Project	55	60	44	25	2	75	65	50	40	2	45	40	60	20	
Resource Demand	300	269	184	105	10	330	260	210	126	6	170	180	225	110	2
Resource Capacity	250	250	200	100	8	250	250	200	100	8	250	250	200	100	8
Capacity Utilization	120%	108%	92%	105%	125%	132%	104%	105%	126%	75%	68%	72%	113%	110%	25%

EXHIBIT 4-9 Aggregate resource planning can be achieved using a simple spreadsheet method based on estimates of resource demands over time. This example spreadsheet uses units of person-years, although smaller time units (quarters or months) are commonly used in practice. The associated chart highlights where capacity is insufficient to handle all of the projects.

Where utilization exceeds 100 percent, there are not sufficient resources to execute all of the projects in the plan on schedule. In fact, to allow for contingencies and to enable responsiveness, planned capacity utilization may be below 100 percent.

In the aggregate planning process, an organization may find that it is in danger of over-committing resources (often by as much as 100 percent or more, according to Wheelwright and Clark, 1992). Therefore the organization must decide in the planning stage which projects are most important to the success of the firm, and pursue those with adequate resources. Other projects may need to be eliminated from the plan or shifted in time.

Project Timing

Determining the timing and sequence of projects, sometimes called *pipeline management,* must consider a number of factors, including:

- *Timing of product introductions:* Generally the sooner a product is brought to market the better; however, launching a product before it is of adequate quality can damage the reputation of the firm.
- *Technology readiness:* The robustness of the underlying technologies plays a critical role in the planning process. A proven, robust technology can be integrated into products much more quickly and reliably.
- *Market readiness:* The sequence of product introductions determines whether early adopters buy the low-end product and may trade up or whether they buy the high-end product offered at a high initial price. Releasing improvements too quickly can frustrate customers who want to keep up; on the other hand, releasing new products too slowly risks lagging behind competitors.
- *Competition:* The anticipated release of competing products may accelerate the timing of development projects.

The Product Plan

The set of projects approved by the planning process, sequenced in time, becomes the *product plan,* as shown earlier in Exhibit 4-2. The plan may include a mix of fundamentally new products, platform projects, and derivative projects of varying size. Product plans are updated on a periodic basis, perhaps quarterly or annually, as part of the firm's strategic planning activity.

Step 4: Complete Pre-Project Planning

Once the project has been approved, but before substantial resources are applied, a pre-project planning activity takes place. This activity involves a small, cross-functional team of people, often known as the *core team.* The Lakes core team consisted of approximately 30 people representing a wide range of technical expertise, marketing, manufacturing, and service functions.

At this point, the earlier opportunity statement may be rewritten as a *product vision statement.* The Lakes concept team began with the following product vision statement:

Develop a networked, mid-range, digital platform for imaging, marking, and finishing.

The objective defined by a product vision statement may be very general. It may not say which specific new technologies should be used, nor does it necessarily specify the goals and constraints of functions such as production and service operations. To provide

EXHIBIT 4-10
Mission statement for the Lakes project. This document summarizes the direction to be followed by the product development team. Many more details are appended to this mission statement, including the environmental goals, service objectives, and specific technologies identified for use in the Lakes platform.

Mission Statement: Multifunctional Office Document Machine	
Product Description	• Networkable, digital machine with copy, print, fax, and scan functions
Benefit Proposition	• Multiple document processing functions in one machine • Connected to office computer network
Key Business Goals	• Support Xerox strategy of leadership in digital office equipment • Serve as platform for all future B&W digital products and solutions • Capture 50% of digital product sales in primary market • Environmentally friendly • First product introduction 4th Q 1997
Primary Market	• Office departments, mid-volume (40–65 ppm, above 42,000 avg. copies/mo.)
Secondary Markets	• Quick-print market • Small "satellite" operations
Assumptions and Constraints	• New product platform • Digital imaging technology • Compatible with CentreWare software • Input devices manufactured in Canada • Output devices manufactured in Brazil • Image processing engine manufactured in both the United States and Europe
Stakeholders	• Purchasers and users • Manufacturing operations • Service operations • Distributors and resellers

clear guidance for the product development organization, generally the team formulates a more detailed definition of the target market and of the assumptions under which the development team will operate. These decisions are captured in a *mission statement*, a summary of which is illustrated in Exhibit 4-10.

Mission Statements

The mission statement may include some or all of the following information:

- *Brief (one-sentence) description of the product:* This description identifies the basic function of the product but avoids implying a specific product concept. It may, in fact, be the product vision statement.

- *Benefit proposition:* This element of the mission statement articulates the critical few reasons a customer would buy the product. To some extent this is a hypothesis, which will be validated during the concept development process.

- *Key business goals:* In addition to the project goals that support the corporate strategy, these goals generally include goals for time, cost, and quality (e.g., timing of the product introduction, desired financial performance, market share targets).

- *Target market(s) for the product:* There may be several target markets for the product. This part of the mission statement identifies the primary market as well as any secondary markets that should be considered in the development effort.
- *Assumptions and constraints that guide the development effort:* Assumptions must be made carefully; although they restrict the range of possible product concepts, they help to maintain a manageable project scope. Information may be attached to the mission statement to document decisions about assumptions and constraints.
- *Stakeholders:* One way to ensure that many of the subtle development issues are addressed is to explicitly list all of the product's stakeholders; that is, all of the groups of people who are affected by the product's success or failure. The stakeholder list begins with the end user (the ultimate external customer) and the external customer who makes the buying decision about the product. Stakeholders also include the customers of the product who reside within the firm, such as the sales force, the service organization, and the production departments. The list of stakeholders serves as a reminder for the team to consider the needs of everyone who will be influenced by the product.

Assumptions and Constraints

In creating the mission statement, the team considers the strategies of several functional areas within the firm. Of the many possible functional strategies to consider, the manufacturing, service, and environmental strategies had the largest influence on the Lakes project. In fact, these strategies guided the core technical developments of the product.

One could reasonably ask why manufacturing, service, and environmental strategies (for example) should be part of the mission statement for a new product. An alternative view is that decisions about these issues should arise from the customer needs for the new product and should not be determined in advance. First, for extremely complex projects, like Lakes, the design of the manufacturing system is a project of similar magnitude to the design of the product itself. As a result, the manufacturing facilities involved in the product need to be identified very early in the process. Second, some product requirements may not be derived strictly from customer needs. For example, most customers will not directly express a need for low environmental impact; however, Xerox chose to adopt a corporate policy of environmentally responsible design. In such cases, the mission statement should reflect such corporate objectives and constraints.

Following are some of the issues that Xerox considered in establishing assumptions and constraints for the Lakes project.

- *Manufacturing:* Even at this very preliminary stage, it is important to consider the capabilities, capacities, and constraints of the manufacturing operations. A broad array of questions may be relevant, including: Which internal production facilities might be used to manufacture and assemble the product? What key suppliers should be involved in the development, and when? Are the existing production systems capable of producing the new technologies that have been identified for the product? For Lakes, Xerox assumed that input devices would be manufactured at production sites in Canada, output devices in Brazil, and the digital image processing engine in both the United States and Europe.
- *Service:* In a business where customer service and service revenue are critical to the success of the firm, it is necessary to also state strategic goals for levels of service

quality. Efforts to improve service include a strategic commitment to designing products that contain few parts, which can be serviced quickly. For Lakes, serviceability goals included reducing both the number of field-replaceable modules required to fully service the machine and the time to install them by an order of magnitude.

- *Environment:* Many corporations today are developing new products with environmental sustainability in mind. The Lakes concept team adopted Xerox's first "zero to land-fill" policy, an aggressive goal even for a leader in environmental design practices such as Xerox. The stated goal was that no components from a Lakes product should ever go to a landfill. All components would be either remanufacturable or recyclable, or both. No parts should be disposed of by customers. The Lakes environmental design strategy also included an energy efficiency goal to be the "most efficient machine in its class."

Staffing and Other Pre-Project Planning Activities

The pre-project planning activity also generally addresses project staffing and leadership. This may involve getting key members of the development staff to "sign up" for a new project; that is, to agree to commit to leading the development of the product or of a critical element of the product. Budgets are also generally established during pre-project planning.

For fundamentally new products, budgets and staffing plans will be for the concept development phase of development only. This is because the details of the project are highly uncertain until the basic concept for the new product has been established. More detailed planning will occur when and if the concept is developed further.

Step 5: Reflect on the Results and the Process

In this final step of the planning and strategy process, the team should ask several questions to assess the quality of both the process and the results. Some suggested questions are:

- Is the opportunity funnel collecting an exciting and diverse set of product opportunities?
- Does the product plan support the competitive strategy of the firm?
- Does the product plan address the most important current opportunities facing the firm?
- Are the total resources allocated to product development sufficient to pursue the firm's competitive strategy?
- Have creative ways of leveraging finite resources been considered, such as the use of product platforms, joint ventures, and partnerships with suppliers?
- Does the core team accept the challenges of the resulting mission statement?
- Are the elements of the mission statement consistent?
- Are the assumptions listed in the mission statement really necessary or is the project overconstrained? Will the development team have the freedom to develop the best possible product?
- How can the product planning process be improved?

Because the mission statement is the handoff to the development team, a "reality check" must be performed before proceeding with the development process. This early stage is the time to remedy known flaws, lest they become more severe and expensive as the development process progresses.

70   *Chapter* 4

This chapter explains the product planning method as a stepwise process, largely for simplicity of the presentation; however, reflection and criticism of consistency and fit should be an ongoing process. Steps in the process can and should be executed simultaneously to make sure that the many plans and decisions are consistent with one another and with the goals, capabilities, and constraints of the firm.

Summary

- Product planning is a periodic process that considers the portfolio of product development projects to be executed.
- Product planning involves a five-step process:

  1. Identify opportunities.
  2. Evaluate and prioritize projects.
  3. Allocate resources and plan timing.
  4. Complete pre-project planning.
  5. Reflect on the results and the process.

- The opportunity funnel collects possibilities for new product platforms, enhancements, and fundamentally new products from several sources within and outside the firm.
- Potential product development projects are evaluated based on the organization's competitive strategy, technological trajectories, and product platform plans.
- A balanced portfolio of development projects may include investments in breakthrough products, new platforms, derivatives, and current product support.
- Aggregate planning ensures that selected projects have adequate resources for successful completion.
- A mission statement for each product development project documents the product description, benefit proposition, business goals, target markets, critical assumptions, and the product's stakeholders.

References and Bibliography

Many current resources are available on the Internet via
www.ulrich-eppinger.net

There are many excellent books on competitive strategy. These selections include discussions related to product planning.

Day, George S., *Market Driven Strategy: Processes for Creating Value,* The Free Press, New York, 1990.

Moore, Geoffrey A., *Crossing the Chasm: Marketing and Selling Technology Products to Mainstream Customers,* third edition, Harper Business, New York, 2014.

Porter, Michael E., *Competitive Advantage: Creating and Sustaining Superior Performance,* The Free Press, New York, 1985.

Treacy, Michael, and Fred Wiersema, *The Discipline of Market Leaders,* Basic Books, New York, 1997.

Wheelwright and Clark discuss several of the dimensions of product planning presented here, including aggregate planning and some mapping methods.

Wheelwright, Steven C., and Kim B. Clark, "Creating Plans to Focus Product Development," *Harvard Business Review,* March–April 1992, pp. 70–82.

Cooper, Edgett, and Kleinschmidt describe a wide range of product portfolio management methods, including financial analysis, scoring techniques, and visual mapping methods.

Cooper, Robert G., Scott J. Edgett, and Elko J. Kleinschmidt, *Portfolio Management for New Products,* second edition, Basic Books, New York, 2001.

Fine relates product planning and competitive strategy to the decisions of supply-chain design and strategic partnerships with suppliers.

Fine, Charles H., *Clockspeed: Winning Control in the Age of Temporary Advantage,* Perseus Books, Reading, MA, 1998.

McGrath emphasizes planning of product platforms and strategy for technology-based products.

McGrath, Michael E., *Product Strategy for High-Technology Companies,* second edition, McGraw-Hill, New York, 2000.

Reinertsen focuses particular attention on the issue of excess utilization of aggregate development capacity.

Reinertsen, Donald G., *Managing the Design Factory: The Product Developer's Toolkit,* The Free Press, New York, 1997.

Marketing texts include a more detailed treatment of market strategy, market analysis, and product planning.

Crawford, C. Merle, and Anthony Di Benedetto, *New Products Management,* eleventh edition, McGraw-Hill, New York, 2014.

Urban, Glen L., and John R. Hauser, *Design and Marketing of New Products,* second edition, Prentice Hall, Englewood Cliffs, NJ, 1993.

Foster developed the S-curve concept and provides many interesting examples from a diverse set of industries.

Foster, Richard N., *Innovation: The Attacker's Advantage,* Summit Books, New York, 1986.

Burgelman and Maidique provide a very good discussion of technology S-curves and stress that these life-cycle curves are not predetermined; rather, they can be influenced by technical development efforts.

Burgelman, Robert A., Clayton M. Christensen, Modesto A. Maidique, and Steven C. Wheelwright, *Strategic Management of Technology and Innovation,* fourth edition, McGraw-Hill, New York, 2003.

Several authors present a more thorough discussion of product platform planning in various industries.

Meyer, Marc H., and Alvin P. Lehnerd, *The Power of Product Platforms,* The Free Press, New York, 1997.

Sanderson, Susan W., and Mustafa Uzumeri, *Managing Product Families,* Irwin, Chicago, 1997.

72   *Chapter* 4

Managers at Motorola and Philips describe their use of several technology roadmapping methods for integrating the planning of technology development and product development.

Groenveld, Pieter, "Roadmapping Integrates Business and Technology," *Research-Technology Management,* Vol. 40, No. 5, Sep./Oct. 1997, pp. 48–55.

Willyard, Charles H., and Cheryl W. McClees, "Motorola's Technology Roadmap Process," *Research Management,* Vol. 30, No. 5, Sep./Oct. 1987, pp. 13–19.

Christensen provides evidence that firms must invest in fundamentally new products, technologies, and markets to remain at the leading edge of their industries.

Christensen, Clayton M., *The Innovator's Dilemma: When New Technologies Cause Great Firms to Fail,* Harvard Business School Press, Boston, 1997.

Exercises

1. Conduct a search using the Internet or published corporate annual reports to identify the corporate strategy of a company in which you might be interested in investing. Learn about the firm's product lines and its newest products. How do these products support the corporate strategy? What types of projects would you expect to see in the product plan?

2. Create a product–technology roadmap illustrating the availability of technologies for a class of products you understand well, such as personal computers.

Thought Questions

1. How might a portfolio of development projects differ if the firm believes a particular product technology is currently at position A or B on the technology S-curve shown below?

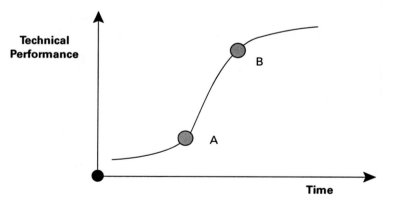

2. How might Xerox be able to address the shortage of mechanical design engineers identified by the aggregate project planning analysis shown in Exhibit 4-9? List five ways Xerox could increase the capacity and five ways to reduce the demand for mechanical design engineers.

CHAPTER FIVE

Identifying Customer Needs

EXHIBIT 5-1
The Nest learning thermostat, which programs itself based on patterns of activity in the home.

Tony Fadell had been a product development leader at Apple for more than a decade, participating in the creation of the iPod portable music player and the iPhone smartphone. After leaving Apple, he contemplated entrepreneurial opportunities and eventually decided to create a better thermostat for control of home heating and cooling systems. Exhibit 5-1 shows the Nest Learning Thermostat, the first product he and his team created from their new company, Nest Labs.

The Nest team aspired to create the best thermostat on the market, and knew that understanding and delivering on customer needs was key to success. The Nest thermostat was extremely well received in the marketplace, and just three years after its formation, Nest Labs was acquired by Google for $3.2 billion, representing a phenomenal financial outcome for the young company.

This chapter presents a method for comprehensively identifying a set of customer needs, and is built around the example of creating a better thermostat.

The goals of the method are to:

- Ensure that the product is focused on customer needs.
- Identify latent or hidden needs as well as explicit needs.
- Provide a fact base for justifying the product specifications.
- Create an archival record of the needs activity of the development process.
- Ensure that no critical customer need is missed or forgotten.
- Develop a common understanding of customer needs among members of the development team.

The philosophy behind the method is to create a high-quality information channel that runs directly between customers in the target market and the developers of the product. This philosophy is built on the premise that those who directly control the details of the product, including the engineers and industrial designers, must interact with customers and experience the *use environment* of the product. Without this direct experience, technical trade-offs are not likely to be made correctly, innovative solutions to customer needs may never be discovered, and the development team may never develop a deep commitment to meeting customer needs.

The process of identifying customer needs is an integral part of the larger product development process and is very closely related to opportunity identification, product planning, concept generation, concept selection, competitive benchmarking, and the establishment of product specifications. The customer-needs activity is shown in Exhibit 5-2 in

EXHIBIT 5-2   The customer-needs activity in relation to other concept development activities.

relation to these other front-end product development activities, which collectively can be thought of as the *concept development* phase.

The concept development process illustrated in Exhibit 5-2 implies a distinction between customer needs and product specifications. This distinction is subtle but important. *Needs* are largely independent of any particular product we might develop; they are not specific to the concept we eventually choose to pursue. A team should be able to identify customer needs without knowing if or how it will eventually address those needs. On the other hand, *specifications* do depend on the concept we select. The specifications for the product we finally choose to develop will depend on what is technically and economically feasible and on what our competitors offer in the marketplace, as well as on customer needs. (See Chapter 6, Product Specifications, for a more detailed discussion of this distinction.) Also note that we choose to use the word *need* to label any attribute of a potential product that is desired by the customer; we do not distinguish here between a want and a need. Other terms used in industrial practice to refer to customer needs include *customer attributes* and *customer requirements*.

The Importance of Latent Needs

Latent needs are those not yet widely recognized by most customers, and not yet fulfilled by existing products. The needs exist, and if fulfilled, would result in greater customer satisfaction, yet they remain largely unknown. For instance, prior to the year 2000, mobile telephones did not contain cameras. Most consumers did not know that they wanted to be able to take photographs with their telephones; however, that need was real, and became a differentiating feature of telephones that fulfilled it. The ability to recognize latent needs is therefore a critical capability in product development, giving firms the ability to create products that surprise and delight customers. Of course, once latent needs are revealed through successful products that fulfill them, they become widely adopted and become "must haves." By 2010, essentially all mobile computing devices could take photographs.

The Process of Identifying Customer Needs

Identifying customer needs is itself a process, for which we present a five-step method. We believe that a little structure goes a long way in facilitating effective product development practices, and we hope and expect that this method will be viewed by those who employ it not as a rigid process but rather as a starting point for continuous improvement and refinement. The five steps are:

1. Gather raw data from customers.
2. Interpret the raw data in terms of customer needs.
3. Organize the needs into a hierarchy of primary, secondary, and (if necessary) tertiary needs.
4. Establish the relative importance of the needs.
5. Reflect on the results and the process.

In this chapter, we treat each of the five steps in turn and illustrate key points with the thermostat example. We chose the thermostat because it is simple enough that the method is not hidden by the complexity of the example; however, note that the same method, with minor adaptation, has been successfully applied to many kinds of products ranging from kitchen utensils costing less than $10 to machine tools costing hundreds of thousands of dollars.

Before beginning the development project, the firm typically specifies a particular market opportunity and lays out the broad constraints and objectives for the project. This information is frequently formalized as a *mission statement* (also sometimes called a *charter* or a *design brief*). The mission statement specifies which direction to go in but generally does not specify a precise destination or a particular way to proceed. The mission statement is the result of the product planning activities described in Chapter 4, Product Planning. The mission statement for a thermostat is shown in Exhibit 5-3.

The thermostat category of products is already relatively well developed. Such products are particularly well suited to a structured process for gathering customer needs. One could reasonably ask whether a structured method is effective for completely new categories of products with which customers have no experience. Satisfying needs is just as important in revolutionary products as in incremental products. A necessary condition for product success is that a product offer perceived benefits to the customer. Products offer benefits when they satisfy needs. This is true whether the product is an incremental variation on an existing product or whether it is a completely new product based on a revolutionary invention. Developing an entirely new category of product is a risky undertaking, and to some extent the only real indication of whether customer needs have been identified correctly is whether customers like the team's first prototypes. Nevertheless, in our opinion, a structured method for gathering data from customers remains useful and can lower the inherent risk in developing a radically new product. Whether or not customers are able to fully articulate their true needs, interaction with customers in the target market will help the development team build a personal understanding of the user's environment and point of view. This information is always useful, even if it does not result in the identification of every need the new product will address.

EXHIBIT 5-3
Mission statement for the thermostat.

Mission Statement: Thermostat Project	
Product Description	• Thermostat for residential use.
Benefit Proposition	• Simple to use, attractive, and saves energy.
Key Business Goals	• Product introduced in fourth quarter of 2012. • 50% gross margin. • 10% share of replacement thermostat market by 2016.
Primary Market	• Residential consumer.
Secondary Markets	• Heating, ventilation, and air conditioning contractors doing residential work.
Assumptions	• Replacement for an existing thermostat. • Compatible with most existing systems and wiring.
Stakeholders	• User • Retailer • Sales force • Service center • Production • Legal department

Step 1: Gather Raw Data from Customers

Consistent with our basic philosophy of creating a high-quality information channel directly from the customer, gathering data involves contact with customers and experience with the use environment of the product. Three methods are commonly used:

1. *Interviews:* One or more development team members discusses needs with a single customer. Interviews are usually conducted in the customer's environment and typically last one to two hours.

2. *Focus groups:* A moderator facilitates a two-hour discussion with a group of 8 to 12 customers. Focus groups are typically conducted in a special room equipped with a transparent mirror allowing several members of the development team to observe the group. In most cases, the moderator is a professional market researcher, but a member of the development team sometimes moderates. The proceedings are usually video recorded. Participants are usually paid a modest fee ($50 to $100 each) for their attendance. The total cost of a focus group, including rental of the room, participant fees, video recording, and refreshments, is about $5,000. In most U.S. cities, firms that recruit participants, moderate focus groups, and/ or rent facilities are listed in directories and search engines under "Market Research."

3. *Observing the product in use:* Watching customers use an existing product or perform a task for which a new product is intended can reveal important details about customer needs. For example, watching a consumer replace an existing thermostat may reveal a mismatch in shapes between the new and old products causing unsightly discontinuities in the wall surface. Observation may be completely passive, without any direct interaction with the customer, or may involve working side by side with a customer, allowing members of the development team to develop firsthand experience using the product. Ideally, team members observe the product in the actual use environment. Procter & Gamble, for example, observes thousands of customers every year in their homes or workplaces to better understand their needs. For some products, such as do-it-yourself tools, actually using the products is simple and natural; for others, such as surgical instruments, the team may have to use the products on surrogate tasks (e.g., cutting fruit instead of human tissue when developing a new scalpel).

Some practitioners also rely on written surveys for gathering raw data. While a Web-based survey is quite useful later in the process, we cannot recommend this approach for initial efforts to identify customer needs; text-based surveys simply do not provide enough information about the use environment of the product, and they are generally ineffective in revealing unanticipated needs.

Research by Griffin and Hauser shows that one 2-hour focus group reveals about the same number of needs as two 1-hour interviews (Griffin and Hauser, 1993). (See Exhibit 5-4.) Because interviews are usually less costly (per hour) than focus groups and because an interview often allows the product development team to experience the use environment of the product, we recommend that interviews be the primary data collection method. Interviews may be supplemented with one or two focus groups as a way to allow top management to observe a group of customers or as a mechanism for sharing a common customer experience (via video) with the members of a larger team. Some practitioners believe that for certain products and customer groups, the interactions among the participants of focus groups can elicit more varied needs than are revealed through interviews, although this belief is not strongly supported by research findings.

78   *Chapter 5*

EXHIBIT 5-4
Comparison of
the percentages
of customer
needs that are
revealed for
focus groups
and interviews
as a function of
the number of
sessions. Note
that a focus
group lasts two
hours, while an
interview lasts
one hour.

Source: Abbie Griffin
and John R. Hauser,
"The Voice of the
Customer," *Marketing
Science*, Vol. 12, No. 1,
Winter 1993, pp. 1–27

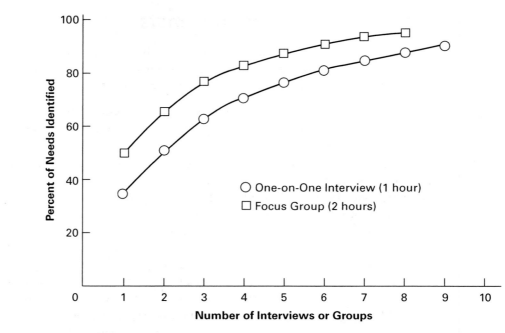

Choosing Customers

Griffin and Hauser also addressed the question of how many customers to interview to reveal most of the customer needs. In one study, they estimated that 90 percent of the customer needs for picnic coolers were revealed after 30 interviews. In another study, they estimated that 98 percent of the customer needs for a piece of office equipment were revealed after 25 hours of data collection in both focus groups and interviews. As a practical guideline for most products, conducting fewer than 10 interviews is probably inadequate and 50 interviews are probably too many; however, interviews can be conducted sequentially and the process can be terminated when no new needs are revealed by additional interviews. These guidelines apply to cases in which the development team is addressing a single market segment. If the team wishes to gather customer needs from multiple distinct segments, then the team may need to conduct 10 or more interviews in each segment. Concept development teams consisting of more than 10 people usually collect data from plenty of customers simply by involving much of the team in the process. For example, if a 10-person team is divided into five pairs and each pair conducts 6 interviews, the team conducts 30 interviews in total.

Needs can be identified more efficiently by interviewing *lead users* and/or extreme users. According to von Hippel, lead users are customers who experience needs months or years ahead of the majority of the market and stand to benefit substantially from product innovations (von Hippel, 1988). These customers are particularly useful sources of data for two reasons: (1) they are often able to articulate their emerging needs, because they have had to struggle with the inadequacies of existing products, and (2) they may have already invented solutions to meet their needs. By focusing a portion of the data collection efforts on lead users, the team may be able to identify needs that, although explicit for lead users, are still latent for the majority of the market. Developing products to meet these latent needs allows a firm to anticipate trends and to leapfrog competitive products.

EXHIBIT 5-5
Customer
selection matrix
for a thermostat
project.

	Lead Users	Users	Retailers
Homeowner	5	5	5
HVAC Contractor	5	5	

Gary Burchill, et al., Concept Engineering, Center for Quality of Management, Cambridge, MA, Document No. ML0080, 1997

Extreme users are those who use the product in unusual ways or who have special needs. For example, extreme users of the thermostat might be people who have limited vision or dexterity or those who need to vary temperatures many times each day. Extreme users can help the team identify needs that may be felt less acutely by the mainstream market, but are nevertheless important opportunities for competitive advantage. For example, entrepreneur Sam Farber created the original Good Grips vegetable peeler in response to the needs of his wife who suffered from arthritis. Her extreme needs proved to be a reflection of the latent need for more ergonomic kitchen tools among mainstream users.

The choice of which customers to interview is complicated when several different groups of people can be considered "the customer." For many products, one person (the buyer) makes the buying decision and another person (the user) actually uses the product. A good approach is to gather data from the end user of the product in all situations, and in cases where other types of customers and stakeholders are clearly important, to gather data from these people as well.

A customer selection matrix is useful for planning exploration of both market and customer variety. Burchill suggests that market segments be listed on the left side of the matrix while the different types of customers are listed across the top (Burchill et al., 1997), as shown in Exhibit 5-5. The number of intended customer contacts is entered in each cell to indicate the depth of coverage.

For industrial and commercial products, actually locating customers is usually a matter of making telephone calls or sending e-mail. In developing such products within an existing firm, a field sales force can often provide names of customers, although the team must be careful about biasing the selection of customers toward those with allegiances to a particular manufacturer. Online directories can be used to identify names of some types of customers for some classes of products (e.g., building contractors or insurance agents). For products that are integral to a customer's job, getting someone to agree to an interview is usually simple; these customers are eager to discuss their needs. For consumer products, customers can also be located through groups on social networks and via e-mail; however, arranging a set of interviews for consumer products generally requires more inquiries than for industrial or commercial products because the benefit of participating in an interview is less direct for these customers.

The Art of Eliciting Customer Needs Data

The techniques we present here are aimed primarily at interviewing end users, but these methods do apply to all of the three data-gathering modes and to all types of stakeholders. The basic approach is to be receptive to information provided by customers and to avoid confrontations or defensive posturing. Gathering needs data is very different from a sales call: the goal is to elicit an honest expression of needs, not to convince a customer of what he or she needs. In most cases customer interactions will be verbal; interviewers ask questions and the customer responds. A prepared interview guide is valuable for structuring this dialogue. Some helpful questions and prompts for use after the interviewers introduce themselves and explain the purpose of the interview are:

- When and why do you use this type of product?
- Walk us through a typical session using the product.
- What do you like about the existing products?
- What do you dislike about the existing products?
- What issues do you consider when purchasing the product?
- What improvements would you make to the product?

Here are some general hints for effective interaction with customers:

- *Go with the flow.* If the customer is providing useful information, do not worry about conforming to the interview guide. The goal is to gather important data on customer needs, not to complete the interview guide in the allotted time.
- *Use visual stimuli and props.* Bring a collection of existing and competitors' products, or even products that are tangentially related to the product under development. At the end of a session, the interviewers might even show some preliminary product concepts to get customers' early reactions to various approaches.
- *Suppress preconceived hypotheses about the product technology.* Frequently, customers will make assumptions about the product concept they expect would meet their needs. In these situations, the interviewers should avoid biasing the discussion with assumptions about how the product will eventually be designed or produced. When customers mention specific technologies or product features, the interviewer should probe for the underlying need the customer believes the suggested solution would satisfy.
- *Have the customer demonstrate the product and/or typical tasks related to the product.* If the interview is conducted in the use environment, a demonstration is usually convenient and invariably reveals new information.
- *Be alert for surprises and the expression of latent needs.* If a customer mentions something surprising, pursue the lead with follow-up questions. Frequently, an unexpected line of questioning will reveal the latent needs, the important dimensions of the customers' needs that are neither fulfilled nor commonly articulated and understood.
- *Watch for nonverbal information.* The process described in the chapter is aimed at developing better physical products. Unfortunately, words are not always the best way to communicate needs related to the physical world. This is particularly true of needs involving the human dimensions of the product, such as comfort, image, or style. The development team must be constantly aware of the nonverbal messages provided by customers. What are their facial expressions? How do they hold competitors' products?

Note that many of our suggested questions and guidelines assume that the customer has some familiarity with products similar to the new product under development. This is almost always true. For example, even before the first programmable thermostats became available, people controlled temperature over the course of the day. Developing an understanding of customer needs as they relate to the general temperature control task would still have been beneficial in developing the first programmable device. Similarly, understanding the needs of customers using other types of household devices such as coffeemakers or microwave ovens can be informative. We can think of no product so revolutionary that there would be no analogous products or tasks from which the development team could learn; however, in gathering needs relating to truly revolutionary products with which customers have no experience, the interview questions should be focused on the task or situation in which the new product will be applied, rather than on the product itself.

Documenting Interactions with Customers

Four methods are commonly used for documenting interactions with customers:

1. *Audio recording:* Making an audio recording of the interview is very easy. Unfortunately, transcribing the recording into text is very time consuming, and hiring someone to do it can be expensive. Also, audio recording has the disadvantage of being intimidating to some customers.

2. *Notes:* Handwritten notes are the most common method of documenting an interview. Designating one person as the primary note taker allows the other person to concentrate on effective questioning. The note taker should strive to capture some of the wording of every customer statement verbatim. These notes, if transcribed immediately after the interview, can be used to create a description of the interview that is very close to an actual transcript. This debriefing immediately after the interview also facilitates sharing of insights between the interviewers.

3. *Video recording:* Video recording is almost always used to document a focus group session. It is also very useful for documenting observations of the customer in the use environment and/or using existing products. The video recording is useful for bringing new team members "up to speed" and is also useful as raw material for presentations to upper management. Multiple viewings of video recordings of customers in action often facilitate the identification of latent customer needs. Video recording is also useful for capturing many aspects of the end user's environment.

4. *Still photography:* Taking photographs provides many of the benefits of video recording, but is usually less intrusive and therefore easier to do while observing customers in the field. Additional advantages of still photography are ease of display of the photos, excellent image quality, and readily available equipment. The primary disadvantage is the relative inability to record dynamic information.

The final result of the data-gathering phase of the process is a set of raw data, usually in the form of *customer statements* but frequently supplemented by video recordings or photographs. A data template implemented in a spreadsheet is useful for organizing these raw data. Exhibit 5-6 shows an example of a portion of such a template. We recommend that the template be filled in as soon as possible after the interaction with the customer and edited by the other development team members present during the interaction. The first column in the main body of the template indicates the question or prompt that elicited the customer data. The second column is a list of verbatim statements the customer made or an observation of a customer action (from a video recording or from direct observation). The third column contains the customer needs implied by the raw data. Some emphasis should be placed on investigating clues that may identify potential latent needs. Such clues may be in the form of humorous remarks, less serious suggestions, frustrations, nonverbal information, or observations and descriptions of the use environment. The symbol (!) is used in Exhibit 5-6 to flag potential latent needs. Techniques for interpreting the raw data in terms of customer needs are given in the next section.

Customer:	Bill Esposito	Interviewer(s):	Jonathan and Lisa
Address:	100 Memorial Drive	Date:	19 January 2015
	Cambridge, MA 02139		
Telephone:	617-864-1274	Currently uses:	Honeywell Model A45
Email:	bespo@zmail.com	Type of user:	Homeowner
Willing to do follow-up?	Yes		

Question/Prompt	Customer Statement	Interpreted Need
Typical uses	I have to manually turn it on and off when it gets too hot or cold.	The thermostat maintains a comfortable temperature without requiring user action.
	Each time I want to change the temperature, I need to adjust both thermostats in the house.	Any user inputs need not be made in multiple locations. (!)
Likes—current model	I like that I can change the temperature if the setting is too high.	The temperature setting is easy to control manually.
	It didn't cost a fortune.	The thermostat is affordable to purchase.
Dislikes—current model	I'm too lazy to learn how to figure it out.	The thermostat requires little or no user instruction or learning.
	I sometimes forget to turn it off when we leave the house.	The thermostat saves energy when no one is home. (!)
	Sometimes the buttons don't register a push and I have to press it repeatedly.	The thermostat definitively registers any user inputs.
Suggested improvements	I would like my iPhone to adjust my thermostat.	The thermostat can be controlled remotely without requiring a special device.
	I like to shift quickly between different options like energy saving or ultra comfort.	The thermostat responds immediately to differences in occupant preferences.

EXHIBIT 5-6   Customer data template filled in with sample customer statements and interpreted needs. (Note that this template represents a partial list from a single interview. A typical interview session may elicit more than 50 customer statements and interpreted needs.)

The final task in step 1 is to write thank-you notes to the customers involved in the process. Invariably, the team will need to solicit further customer information, so developing and maintaining a good rapport with a set of users is important.

Step 2: Interpret Raw Data in Terms of Customer Needs

Customer needs are expressed as written statements and are the result of interpreting the need underlying the raw data gathered from the customers. Each statement or observation (as listed in the second column of the data template) may be translated into any number of customer needs. Griffin and Hauser found that multiple analysts may translate the same interview notes into different needs, so it is useful to have more than one team member conducting the translation process. Later in this section, we provide five guidelines for writing needs statements. The first two guidelines are fundamental and are critical to effective translation; the remaining three guidelines ensure consistency of phrasing and style across all needs statements. Exhibit 5-7 provides examples to illustrate each guideline.

Product Design and Development, Sixth Edition   **65**

Identifying Customer Needs   **83**

Guideline	Customer Statement	Needs Statement— Right	Needs Statement— Wrong
"What" not "How"	I would like my iPhone to adjust my thermostat.	The thermostat can be controlled remotely without requiring a special device.	The thermostat is accompanied by a downloadable iPhone app.
Specificity	I have different heating and cooling systems.	The thermostat can control separate heating and cooling systems.	The thermostat is versatile.
Positive not negative	I get tired of standing in front of my thermostat to program it.	The thermostat can be programmed from a comfortable position.	The thermostat does not require me to stand in front of it for programming.
An attribute of the product	I have to manually override the program if I'm home when I shouldn't be.	The thermostat automatically responds to an occupant's presence.	An occupant's presence triggers the thermostat to automatically change modes.
Avoid "must" and "should"	I'm worried about how secure my thermostat would be if it were accessible online.	The thermostat controls are secure from unauthorized access.	The thermostat must be secure from unauthorized access.

EXHIBIT 5-7   Examples illustrating the guidelines for writing needs statements.

- *Express the need in terms of **what** the product has to do, not in terms of **how** it might do it.* Customers often express their preferences by describing a solution concept or an implementation approach; however, the needs statement should be expressed in terms independent of a particular technological solution.
- *Express the need as specifically as the raw data.* Needs can be expressed at many different levels of detail. To avoid loss of information, express the need at the same level of detail as the raw data.
- *Use positive, not negative, phrasing.* Subsequent translation of a need into a product specification is easier if the need is expressed as a positive statement. This is not a rigid guideline, because sometimes positive phrasing is difficult and awkward. For example, one of the needs statements in Exhibit 5-6 is "The thermostat does not require replacing batteries." This need is more naturally expressed in a negative form.
- *Express the need as an attribute of the product.* Wording needs as statements about the product ensures consistency and facilitates subsequent translation into product specifications. Not all needs can be cleanly expressed as attributes of the product, however, and in most of these cases the needs can be expressed as attributes of the user of the product (e.g., "An occupant's presence triggers the thermostat to automatically change modes.").
- *Avoid the words **must** and **should.*** The words *must* and *should* imply a level of importance for the need. Rather than casually assigning a binary importance rating (*must* versus *should*) to the needs at this point, we recommend deferring the assessment of the importance of each need until step 4.

The list of customer needs is the superset of all the needs elicited from all the interviewed customers in the target market. Some needs may not be technologically realizable.

The constraints of technical and economic feasibility are incorporated into the process of establishing product specifications in subsequent development steps. (See Chapter 6, Product Specifications.) In some cases, customers will have expressed conflicting needs. At this point in the process the team does not attempt to resolve such conflicts, but simply documents both needs. Deciding how to address conflicting needs is one of the challenges of the subsequent concept development activities.

Step 3: Organize the Needs into a Hierarchy

The result of steps 1 and 2 is generally a list of 50 to 300 *needs statements.* Such a large number of detailed needs is awkward to work with and difficult to summarize for use in subsequent development activities. The goal of step 3 is to organize these needs into a useful hierarchical list. The list will typically consist of a set of *primary needs,* each one of which will be further characterized by a set of *secondary needs.* In cases of very complex products, the secondary needs may be broken down into tertiary needs as well. The primary needs are the most general needs, while the secondary and tertiary needs express needs in more detail. Exhibit 5-8 shows the resulting hierarchical list of needs for the thermostat example. In this instance, there are 15 primary needs and 49 secondary needs.

The procedure for organizing the needs into a hierarchical list is intuitive, and many teams can successfully complete the task without detailed instructions. For completeness, we provide a step-by-step procedure here. This activity is best performed on a wall or a large table by a small group of team members.

1. *Print or write each needs statement on a separate card or self-stick note.* A print macro can be easily written to print the needs statements directly from the data template. A nice feature of this approach is that the need can be printed in a large font in the center of the card and then the original customer statement and other relevant information can be printed in a small font at the bottom of the card for easy reference. Four cards can be cut from a standard printed sheet.

2. *Eliminate redundant statements.* Those cards expressing redundant needs statements can be stapled together and treated as a single card. Be careful to consolidate only those statements that are identical in meaning.

3. *Group the cards according to the similarity of the needs they express.* At this point, the team should attempt to create groups of roughly three to seven cards that express similar needs. The logic by which groups are created deserves special attention. Novice development teams often create groups according to a technological perspective, clustering needs relating to, for example, materials, packaging, or power. Or they create groups according to assumed components such as enclosure, display, dial, and software. Both of these approaches are dangerous. Recall that the goal of the process is to create a description of the needs of the customer. For this reason, the groupings should be consistent with the way customers think about their needs and not with the way the development team thinks about the product. The groups should correspond to needs customers would view as similar. In fact, some practitioners use a process in which customers actually organize the needs statements.

4. *For each group, choose a label.* The label is itself a statement of need that generalizes all of the needs in the group. It can be selected from one of the needs in the group, or the team can write a new needs statement.

**   **The thermostat is easy to install.**
***   The thermostat works with my existing heating and/or cooling system.
**   The thermostat installation is an easy do-it-yourself project for a novice.
**   The thermostat can control separate heating and cooling systems.
*   The thermostat can be installed without special tools.
  The thermostat is easily purchased.

*   **The thermostat lasts a long time.**
  The thermostat is safe to bump into.
  The thermostat resists dirt and dust.
!   The thermostat exterior surfaces do not fade or discolor over time.
  The thermostat is recyclable at end of life.

***   **The thermostat is easy to use.**
**   The thermostat user interaction is easy to understand.
*   The thermostat is easy to learn to use.
*   The thermostat does not place significant demands on user memory.
!   The thermostat can be programmed from a comfortable position.
  The thermostat can be controlled remotely without requiring a special device.
!   The thermostat works pretty well right out of the box with no set up.
  The thermostat's behavior is easy to change.
  The thermostat is easy to control manually.
  The thermostat display is easy to read from a distance.
  The thermostat display can be read clearly in all conditions.
  The thermostat's controls accommodate users with limited dexterity.
  The thermostat accommodates different conventions for temperature scales.
  The thermostat accommodates different preferences for representing time and date.

**   **The thermostat controls are precise.**
**   The thermostat maintains temperature accurately.
  The thermostat minimizes unintended variability in temperature.
  The thermostat allows temperatures to be specified precisely.

***   **The thermostat is smart.**
***   The thermostat can adjust temperature during the day according to user preferences.
**   The thermostat can be programmed to a precise schedule.
!   The thermostat automatically responds to occupancy.
!   The thermostat prevents pipes from freezing in cold months.
  The thermostat alerts the user when a problem arises.
  The thermostat does not require users to set time or date.
  The thermostat adjusts automatically to the seasons.

*   **The thermostat is personal.**
*   The thermostat accommodates different user preferences for comfort.
  The thermostat accommodates different user preferences for energy efficiency.
  The thermostat controls are secure from unauthorized access.
  The thermostat provides useful information.

***   **The thermostat is a good investment.**
**   The thermostat is affordable to purchase.
***   The thermostat saves energy.
*   The thermostat tracks cost savings.

**   **The thermostat is reliable.**
  The thermostat does not require replacing batteries.
  The thermostat works normally when electric power is suspended.

EXHIBIT 5-8   Hierarchical list of primary and secondary customer needs for the thermostat. Importance ratings for the secondary needs are indicated by the number of *'s, with *** denoting critically important needs. Latent needs are denoted by !.

     5. *Consider creating supergroups consisting of two to five groups.* If there are fewer than 20 groups, then a two-level hierarchy is probably sufficient to organize the data. In this case, the group labels are primary needs and the group members are secondary needs; however, if there are more than 20 groups, the team may consider creating supergroups, and therefore a third level in the hierarchy. The process of creating supergroups is identical to the process of creating groups. As with the previous step, cluster groups according to similarity of the need they express and then create or select a supergroup label. These supergroup labels become the primary needs, the group labels become the secondary needs, and the members of the groups become tertiary needs.

6. *Review and edit the organized needs statements.* There is no single correct arrangement of needs in a hierarchy. At this point, the team may wish to consider alternative groupings or labels and may engage another team to suggest alternative arrangements.

The process is more complicated when the team attempts to reflect the needs of two or more distinct market segments. There are at least two approaches that can be taken to address this challenge. First, the team can label each need with the segment (and possibly the name) of the customer from whom the need was elicited. This way, differences in needs across segments can be observed directly. One practical visual technique for this labeling is to use different colors of paper for the cards on which the needs statements are written, with each color corresponding to a different market segment. The other approach to multiple market segments is to perform the clustering process separately for each market segment. Using this approach, the team can observe differences both in the needs themselves and in the ways in which these needs are best organized. We recommend that the team adopt this parallel, independent approach when the segments are very different in their needs and when there is some doubt about the ability of the team to address the different segments with the same product.

Step 4: Establish the Relative Importance of the Needs

The hierarchical list alone does not provide any information on the relative importance that customers place on different needs. Yet the development team will have to make trade-offs and allocate resources in designing the product. A sense of the relative importance of the various needs is essential to making these trade-offs correctly. Step 4 in the needs process establishes the relative importance of the customer needs identified in steps 1 through 3. The outcome of this step is a numerical importance weighting for a subset of the needs. There are two basic approaches to the task: (1) relying on the consensus of the team members based on their experience with customers, or (2) basing the importance assessment on further customer surveys. The obvious trade-off between the two approaches is cost and speed versus accuracy: the team can make an educated assessment of the relative importance of the needs in one meeting, while a customer survey generally takes a week or more. In most cases we believe the customer survey is important and worth the time required to complete it. Other development tasks, such as concept generation and analysis of competitive products, can begin before the relative importance surveys are complete.

At this point the team should have developed a rapport with a group of customers. These same customers can be surveyed to rate the relative importance of the needs that have been identified. The survey can be done in person, by telephone, via the Internet, or by mail. Few customers will respond to a survey asking them to evaluate the importance of 100 needs, so typically the team will work with only a subset of the needs. A practical limit on how many needs can be addressed in a customer survey is about 50. This limit is not too severe, however, because many of the needs are either obviously important (e.g., The thermostat maintains temperature accurately) or are easy to implement (e.g., The thermostat allows temperatures to be specified precisely). The team can therefore limit the scope of the survey by querying customers only about needs that are likely to give rise to difficult technical

---

Thermostat Survey

For each of the following thermostat features, please indicate on a scale of 1 to 5 how important the feature is to you. Please use the following scale:

1. Feature is undesirable. I would not consider a product with this feature.
2. Feature is not important, but I would not mind having it.
3. Feature would be nice to have, but is not necessary.
4. Feature is highly desirable, but I would consider a product without it.
5. Feature is critical. I would not consider a product without this feature.

Also indicate by checking the box to the right if you feel that the feature is unique, exciting, and/or unexpected.

Importance of feature on scale of 1 to 5	Check box if feature is unique, exciting, and/or unexpected.
_____ The thermostat does not require the user to set time or date.	❏
_____ The thermostat does not require replacing batteries.	❏
_____ The thermostat adjusts automatically to the seasons.	❏
_____ The thermostat accommodates different preferences for representing date and time.	❏

And so forth.

EXHIBIT 5-9   Example importance survey (partial).

trade-offs or costly features in the product design. Such needs would include, for instance, the need to avoid replacing batteries, or the need to not have to enter time or date. Alternatively the team could develop a set of surveys to ask a variety of customers each about different subsets of the needs list. There are many survey designs for establishing the relative importance of customer needs. One good design is illustrated by the portion of the thermostat survey shown in Exhibit 5-9. In addition to asking for importance ratings, this survey asks the respondent to explicitly identify the needs that are unique or unexpected. This information can be used to help the team identify latent needs.

The survey responses for each needs statement can be characterized in a variety of ways: by the mean, by the standard deviation, or by the number of responses in each category. The responses can then be used to assign an importance weighting to the needs statements. The same scale of 1 to 5 can be used to summarize the importance data. The needs in Exhibit 5-8 are rated according to the survey data, with the importance ratings denoted by the number of *'s next to each needs statement and the latent needs denoted by !. Note that no critical needs are also latent needs. This is because if a need were critical, customers would not be surprised or excited by it; they would expect it to be met.

Step 5: Reflect on the Results and the Process

The final step in the method is to reflect on the results and the process. While the process of identifying customer needs can be usefully structured, it is not an exact science. The team must challenge its results to verify that they are consistent with the knowledge and intuition the team has developed through many hours of interaction with customers. Some questions to ask include:

- Have we interacted with all of the important types of customers in our target market?
- Are we able to see beyond needs related only to existing products to capture the latent needs of our target customers?

- Are there areas of inquiry we should pursue in follow-up interviews or surveys?
- Which of the customers we spoke to would be good participants in our ongoing development efforts?
- What do we know now that we didn't know when we started? Are we surprised by any of the needs?
- Did we involve everyone within our own organization who needs to deeply understand customer needs?
- How might we improve the process in future efforts?

A good way to summarize the results of the process is to list the most important needs and the latent needs. For instance, the most important needs identified are:

- The thermostat is easy to use.
- The thermostat can adjust temperature during the day according to user preferences.
- The thermostat works with my existing heating and/or cooling system.
- The thermostat reduces energy consumption.

The latent needs are:

- The thermostat can be programmed from a comfortable position.
- The thermostat works pretty well right out of the box with no set up.
- The thermostat automatically responds to occupancy.
- The thermostat exterior surfaces do not fade or discolor over time.
- The thermostat prevents pipes from freezing in cold months.

The important needs are an excellent reminder of the critical few needs that must be addressed for a great product, and the latent needs provide insights that can drive the creative process of generating product concepts.

Summary

Identifying customer needs is an integral part of the concept development phase of the product development process. The resulting customer needs are used to guide the team in establishing product specifications, generating product concepts, and selecting a product concept for further development.

- The process of identifying customer needs includes five steps:

    1. Gather raw data from customers.
    2. Interpret the raw data in terms of customer needs.
    3. Organize the needs into a hierarchy.
    4. Establish the relative importance of the needs.
    5. Reflect on the results and the process.

- Creating a high-quality information channel from customers to the product developers ensures that those who directly control the details of the product, including the product designers, fully understand the needs of the customer.

- Lead users are a good source of customer needs because they experience new needs months or years ahead of most customers and because they stand to benefit substantially from new product innovations. Furthermore, they are frequently able to articulate their needs more clearly than typical customers. Extreme users have special needs that may reflect latent needs among mainstream users.

- Latent needs may be even more important than explicit needs in determining customer satisfaction. Latent needs are those that many customers recognize as important in a final product but do not or cannot articulate in advance.

- Customer needs should be expressed in terms of what the product has to do, not in terms of how the product might be implemented. Adherence to this principle leaves the development team with maximum flexibility to generate and select product concepts.

- The key benefits of the method are ensuring that the product is focused on customer needs and that no critical customer need is forgotten; developing a clear understanding among members of the development team of the needs of the customers in the target market; developing a fact base to be used in generating concepts, selecting a product concept, and establishing product specifications; and creating an archival record of the needs phase of the development process.

References and Bibliography

Many current resources are available on the Internet via
www.ulrich-eppinger.net

Concept engineering is a method developed by Burchill at MIT in collaboration with the Center for Quality of Management. This chapter benefits from our observations of the development and application of concept engineering. For a complete and detailed description of concept engineering, see:

> Burchill, Gary, et al., *Concept Engineering,* Center for Quality of Management, Cambridge, MA, Document No. ML0080, 1997.

The research by Griffin and Hauser validates different methods for extracting needs from interview data. Their study of the fraction of needs identified as a function of the number of customers interviewed is particularly interesting.

> Griffin, Abbie, and John R. Hauser, "The Voice of the Customer," *Marketing Science,* Vol. 12, No. 1, Winter 1993, pp. 1–27.

Kinnear and Taylor thoroughly discuss data collection methods and survey design.

> Kinnear, Thomas C., and James R. Taylor, *Marketing Research: An Applied Approach,* fifth edition, McGraw-Hill, New York, 1995.

Norman has written extensively on user needs, especially as related to the cognitive challenges of using products.

> Norman, Donald A., *The Design of Everyday Things,* Doubleday, New York, 1990.

Payne's book is a detailed and interesting discussion of how to pose questions in surveys.

> Payne, Stanley L., *The Art of Asking Questions,* Princeton University Press, Princeton, NJ, 1980.

Total quality management (TQM) provides a valuable perspective on how identifying customer needs fits into an overall effort to improve the quality of goods and services.

    Shiba, Shoji, Alan Graham, and David Walden, *A New American TQM: Four Practical Revolutions in Management,* Productivity Press, Cambridge, MA, and The Center for Quality of Management, Cambridge, MA, 1993.

Urban and Hauser provide a thorough discussion of how to create hierarchies of needs (along with many other topics).

    Urban, Glen L., and John R. Hauser, *Design and Marketing of New Products,* second edition, Prentice Hall, Englewood Cliffs, NJ, 1993.

Von Hippel describes many years of research on the role of lead users in innovation. He provides useful guidelines for identifying lead users.

    von Hippel, Eric, *The Sources of Innovation,* Oxford University Press, New York, 1988.

Exercises

1. Translate the following customer statements about a student book bag into proper needs statements:

   a. "See how the leather on the bottom of the bag is all scratched; it's ugly."
   b. "When I'm standing in line at the cashier trying to find my checkbook while balancing my bag on my knee, I feel like a stork."
   c. "This bag is my life; if I lose it I'm in big trouble."
   d. "There's nothing worse than a banana that's been squished by the edge of a textbook."
   e. "I never use both straps on my knapsack; I just sling it over one shoulder."

2. Observe someone performing an everyday task. (Ideally, you should choose a task for which you can observe different users performing the task repeatedly.) Identify frustrations and difficulties encountered by these people. Identify the latent customer needs.

3. Choose a product that continually annoys you. Identify the needs the developers of this product missed. Why do you think these needs were not met? Do you think the developers deliberately ignored these needs?

Thought Questions

1. One of the reasons the method is effective is that it involves the entire development team. Unfortunately, the method can become unwieldy with a team of more than 10 people. How might you modify the method to maximize involvement yet maintain a focused and decisive effort given a large development team?

2. Can the process of identifying customer needs lead to the creation of innovative product concepts? In what ways? Could a structured process of identifying customer needs lead to a fundamentally new product concept like the Post-it Note?

CHAPTER SIX

Product Specifications

Courtesy of Specialized Bicycle Components

EXHIBIT 6-1
One of Specialized's existing mountain bikes with a suspension fork.

Specialized Bicycle Components was interested in developing a new front suspension fork for the mountain bike market. Although the firm was already selling suspension forks on its bicycles (Exhibit 6-1), it was interested in exploring designs that would provide higher value for the recreational cyclist.

The development team had spent a great deal of time identifying customer needs. In addition to logging many hours of riding on suspended bikes themselves, the members of the team had interviewed lead users at mountain bike races and recreational cyclists on local trails, and they also had spent time working with dealers in their stores. As a result of this process they had assembled a list of customer needs. They now faced several challenges:

- How could the relatively subjective customer needs be translated into precise targets for the remaining development effort?
- How could the team and its senior management agree on what would constitute success or failure of the resulting product design?
- How could the team develop confidence that its intended product would garner a substantial share of the suspension fork market?
- How could the team resolve the inevitable trade-offs among product characteristics like cost and weight?

This chapter presents a method for establishing product specifications. We assume that the customer needs are already documented as described in Chapter 5, Identifying Customer Needs. The method employs several simple information systems, all of which can be constructed using conventional spreadsheet software.

What Are Specifications?

Customer needs are generally expressed in the "language of the customer." The primary customer needs for the suspension fork are listed in Exhibit 6-2. Customer needs such as "the suspension is easy to install" or "the suspension enables high-speed descents on bumpy trails" are typical in terms of the subjective quality of the expressions; however, while such expressions are helpful in developing a clear sense of the issues of interest to customers, they provide little specific guidance about how to design and engineer the product. They simply leave too much margin for subjective interpretation. For this reason, development teams usually establish a set of specifications, which spell out in precise, measurable detail *what* the product has to do. Product specifications do not tell the team *how* to address the customer needs, but they do represent an unambiguous agreement on what the team will attempt to achieve to satisfy the customer needs. For example, in contrast to the customer need that "the suspension is easy to install," the corresponding specification might be that "the average time to assemble the fork to the frame is less than 75 seconds."

We intend the term *product specifications* to mean the precise description of what the product has to do. Some firms use the terms "product requirements" or "engineering characteristics" in this way. Other firms use "specifications" or "technical specifications" to refer to key design variables of the product such as the oil viscosity or spring constant of the suspension system. These are just differences in terminology. For clarity, let us be

EXHIBIT 6-2
Customer needs for the suspension fork and their relative importance (shown in a convenient spreadsheet format).

No.		Need	Imp.
1	The suspension	reduces vibration to the hands.	3
2	The suspension	allows easy traversal of slow, difficult terrain.	2
3	The suspension	enables high-speed descents on bumpy trails.	5
4	The suspension	allows sensitivity adjustment.	3
5	The suspension	preserves the steering characteristics of the bike.	4
6	The suspension	remains rigid during hard cornering.	4
7	The suspension	is lightweight.	4
8	The suspension	provides stiff mounting points for the brakes.	2
9	The suspension	fits a wide variety of bikes, wheels, and tires.	5
10	The suspension	is easy to install.	1
11	The suspension	works with fenders.	1
12	The suspension	instills pride.	5
13	The suspension	is affordable for an amateur enthusiast.	5
14	The suspension	is not contaminated by water.	5
15	The suspension	is not contaminated by grunge.	5
16	The suspension	can be easily accessed for maintenance.	3
17	The suspension	allows easy replacement of worn parts.	1
18	The suspension	can be maintained with readily available tools.	3
19	The suspension	lasts a long time.	5
20	The suspension	is safe in a crash.	5

precise about a few definitions. A *specification* (singular) consists of a *metric* and a *value*. For example, "average time to assemble" is a metric, while "less than 75 seconds" is the value of this metric. Note that the value may take on several forms, including a particular number, a range, or an inequality. Values are always labeled with the appropriate units (e.g., seconds, kilograms, joules). Together, the metric and value form a specification. The *product specifications* (plural) are simply the set of the individual specifications.

When Are Specifications Established?

In an ideal world, the team would establish the product specifications once early in the development process and then proceed to design and engineer the product to exactly meet those specifications. For some products, such as soap or soup, this approach works quite well; the technologists on the team can reliably concoct a formulation that satisfies almost any reasonable specifications; however, for technology-intensive products this is rarely possible. For such products, specifications are established at least twice. Immediately after identifying the customer needs, the team sets *target specifications*. These specifications represent the hopes and aspirations of the team, but they are established before the team knows what constraints the product technology will place on what

EXHIBIT 6-3   The concept development process. The target specifications are set early in the process, but setting the final specifications must wait until after the product concept has been selected.

can be achieved. The team's efforts may fail to meet some of these specifications and may exceed others, depending on the product concept the team eventually selects. For this reason, the target specifications must be refined after a product concept has been selected. The team revisits the specifications while assessing the actual technological constraints and the expected production costs. To set the *final specifications,* the team must frequently make hard trade-offs among different desirable characteristics of the product. For simplicity, we present a two-stage process for establishing specifications, but we note that in some organizations specifications are revisited many times throughout the development process.

The two stages in which specifications are established are shown as part of the concept development process in Exhibit 6-3. Note that the final specifications are one of the key elements of the development plan, which is usually documented in the project's *contract book.* The contract book (described in Chapter 19, Managing Projects) specifies what the team agrees to achieve, the project schedule, the required resources, and the economic implications for the business. The list of product specifications is also one of the key information systems used by the team throughout the development process.

This chapter presents two methods: the first is for establishing the target specifications and the second is for setting the final specifications after the product concept has been selected.

Establishing Target Specifications

As Exhibit 6-3 illustrates, the target specifications are established after the customer needs have been identified but before product concepts have been generated and the most promising one(s) selected. An arbitrary setting of the specifications may not be technically feasible. For example, in designing a suspension fork, the team cannot assume in advance that it will be able to achieve simultaneously a mass of 1 kilogram, a manufacturing cost of $30, and the best descent time on the test track, as these are three quite aggressive specifications. Actually meeting the specifications established at this point is contingent upon the details of the product concept the team eventually selects. For this reason, such preliminary specifications are labeled "target specifications." They are the goals of the development team, describing a product that the team believes would succeed in the marketplace. Later these specifications will be refined based on the limitations of the product concept actually selected.

The process of establishing the target specifications contains four steps:

1. Prepare the list of metrics.
2. Collect competitive benchmarking information.
3. Set ideal and marginally acceptable target values.
4. Reflect on the results and the process.

Step 1: Prepare the List of Metrics

The most useful metrics are those that reflect as directly as possible the degree to which the product satisfies the customer needs. The relationship between needs and metrics is central to the entire concept of specifications. The working assumption is that a translation from customer needs to a set of precise, measurable specifications is possible and that meeting specifications will therefore lead to satisfaction of the associated customer needs.

A list of metrics is shown in Exhibit 6-4. A good way to generate the list of metrics is to contemplate each need in turn and to consider what precise, measurable characteristic of the product will reflect the degree to which the product satisfies that need. In the ideal case, there is one and only one metric for each need. In practice, this is frequently not possible.

For example, consider the need that the suspension be "easy to install." The team may conclude that this need is largely captured by measuring the time required for assembly of the fork to the frame; however, note the possible subtleties in this translation. Is assembly time really identical to ease of installation? The installation could be extremely fast but require an awkward and painful set of finger actions, which ultimately may lead to worker injury or dealer frustration. Because of the imprecise nature of the translation process, those establishing the specifications should have been directly involved in identifying the customer needs. In this way the team can rely on its understanding of the meaning of each need statement derived from firsthand interactions with customers.

The need for the fork to reduce vibration to the user's hands may be even more difficult to translate into a single metric, because there are many different conditions under which vibration can be transmitted, including small bumps on level roads and big bumps on rough trails. The team may conclude that several metrics are required to capture this need, including, for example, the metrics "attenuation from dropout to handlebar at 10 Hz" and "maximum value from the Monster." (The "Monster" is a suspension test developed by *Mountain Bike* magazine.)

A simple needs-metrics matrix represents the relationship between needs and metrics. An example needs-metrics matrix is shown in Exhibit 6-5. The rows of the matrix correspond to the customer needs, and the columns of the matrix correspond to the metrics. A mark in a cell of the matrix means that the need and the metric associated with the cell are related; performance relative to the metric will influence the degree to which the product satisfies the customer need. This matrix is a key element of the *House of Quality,* a graphical technique used in *Quality Function Deployment,* or *QFD* (Hauser and Clausing, 1988). In many cases, we find the information in the needs-metrics matrix is just as easily communicated by listing the numbers of the needs related to each metric alongside the list of metrics (the second column in Exhibit 6-4). There are some cases, however, in which the mapping from needs to metrics is complex, and the matrix can be quite useful for representing this mapping.

Metric No.	Need Nos.	Metric	Imp.	Units
1	1, 3	Attenuation from dropout to handlebar at 10 Hz	3	dB
2	2, 6	Spring preload	3	N
3	1, 3	Maximum value from the Monster	5	g
4	1, 3	Minimum descent time on test track	5	s
5	4	Damping coefficient adjustment range	3	N-s/m
6	5	Maximum travel (26-in. wheel)	3	mm
7	5	Rake offset	3	mm
8	6	Lateral stiffness at the tip	3	kN/m
9	7	Total mass	4	kg
10	8	Lateral stiffness at brake pivots	2	kN/m
11	9	Headset sizes	5	in.
12	9	Steertube length	5	mm
13	9	Wheel sizes	5	List
14	9	Maximum tire width	5	in.
15	10	Time to assemble to frame	1	s
16	11	Fender compatibility	1	List
17	12	Instills pride	5	Subj.
18	13	Unit manufacturing cost	5	US$
19	14	Time in spray chamber without water entry	5	s
20	15	Cycles in mud chamber without contamination	5	k-cycles
21	16, 17	Time to disassemble/assemble for maintenance	3	s
22	17, 18	Special tools required for maintenance	3	List
23	19	UV test duration to degrade rubber parts	5	hr
24	19	Monster cycles to failure	5	Cycles
25	20	Japan Industrial Standards test	5	Binary
26	20	Bending strength (frontal loading)	5	kN

EXHIBIT 6-4   List of metrics for the suspension. The relative importance of each metric and the units for the metric are also shown. "Subj." is an abbreviation indicating that a metric is subjective.

A few guidelines should be considered when constructing the list of metrics:

- *Metrics should be complete.* Ideally each customer need would correspond to a single metric, and the value of that metric would correlate perfectly with satisfaction of that need. In practice, several metrics may be necessary to completely reflect a single customer need.

- *Metrics should be dependent, not independent, variables.* This guideline is a variant of the *what-not-how principle* introduced in Chapter 5. As do customer needs, specifications also indicate *what* the product must do, but not *how* the specifications will

Need	1 Attenuation from dropout to handlebar at 10 Hz	2 Spring preload	3 Maximum value from the Monster	4 Minimum descent time on test track	5 Damping coefficient adjustment range	6 Maximum travel (26-in. wheel)	7 Rake offset	8 Lateral stiffness at the tip	9 Total mass	10 Lateral stiffness at brake pivots	11 Headset sizes	12 Steertube length	13 Wheel sizes	14 Maximum tire width	15 Time to assemble to frame	16 Fender compatibility	17 Instills pride	18 Unit manufacturing cost	19 Time in spray chamber without water entry	20 Cycles in mud chamber without contamination	21 Time to disassemble/assemble for maintenance	22 Special tools required for maintenance	23 UV test duration to degrade rubber parts	24 Monster cycles to failure	25 Japan Industrial Standards test	26 Bending strength (frontal loading)
1 Reduces vibration to the hands	●		●	●																						
2 Allows easy traversal of slow, difficult terrain		●																								
3 Enables high-speed descents on bumpy trails	●		●	●																						
4 Allows sensitivity adjustment					●																					
5 Preserves the steering characteristics of the bike						●	●																			
6 Remains rigid during hard cornering	●							●																		
7 Is lightweight									●																	
8 Provides stiff mounting points for the brakes										●																
9 Fits a wide variety of bikes, wheels, and tires											●	●	●	●												
10 Is easy to install															●											
11 Works with fenders																●										
12 Instills pride																	●									
13 Is affordable for an amateur enthusiast																		●								
14 Is not contaminated by water																			●							
15 Is not contaminated by grunge																				●						
16 Can be easily accessed for maintenance																					●					
17 Allows easy replacement of worn parts																					●	●				
18 Can be maintained with readily available tools																						●				
19 Lasts a long time																							●	●		
20 Is safe in a crash																									●	●

EXHIBIT 6-5 The needs-metrics matrix.

be achieved. Designers use many types of variables in product development; some are *dependent,* such as the mass of the fork, and some are *independent,* such as the material used for the fork. In other words, designers cannot control mass directly because it arises from other independent decisions the designers will make, such as dimensions and materials choices. Metrics specify the overall performance of a product and should therefore be the dependent variables (i.e., the performance measures or output variables) in the design problem. By using dependent variables for the specifications, designers are left with the freedom to achieve the specifications using the best approach possible.

- *Metrics should be practical.* It does not serve the team to devise a metric for a bicycle suspension that can only be measured by a scientific laboratory at a cost of $100,000. Ideally, metrics will be directly observable or analyzable properties of the product that can be easily evaluated by the team.

- *Some needs cannot easily be translated into quantifiable metrics.* The need that the suspension instills pride may be quite critical to success in the fashion-conscious mountain bike market, but how can pride be quantified? In these cases, the team simply repeats the need statement as a specification and notes that the metric is subjective. (We indicate this by entering "Subj." in the units column.) However, the team still has to decide how to confirm that the specification is satisfied; for example, by a panel of customers.

- *The metrics should include the popular criteria for comparison in the marketplace.* Many customers in various markets buy products based on independently published evaluations. Such evaluations are found, for example, in *Popular Science, Consumer Reports,* on various Internet sites, or, in our case, in *Bicycling* and *Mountain Bike* magazines. If the team knows that its product will be evaluated by the trade media and knows what the evaluation criteria will be, then it should include metrics corresponding to these criteria. *Mountain Bike* magazine uses a test machine called the Monster, which measures the vertical acceleration (in g's) of the handlebars as a bicycle equipped with the fork runs over a block 50 millimeters tall. For this reason, the team included "maximum value from the Monster" as a metric. If the team cannot find a relationship between the criteria used by the media and the customer needs it has identified, then it should ensure that a need has not been overlooked and/or should work with the media to revise the criteria. In a few cases, the team may conclude that high performance in the media evaluations is in itself a customer need and choose to include a metric used by the media that has little intrinsic technical merit.

In addition to denoting the needs related to each metric, Exhibit 6-4 contains the units of measurement and an importance rating for each metric. The units of measurement are most commonly conventional engineering units such as kilograms and seconds; however, some metrics will not lend themselves to numerical values. The need that the suspension "works with fenders" is best translated into a specification listing the models of fenders with which the fork is compatible. In this case, the value of the metric is actually a list of fenders rather than a number. For the metric involving the standard safety test, the value is pass/fail. (We indicate these two cases by entering "List" and "Binary" in the units column.)

The importance rating of a metric is derived from the importance ratings of the needs it reflects. For cases in which a metric maps directly to a single need, the importance rating of the need becomes the importance rating of the metric. For cases in which a metric is related to more than one need, the importance of the metric is determined by considering the importances of the needs to which it relates and the nature of these relationships. We believe that there are enough subtleties in this process that importance weightings can best be determined through discussion among the team members, rather than through a formal algorithm. When there are relatively few specifications and establishing the relative importance of these specifications is critically important, *conjoint analysis* may be useful. Conjoint analysis is described briefly later in this chapter and publications explaining the technique are referenced at the end of the chapter.

Step 2: Collect Competitive Benchmarking Information

Unless the team expects to enjoy a total monopoly, the relationship of the new product to competitive products is paramount in determining commercial success. While the team will have entered the product development process with some idea of how it wishes to compete in the marketplace, the target specifications are the language the team uses to discuss and agree on the detailed positioning of its product relative to existing products, both its own and competitors'. Information on competing products must be gathered to support these positioning decisions.

An example of a competitive benchmarking chart is shown in Exhibit 6-6. The columns of the chart correspond to the competitive products and the rows are the metrics established in step 1. Note that the competitive benchmarking chart can be constructed as a simple appendage to the spreadsheet containing the list of metrics. (This information is one of the "rooms" in the *House of Quality*, described by Hauser and Clausing.)

The benchmarking chart is conceptually very simple. For each competitive product, the values of the metrics are simply entered down a column. Gathering these data can be very time consuming, involving (at the least) purchasing, testing, disassembling, and estimating the production costs of the most important competitive products; however, this investment of time is essential, as no product development team can expect to succeed without having this type of information. A word of warning: Sometimes the data contained in competitors' catalogs and supporting literature are not accurate. Where possible, values of the key metrics should be verified by independent testing or observation.

An alternative competitive benchmarking chart can be constructed with rows corresponding to the customer needs and columns corresponding to the competitive products (see Exhibit 6-7). This chart is used to compare customers' perceptions of the relative degree to which the products satisfy their needs. Constructing this chart requires collecting customer perception data, which can also be very expensive and time consuming. Some techniques for measuring customers' perceptions of satisfaction of needs are contained in a book by Urban and Hauser (1993). Both charts can be useful and any discrepancies between the two are instructive. At a minimum, a chart showing the competitive values of the metrics (Exhibit 6-6) should be created.

Step 3: Set Ideal and Marginally Acceptable Target Values

In this step, the team synthesizes the available information to actually set the *target values* for the metrics. Two types of target value are useful: an *ideal value* and a *marginally acceptable value*. The ideal value is the best result the team could hope for. The marginally acceptable value is the value of the metric that would just barely make the product commercially viable. Both of these targets are useful in guiding the subsequent stages of concept generation and concept selection, and for refining the specifications after the product concept has been selected.

There are five ways to express the values of the metrics:

- *At least X:* These specifications establish targets for the lower bound on a metric, but higher is still better. For example, the value of the brake mounting stiffness is specified to be at least 325 kilonewtons/meter.

- *At most X:* These specifications establish targets for the upper bound on a metric, with smaller values being better. For example, the value for the mass of the suspension fork is set to be at most 1.4 kilograms.

100   *Chapter 6*

Metric No.	Need Nos.	Metric	Imp.	Units	ST Tritrack	Maniray 2	Rox Tahx Quadra	Rox Tahx Ti 21	Tonka Pro	Gunhill Head Shox
1	1, 3	Attenuation from dropout to handlebar at 10 Hz	3	dB	8	15	10	15	9	13
2	2, 6	Spring preload	3	N	550	760	500	710	480	680
3	1, 3	Maximum value from the Monster	5	g	3.6	3.2	3.7	3.3	3.7	3.4
4	1, 3	Minimum descent time on test track	5	s	13	11.3	12.6	11.2	13.2	11
5	4	Damping coefficient adjustment range	3	N-s/m	0	0	0	200	0	0
6	5	Maximum travel (26-in. wheel)	3	mm	28	48	43	46	33	38
7	5	Rake offset	3	mm	41.5	39	38	38	43.2	39
8	6	Lateral stiffness at the tip	3	kN/m	59	110	85	85	65	130
9	7	Total mass	4	kg	1.409	1.385	1.409	1.364	1.222	1.100
10	8	Lateral stiffness at brake pivots	2	kN/m	295	550	425	425	325	650
11	9	Headset sizes	5	in.	1.000 1.125	1.000 1.125 1.250	1.000 1.125	1.000 1.125 1.250	1.000 1.125	NA
12	9	Steertube length	5	mm	150 180 210 230 255	140 165 190 215	150 170 190 210	150 170 190 210 230	150 190 210 220	NA
13	9	Wheel sizes	5	List	26 in.	26 in.	26 in.	26 in. 700C	26 in.	26 in.

EXHIBIT 6-6   Competitive benchmarking chart based on metrics.

- *Between X and Y:* These specifications establish both upper and lower bounds for the value of a metric. For example, the value for the spring preload is set to be between 480 and 800 newtons. Any more and the suspension is harsh; any less and the suspension is too bouncy.
- *Exactly X:* These specifications establish a target of a particular value of a metric, with any deviation degrading performance. For example, the ideal value for the rake offset metric is set to 38 millimeters. This type of specification is to be avoided if possible because such specifications substantially constrain the design. Often, upon reconsideration, the team realizes that what initially appears as an "exactly X" specification can be expressed as a "between X and Y" specification.
- *A set of discrete values:* Some metrics will have values corresponding to several discrete choices. For example, the headset diameters are 1.000, 1.125, or 1.250 inches. (Industry practice is to use English units for these and several other critical bicycle dimensions.)

Metric No.	Need Nos.	Metric	Imp.	Units	ST Tritrack	Maniray 2	Rox Tahx Quadra	Rox Tahx Ti 21	Tonka Pro	Gunhill Head Shox
14	9	Maximum tire width	5	in.	1.5	1.75	1.5	1.75	1.5	1.5
15	10	Time to assemble to frame	1	s	35	35	45	45	35	85
16	11	Fender compatibility	1	List	Zefal	None	None	None	None	All
17	12	Instills pride	5	Subj.	1	4	3	5	3	5
18	13	Unit manufacturing cost	5	US$	65	105	85	115	80	100
19	14	Time in spray chamber without water entry	5	s	1300	2900	>3600	>3600	2300	>3600
20	15	Cycles in mud chamber without contamination	5	k-cycles	15	19	15	25	18	35
21	16, 17	Time to disassemble/ assemble for maintenance	3	s	160	245	215	245	200	425
22	17, 18	Special tools required for maintenance	3	List	Hex	Hex	Hex	Hex	Long hex	Hex, pin wrench
23	19	UV test duration to degrade rubber parts	5	hr	400+	250	400+	400+	400+	250
24	19	Monster cycles to failure	5	Cycles	500k+	500k+	500k+	480k	500k+	330k
25	20	Japan Industrial Standards test	5	Binary	Pass	Pass	Pass	Pass	Pass	Pass
26	20	Bending strength (frontal loading)	5	kN	5.5	8.9	7.5	7.5	6.2	10.2

EXHIBIT 6-6 *Continued*

The desirable range of values for one metric may depend on another. In other words, we may wish to express a target as, for example, "the fork tip lateral stiffness is no more than 20 percent of the lateral stiffness at the brake pivots." In applications where the team feels this level of complexity is warranted, such targets can easily be included, although we recommend that this level of complexity not be introduced until the final phase of the specifications process.

Using these five different types of expressions for values of the metrics, the team sets the target specifications. The team simply proceeds down the list of metrics and assigns both the marginally acceptable and ideal target values for each metric. These decisions are facilitated by the metric-based competitive benchmarking chart shown in Exhibit 6-6. To set the target values, the team has many considerations, including the capability of competing products available at the time, competitors' future product capabilities (if these are predictable), and the product's mission statement and target market segment. Exhibit 6-8 shows the targets assigned for the suspension fork.

No.	Need	Imp.	ST Tritrack	Maniray 2	Rox Tahx Quadra	Rox Tahx Ti 21	Tonka Pro	Gunhill Head Shox
1	Reduces vibration to the hands	3	•	••••	••	•••••	••	•••
2	Allows easy traversal of slow, difficult terrain	2	••	••••	•••	•••••	•••	•••••
3	Enables high-speed descents on bumpy trails	5	•	•••••	••	•••••	••	•••
4	Allows sensitivity adjustment	3	•	••••	••	•••••	••	•••
5	Preserves the steering characteristics of the bike	4	••••	••	•	••	•••••	•••••
6	Remains rigid during hard cornering	4	•	•••	•	•••••	•	•••••
7	Is lightweight	4	•	•••	•	•••	••••	•••••
8	Provides stiff mounting points for the brakes	2	•	••••	•••	•••	•••••	••
9	Fits a wide variety of bikes, wheels, and tires	5	••••	•••••	•••	•••••	•••	•
10	Is easy to install	1	••••	•••••	••••	••••	•••••	•
11	Works with fenders	1	•••	•	•	•	•	•••••
12	Instills pride	5	•	••••	•••	•••••	•••	•••••
13	Is affordable for an amateur enthusiast	5	•••••	•	•••	•	•••	••
14	Is not contaminated by water	5	•	•••	••••	••••	••	•••••
15	Is not contaminated by grunge	5	•	•••	•	••••	••	•••••
16	Can be easily accessed for maintenance	3	••••	•••••	••••	••••	•••••	•
17	Allows easy replacement of worn parts	1	••••	•••••	••••	••••	•••••	•
18	Can be maintained with readily available tools	3	•••••	•••••	•••••	•••••	••	•
19	Lasts a long time	5	•••••	•••••	•••••	•••	•••••	•
20	Is safe in a crash	5	•••••	•••••	•••••	•••••	•••••	•••••

EXHIBIT 6-7 Competitive benchmarking chart based on perceived satisfaction of needs. (Scoring more "dots" corresponds to greater perceived satisfaction of the need.)

Because most of the values are expressed in terms of bounds (upper or lower or both), the team is establishing the boundaries of the competitively viable product space. The team hopes that the product will meet some of the ideal targets but is confident that a product can be commercially viable even if it exhibits one or more marginally acceptable characteristics. Note that these specifications are preliminary because until a product concept is chosen and some of the design details are worked out, many of the exact trade-offs are uncertain.

Step 4: Reflect on the Results and the Process

The team may require some iteration to agree on the targets. Reflection after each iteration helps to ensure that the results are consistent with the goals of the project. Questions to consider include:

- Are members of the team "gaming"? For example, is the key marketing representative insisting that an aggressive value is required for a particular metric in the hopes that by setting a high goal, the team will actually achieve more than if his or her true, and more lenient, beliefs were expressed?

- Should the team consider offering multiple products or at least multiple options for the product to best match the particular needs of more than one market segment, or will one "average" product suffice?

- Are any specifications missing? Do the specifications reflect the characteristics that will dictate commercial success?

Once the targets have been set, the team can proceed to generate solution concepts. The target specifications then can be used to help the team select a concept and will help the team know when a concept is commercially viable. (See Chapter 7, Concept Generation, and Chapter 8, Concept Selection.)

Setting the Final Specifications

As the team finalizes the choice of a concept and prepares for subsequent design and development, the specifications are revisited. Specifications that originally were only targets expressed as broad ranges of values are now refined and made more precise.

Finalizing the specifications is difficult because of trade-offs—inverse relationships between two specifications that are inherent in the selected product concept. Trade-offs frequently occur between different technical performance metrics and almost always occur between technical performance metrics and production cost. There may also be trade-offs between product performance and development time or cost. For example, one trade-off is between brake mounting stiffness and mass of the fork. Because of the basic mechanics of the fork structure, these specifications are inversely related, assuming other factors are held constant. Another trade-off is between cost and mass. For a given concept, the team may be able to reduce the mass of the fork by making some parts out of titanium instead of steel. Unfortunately, decreasing the mass in this way will most likely increase the manufacturing cost of the product. The difficult part of refining the specifications is choosing how such trade-offs will be resolved.

Metric No.	Need Nos.	Metric	Imp.	Units	Marginal Value	Ideal Value
1	1, 3	Attenuation from dropout to handlebar at 10 Hz	3	dB	>10	>15
2	2, 6	Spring preload	3	N	480–800	650–700
3	1, 3	Maximum value from the Monster	5	g	<3.5	<3.2
4	1, 3	Minimum descent time on test track	5	s	<13.0	<11.0
5	4	Damping coefficient adjustment range	3	N-s/m	0	>200
6	5	Maximum travel (26-in. wheel)	3	mm	33–50	45
7	5	Rake offset	3	mm	37–45	38
8	6	Lateral stiffness at the tip	3	kN/m	>65	>130
9	7	Total mass	4	kg	<1.4	<1.1
10	8	Lateral stiffness at brake pivots	2	kN/m	>325	>650
11	9	Headset sizes	5	in.	1.000 1.125	1.000 1.125 1.250
12	9	Steertube length	5	mm	150 170 190 210	150 170 190 210 230
13	9	Wheel sizes	5	List	26 in.	26 in. 700C
14	9	Maximum tire width	5	in.	>1.5	>1.75
15	10	Time to assemble to frame	1	s	<60	<35
16	11	Fender compatibility	1	List	None	All
17	12	Instills pride	5	Subj.	>3	>5
18	13	Unit manufacturing cost	5	US$	<85	<65
19	14	Time in spray chamber without water entry	5	s	>2300	>3600
20	15	Cycles in mud chamber without contamination	5	k-cycles	>15	>35
21	16, 17	Time to disassemble/assemble for maintenance	3	s	<300	<160
22	17, 18	Special tools required for maintenance	3	List	Hex	Hex
23	19	UV test duration to degrade rubber parts	5	hr	>250	>450
24	19	Monster cycles to failure	5	Cycles	>300k	>500k
25	20	Japan Industrial Standards test	5	Binary	Pass	Pass
26	20	Bending strength (frontal loading)	5	kN	>7.0	>10.0

EXHIBIT 6-8 The target specifications. Like the other information systems, this one is easily encoded with a spreadsheet as a simple extension to the list of specifications.

Here, we propose a five-step process:

1. Develop technical models of the product.
2. Develop a cost model of the product.
3. Refine the specifications, making trade-offs where necessary.
4. Flow down the specifications as appropriate.
5. Reflect on the results and the process.

Step 1: Develop Technical Models of the Product

A *technical model* of the product is a tool for predicting the values of the metrics for a particular set of design decisions. We intend the term *models* to refer to both analytical and physical approximations of the product. (See Chapter 14, Prototyping, for further discussion of such models.)

At this point, the team had chosen an oil-damped coil spring concept for the suspension fork. The design decisions facing the team included details such as the materials for the structural components, the orifice diameter and oil viscosity for the damper, and the spring constant. Three models linking such design decisions to the performance metrics are shown in conceptual form in Exhibit 6-9. Such models can be used to predict the product's performance along a number of dimensions. The inputs to these models are the independent design variables associated with the product concept, such as oil viscosity, orifice diameter, spring constant, and geometry. The outputs of the model are the values of the metrics, such as attenuation, stiffness, and fatigue life.

Ideally, the team will be able to accurately model the product analytically, perhaps by implementing the model equations in a spreadsheet or computer simulation. Such a model allows the team to predict rapidly what type of performance can be expected from a particular choice of design variables, without costly physical experimentation. In most cases, such analytical models will be available for only a small subset of the metrics. For example, the team was able to model attenuation analytically, based on the engineers' knowledge of dynamic systems.

Several independent models, each corresponding to a subset of the metrics, may be more manageable than one large integrated model. For example, the team developed a separate analytical model for the brake mounting stiffness that was completely independent of the dynamic model used to predict vibration attenuation. In some cases, no analytical models will be available at all. For example, the team was not able to model analytically the fatigue performance of the suspension, so physical models were built and tested. It is generally necessary to actually build a variety of different physical mock-ups or prototypes to explore the implications of several combinations of design variables. To reduce the number of models that must be constructed, it is useful to employ design-of-experiments (DOE) techniques, which can minimize the number of experiments required to explore the design space. (See Chapter 15, Robust Design, for a summary of DOE methods.)

Armed with these technical models, the team can predict whether any particular set of specifications (such as the ideal target values) is technically feasible by exploring different combinations of design variables. This type of modeling and analysis prevents the team from setting a combination of specifications that cannot be achieved using the available latitude in the product concept.

EXHIBIT 6-9 Models used to assess technical feasibility. Technical models may be analytical or physical approximations of the product concept.

Note that a technical model is almost always unique to a particular product concept. One of the models illustrated in Exhibit 6-9 is for an oil-damped suspension system; the model would be substantially different if the team had selected a concept employing a rubber suspension element. Thus, the modeling step can only be performed after the concept has been chosen.

Step 2: Develop a Cost Model of the Product

The goal of this step of the process is to make sure that the product can be produced at the *target cost*. The target cost is the manufacturing cost at which the company and its distribution partners can make adequate profits while still offering the product to the end customer at a competitive price. The appendix to this chapter provides an explanation of target costing. It is at this point that the team attempts to discover, for example, how much it will have to sacrifice in manufacturing cost to save 50 grams of mass.

For most products, the first estimates of manufacturing costs are completed by drafting a *bill of materials* (a list of all the parts) and estimating a purchase price or fabrication cost for each part. At this point in the development process the team does not generally know all of the components that will be in the product, but the team nevertheless makes an attempt to list the components it expects will be required. While early estimates generally focus on the cost of components, the team will usually make a rough estimate of assembly and other manufacturing costs (e.g., overhead) at this point as well. Efforts to develop these early cost estimates involve soliciting cost estimates from vendors and estimating the production costs of the components the firm will make itself. This process

Component	Qty/ Fork	High ($ ea.)	Low ($ ea.)	High Total ($/fork)	Low Total ($/fork)
Steertube	1	2.50	2.00	2.50	2.00
Crown	1	4.00	3.00	4.00	3.00
Boot	2	1.00	0.75	2.00	1.50
Lower tube	2	3.00	2.00	6.00	4.00
Lower tube top cover	2	2.00	1.50	4.00	3.00
Main lip seal	2	1.50	1.40	3.00	2.80
Slide bushing	4	0.20	0.18	0.80	0.72
Slide bushing spacer	2	0.50	0.40	1.00	0.80
Lower tube plug	2	0.50	0.35	1.00	0.70
Upper tube	2	5.50	4.00	11.00	8.00
Upper tube top cap	2	3.00	2.50	6.00	5.00
Upper tube adjustment knob	2	2.00	1.75	4.00	3.50
Adjustment shaft	2	4.00	3.00	8.00	6.00
Spring	2	3.00	2.50	6.00	5.00
Upper tube orifice cap	1	3.00	2.25	3.00	2.25
Orifice springs	4	0.50	0.40	2.00	1.60
Brake studs	2	0.40	0.35	0.80	0.70
Brake brace bolt	2	0.25	0.20	0.50	0.40
Brake brace	1	5.00	3.50	5.00	3.50
Oil (liters)	0.1	2.50	2.00	0.25	0.20
Misc. snap rings, o-rings	10	0.15	0.10	1.50	1.00
Decals	4	0.25	0.15	1.00	0.60
Assembly at $20/hr		30 min	20 min	10.00	6.67
Overhead at 25% of direct cost				20.84	15.74
Total				$104.19	$78.68

EXHIBIT 6-10 A bill of materials with cost estimates. This simple cost model allows early cost estimates to facilitate realistic trade-offs in the product specifications.

is often facilitated by a purchasing expert and a production engineer. A bill-of-materials cost model is shown in Exhibit 6-10 for the suspension fork. (See Chapter 13, Design for Manufacturing, for more details on estimating manufacturing cost.)

A useful way to record cost information is to list figures for the high and low estimates of each item. This helps the team to understand the range of uncertainty in the estimates. The bill of materials is typically used iteratively: the team performs a "what-if" cost analysis for a set of design decisions and then revises these decisions based on what it learns. The bill of materials is itself a kind of performance model, but instead of predicting the value of a technical performance metric, it predicts cost performance. The bill of materials remains useful throughout the development process and is updated regularly (as frequently as once each week) to reflect the current status of the estimated manufacturing cost.

At this point in the development process, teams developing complex products containing hundreds or thousands of parts will not generally be able to include every part in the bill of materials. Instead, the team will list the major components and subsystems and place bounds on their costs based on past experience or on the judgment of suppliers.

108   *Chapter 6*

Step 3: Refine the Specifications, Making Trade-Offs Where Necessary

Once the team has constructed technical performance models where possible and constructed a preliminary cost model, these tools can be used to develop final specifications. Finalizing specifications can be accomplished in a group session in which feasible combinations of values are determined through the use of the technical models and then the cost implications are explored. In an iterative fashion, the team converges on the specifications that will most favorably position the product relative to the competition, will best satisfy the customer needs, and will ensure adequate profits.

One important tool for supporting this decision-making process is the *competitive map*. An example competitive map is shown in Exhibit 6-11. This map is simply a scatter plot of the competitive products along two dimensions selected from the set of metrics and is sometimes called a trade-off map. The map displayed in Exhibit 6-11 shows estimated manufacturing cost versus score on the Monster test. The regions defined by the marginal and ideal values of the specifications are shown on the map. This map is particularly useful in showing that all of the high-performance suspensions (low Monster scores) have high estimated manufacturing costs. Armed with technical performance models and a cost model, the team can assess whether or not it will be able to "beat the trade-off" exhibited in the competitive map.

EXHIBIT 6-11   A competitive map showing estimated manufacturing cost versus score on the Monster test. Trade-off curves for two suspension concepts are also drawn on this map.

These maps can be constructed directly from the data contained in the competitive benchmarking chart using the plotting feature of the spreadsheet software. Generally, the team will prepare three or four such maps corresponding to a handful of critical metrics. Additional maps may be created as needed to support subsequent decision making.

The competitive map is used to position the new product relative to the competition. Trade-off curves, showing performance of the product concept for a range of design variables, can be drawn directly on the competitive map, as shown in Exhibit 6-11. Using the technical and cost models of the product and the competitive maps, the team can refine the specifications to both satisfy the inherent constraints of the product concept and make the trade-offs in a way that will provide a performance advantage relative to the competitive products. The final specifications for the suspension fork are shown in Exhibit 6-12.

For relatively mature product categories in which competition is based on performance relative to a handful of well-understood performance metrics, *conjoint analysis* may be useful in refining product specifications. Conjoint analysis uses customer survey data to construct a model of customer preference. Essentially, each respondent in a sample of potential customers is repeatedly asked to evaluate hypothetical products characterized by a set of attributes. These attributes must generally be metrics that are easily understood by customers (e.g., fuel economy and price for automobiles). Subjective attributes (e.g., styling) can be represented graphically. The hypothetical products are constructed using the statistical techniques of experimental design. Using customer responses, conjoint analysis infers the relative importance of each attribute to the customer. These data can then be used to predict which product a customer would choose when offered a hypothetical set of alternatives. By using these predictions for all of the customers in a sample, the market share of each product in the set of alternatives can be forecast. Using this approach, the specification values that maximize market share can be estimated. The details of conjoint analysis are fairly straightforward, but beyond the scope of this chapter. Relevant references are listed at the end of the chapter.

Step 4: Flow Down the Specifications as Appropriate

This chapter focuses on the specifications for a relatively simple component designed by a single, relatively small development team. Establishing specifications takes on additional importance and is substantially more challenging when developing a highly complex product consisting of multiple subsystems designed by multiple development teams. In such a context, specifications are used to define the development objectives of each of the subsystems as well as for the product as a whole. The challenge in this case is to *flow down* the overall specifications to specifications for each subsystem. For example, the overall specifications for an automobile contain metrics like fuel economy, 0–100 kilometer/ hour acceleration time, and turning radius; however, specifications must also be created for the several dozen major subsystems that make up the automobile, including the body, engine, transmission, braking system, and suspension. The specifications for the engine include metrics like peak power, peak torque, and fuel consumption at peak efficiency. One challenge in the flow-down process is to ensure that the subsystem specifications in fact reflect the overall product specifications—that if specifications for the subsystems are achieved, the overall product specifications will be achieved. A second challenge is to ensure that certain specifications for different subsystems are equally

EXHIBIT 6-12
The final specifications.

No.	Metric	Unit	Value
1	Attenuation from dropout to handlebar at 10 Hz	dB>	12
2	Spring preload	N	600–650
3	Maximum value from the Monster	g	<3.4
4	Minimum descent time on test track	s	<11.5
5	Damping coefficient adjustment range	N-s/m	>100
6	Maximum travel (26-in. wheel)	mm	43
7	Rake offset	mm	38
8	Lateral stiffness at the tip	kN/m	>75
9	Total mass	kg	<1.4
10	Lateral stiffness at brake pivots	kN/m	>425
11	Headset sizes	in.	1.000 1.125
12	Steertube length	mm	150 170 190 210 230
13	Wheel sizes	List	26 in.
14	Maximum tire width	in.	>1.75
15	Time to assemble to frame	s	<45
16	Fender compatibility	List	Zefal
17	Instills pride	Subj.	>4
18	Unit manufacturing cost	US$	<80
19	Time in spray chamber without water entry	s	>3600
20	Cycles in mud chamber without contamination	k-cycles	>25
21	Time to disassemble/assemble for maintenance	s	<200
22	Special tools required for maintenance	List	Hex
23	UV test duration to degrade rubber parts	hr	>450
24	Monster cycles to failure	Cycles	>500k
25	Japan Industrial Standards test	Binary	Pass
26	Bending strength (frontal loading)	kN	>10.0

difficult to meet. That is, for example, that the mass specification for the engine is not inordinately more difficult to meet than is the mass specification for the body. Otherwise, the cost of the product will likely be higher than necessary.

Some overall component specifications can be established through *budget allocations*. For example, specifications for manufacturing cost, mass, and power consumption can be allocated to subsystems with the confidence that the overall cost, mass, and power consumption of the product will simply be the sum of these quantities for each subsystem.

To some extent, geometric volume can be allocated this way as well. Other component specifications must be established through a more complex understanding of how subsystem performance relates to overall product performance. For example, fuel efficiency is a relatively complex function of vehicle mass, rolling resistance, aerodynamic drag coefficient, frontal area, and engine efficiency. Establishing specifications for the body, tires, and engine requires a model of how these variables relate to overall fuel efficiency.

A comprehensive treatment of flowing down specifications for complex products is beyond the scope of this chapter, and in fact is a major focus of the field of *systems engineering*. We refer the reader to books on this subject in the reference list.

Step 5: Reflect on the Results and the Process

As always, the final step in the method is to reflect on the outcome and the process. Some questions the team may want to consider are:

- Is the product a winner? The product concept should allow the team to actually set the specifications so that the product will meet the customer needs and excel competitively. If not, then the team should return to the concept generation and selection phase or abandon the project.

- How much uncertainty is there in the technical and cost models? If competitive success is dictated by metrics around which much uncertainty remains, the team may wish to refine the technical or cost models to increase confidence in meeting the specifications.

- Is the concept chosen by the team best suited to the target market, or could it be best applied in another market (say, the low end or high end instead of the middle)? The selected concept may actually be too good. If the team has generated a concept that is dramatically superior to the competitive products, it may wish to consider employing the concept in a more demanding, and potentially more profitable, market segment.

- Should the firm initiate a formal effort to develop better technical models of some aspect of the product's performance for future use? Sometimes the team will discover that it does not really understand the underlying product technology well enough to create useful performance models. In such circumstances, an engineering effort to develop better understanding and models may be useful in subsequent development projects.

Summary

Customer needs are generally expressed in the "language of the customer." To provide specific guidance about how to design and engineer a product, development teams establish a set of specifications, which spell out in precise, measurable detail what the product has to do to be commercially successful. The specifications must reflect the customer needs, differentiate the product from the competitive products, and be technically and economically realizable.

- Specifications are typically established at least twice. Immediately after identifying the customer needs, the team sets *target specifications*. After concept selection and testing, the team develops *final specifications*.

- Target specifications represent the hopes and aspirations of the team, but they are established before the team knows the constraints the product technology will place on what can be achieved. The team's efforts may fail to meet some of these specifications and may exceed others, depending on the details of the product concept the team eventually selects.

- The process of establishing the target specifications entails four steps:

  1. Prepare the list of metrics.
  2. Collect competitive benchmarking information.
  3. Set *ideal* and *marginally acceptable* target values.
  4. Reflect on the results and the process.

- Final specifications are developed by assessing the actual technological constraints and the expected production costs using analytical and physical models. During this refinement phase the team must make difficult trade-offs among various desirable characteristics of the product.

- The five-step process for refining the specifications is:

  1. Develop technical models of the product.
  2. Develop a cost model of the product.
  3. Refine the specifications, making trade-offs where necessary.
  4. Flow down the specifications as appropriate.
  5. Reflect on the results and the process.

- The specifications process is facilitated by several simple information systems that can easily be created using conventional spreadsheet software. Tools such as the list of metrics, the needs-metrics matrix, the competitive benchmarking charts, and the competitive maps all support the team's decision making by providing the team with a way to represent and discuss the specifications.

- Because of the need to utilize the best possible knowledge of the market, the customers, the core product technology, and the cost implications of design alternatives, the specifications process requires active participation from team members representing the marketing, design, and manufacturing functions of the enterprise.

References and Bibliography

Many current resources are available on the Internet via
www.ulrich-eppinger.net

The process of translating customer needs into a set of specifications is also accomplished by the Quality Function Deployment (QFD) method. The key ideas behind QFD and the House of Quality are clearly presented by Hauser and Clausing in a popular article.

Hauser, John, and Don Clausing, "The House of Quality," *Harvard Business Review*, Vol. 66, No. 3, May–June 1988, pp. 63–73.

Urban and Hauser present several techniques for selecting combinations of product attributes to maximize customer satisfaction. Some of these techniques can serve as powerful analytical support for the general method described in this chapter.

Urban, Glen, and John Hauser, *Design and Marketing of New Products,* second edition, Prentice Hall, Englewood Cliffs, NJ, 1993.

Ramaswamy and Ulrich treat the use of engineering models in setting specifications in detail. They also identify some of the weaknesses in the conventional House of Quality method.
Ramaswamy, Rajan, and Karl Ulrich, "Augmenting the House of Quality with Engineering Models," *Research in Engineering Design,* Vol. 5, 1994, pp. 70–79.

Most marketing research textbooks discuss conjoint analysis. Here are two references.
Aaker, David A., V. Kumar, and George S. Day, *Marketing Research,* sixth edition, John Wiley & Sons, New York, 1997.
Conjoint Analysis: A Guide for Designing and Interpreting Conjoint Studies, American Marketing Association, June 1992.

Systems engineering and the flow down of specifications are treated comprehensively in the following books.
Systems Engineering Handbook: A Guide for System Life Cycle Processes and Activities, International Council on Systems Engineering, October 2011.
Rechtin, Eberhardt, and Mark W. Maier, *The Art of Systems Architecting,* second edition, CRC Press, Boca Raton, FL, 2000.

More detail on the use of target costing is available in this article by Cooper and Slagmulder.
Cooper, Robin, and Regine Slagmulder, "Develop Profitable New Products with Target Costing," *Sloan Management Review,* Vol. 40, No. 4, Summer 1999, pp. 23–33.

Exercises

1. List a set of metrics corresponding to the need that a pen write smoothly.
2. Devise a metric and a corresponding test for the need that a roofing material last many years.
3. Some of the same metrics seem to be involved in trade-offs for many different products. What are some examples of such metrics?

Thought Questions

1. How might you establish precise and measurable specifications for intangible needs such as "the front suspension looks great"?
2. Why are some customer needs difficult to map to a single metric?
3. How might you explain a situation in which customers' perceptions of the competitive products (as in Exhibit 6-7) are not consistent with the values of the metrics for those same products (as in Exhibit 6-6)?
4. Can poor performance relative to one specification always be compensated for by high performance on other specifications? If so, how can there ever really be a "marginally acceptable" value for a metric?
5. Why should independent design variables not be used as metrics?

114   *Chapter 6*

Appendix

Target Costing

Target costing is a simple idea: set the value of the manufacturing cost specification based on the price the company hopes the end user will pay for the product and on the profit margins that are required for each stage in the distribution channel. For example, assume Specialized wishes to sell its suspension fork to its customers through bicycle shops. If the price it expected the customer to pay was $250 and if bicycle shops normally expect a gross profit margin of 45 percent on components, then Specialized would have to sell its fork to bicycle shops for $(1 - 0.45) \cdot 250 = \$137.50$. If Specialized wishes to earn a gross margin of at least 40 percent on its components, then its unit manufacturing cost must be less than $(1 - 0.40) \cdot 137.50 = \$82.50$.

Target costing is the reverse of the *cost-plus* approach to pricing. The cost-plus approach begins with what the firm expects its manufacturing costs to be and then sets its prices by adding its expected profit margin to the cost. This approach ignores the realities of competitive markets, in which prices are driven by market and customer factors. Target costing is a mechanism for ensuring that specifications are set in a way that allows the product to be competitively priced in the marketplace.

Some products are sold directly by a manufacturer to end users of the product. Frequently, products are distributed through one or more intermediate stages, such as distributors and retailers. Exhibit 6-13 provides some approximate values of gross profit margins for different product categories.

Let *M* be the gross profit *margin* of a stage in the distribution channel.

$$M = \frac{(P - C)}{P}$$

where *P* is the price this stage charges its customers and *C* is the cost this stage pays for the product it sells. (Note that *mark-up* is similar to margin, but is defined slightly differently as $P/C - 1$, so that a margin of 50 percent is equivalent to a mark-up of 100 percent.)

Target cost, *C,* is given by the following expression:

$$C = P \prod_{i=1}^{n}(1 - M_i)$$

where *P* is the price paid by the end user, *n* is the number of stages in the distribution channel, and M_i is the margin of the *i*th stage.

EXAMPLE

Assume the end user price, *P,* equals $250.

If the product is sold directly to the end user by the manufacturer, and the desired gross profit margin of the manufacturer, M_m, equals 0.40, then the target cost is

$$C = P(1 - M_m) = \$250 \,(1 - 0.40) = \$150$$

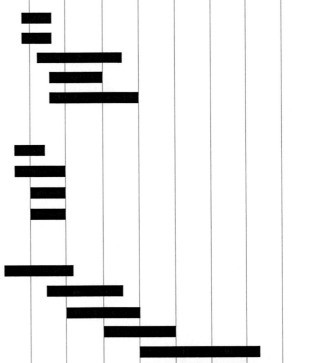

EXHIBIT 6-13 Approximate margins for manufacturers, wholesalers, distributors, sales representatives, and retailers. Note that these values are quite approximate. Actual margins depend on many idiosyncratic factors, including competitive intensity, the volume of units sold, and the level of customer support required. Sales representatives are paid by commission and are not strictly part of the distribution channel; however, the team may wish to account for commissions in its analysis of target cost.

If the product is sold through a retailer, and the desired gross profit margin for the retailer, M_r, equals 0.45, then

$$C = P(1 - M_m)(1 - M_r)$$
$$= \$250\,(1 - 0.40)(1 - 0.45) = \$82.50$$

If the product is sold through a distributor and a retailer, and the desired gross profit margin for the distributor, M_d, equals 0.20, then

$$C = P(1 - M_m)(1 - M_d)(1 - M_r) = \$250\,(1 - 0.40)(1 - 0.20)(1 - 0.45) = \$66.00$$

CHAPTER SEVEN

Concept Generation

EXHIBIT 7-1
A cordless electric roofing nailer.

The president of Stanley-Bostitch commissioned a team to develop a new handheld nailer for the roofing market. The product that eventually resulted from the effort is shown in Exhibit 7-1. The mission of the team was to consider broadly alternative product concepts, assuming only that the tool would employ conventional nails as the basic fastening technology. After identifying a set of customer needs and establishing target product specifications, the team faced the following questions:

- What existing solution concepts, if any, could be successfully adapted for this application?
- What new concepts might satisfy the established needs and specifications?
- What methods can be used to facilitate the concept generation process?

The Activity of Concept Generation

A product concept is an approximate description of the technology, working principles, and form of the product. It is a concise description of how the product will satisfy the customer needs. A concept is usually expressed as a sketch or as a rough three-dimensional model and is often accompanied by a brief textual description. The degree to which a product satisfies customers and can be successfully commercialized depends to a large measure on the quality of the underlying concept. A good concept is sometimes poorly implemented in subsequent development phases, but a poor concept can rarely be manipulated to achieve commercial success. Fortunately, concept generation is relatively inexpensive and can be done relatively quickly in comparison to the rest of the development process. For example, concept generation had typically consumed less than 5 percent of the budget and 15 percent of the development time in previous nailer development efforts. Because the concept generation activity is not costly, there is no excuse for a lack of diligence and care in executing a sound concept generation method.

The concept generation process begins with a set of customer needs and target specifications and results in a set of product concepts from which the team will make a final selection. The relation of concept generation to the other concept development activities is shown in Exhibit 7-2. In most cases, an effective development team will generate hundreds of concepts, of which 5 to 20 will merit serious consideration during the concept selection activity.

EXHIBIT 7-2   Concept generation is an integral part of the concept development phase.

Good concept generation leaves the team with confidence that the full space of alternatives has been explored. Thorough exploration of alternatives early in the development process greatly reduces the likelihood that the team will stumble upon a superior concept late in the development process or that a competitor will introduce a product with dramatically better performance than the product under development.

Structured Approaches Reduce the Likelihood of Costly Problems

Common dysfunctions exhibited by development teams during concept generation include:

- Consideration of only one or two alternatives, often proposed by the most assertive members of the team.
- Failure to consider carefully the usefulness of concepts employed by other firms in related and unrelated products.
- Involvement of only one or two people in the process, resulting in lack of confidence and commitment by the rest of the team.
- Ineffective integration of promising partial solutions.
- Failure to consider entire categories of solutions.

A structured approach to concept generation reduces the incidence of these problems by encouraging the gathering of information from many disparate information sources, by guiding the team in the thorough exploration of alternatives, and by providing a mechanism for integrating partial solutions. A structured method also provides a step-by-step procedure for those members of the team who may be less experienced in design-intensive activities, allowing them to participate actively in the process.

A Five-Step Method

This chapter presents a five-step concept generation method. The method, outlined in Exhibit 7-3, breaks a complex problem into simpler subproblems. Solution concepts are then identified for the subproblems by external and internal search procedures. Classification trees and concept combination tables are then used to systematically explore the space of solution concepts and to integrate the subproblem solutions into a total solution. Finally, the team takes a step back to reflect on the validity and applicability of the results, as well as on the process used.

This chapter will follow the recommended method and will describe each of the five steps in detail. Although we present the method in a linear sequence, concept generation is almost always iterative. Like our other development methods, these steps are intended to be a baseline from which product development teams can develop and refine their own unique problem-solving style.

Our presentation of the method is focused primarily on the overall concept for a new product; however, the method can and should be used at several different points in the development process. The process is useful not only for overall product concepts but also for concepts for subsystems and specific components as well. Also note that while the example in this chapter involves a relatively technical product, the same basic approach can be applied to nearly any product.

EXHIBIT 7-3
The five-step concept generation method.

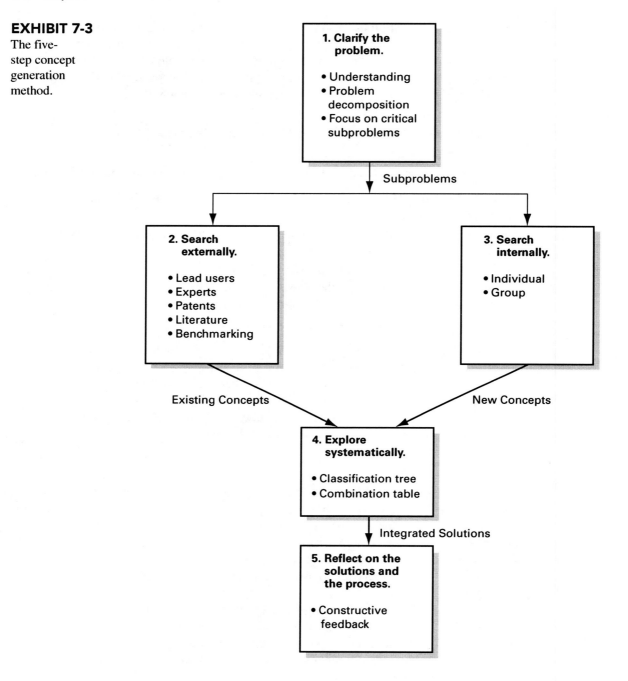

Step 1: Clarify the Problem

Clarifying the problem consists of developing a general understanding and then breaking the problem down into subproblems if necessary.

The mission statement for the project, the customer needs list, and the preliminary product specification are the ideal inputs to the concept generation process, although often these pieces of information are still being refined as the concept generation phase begins. Ideally the team has been involved both in the identification of the customer needs and in the setting of the target product specifications. Those members of the team who were not involved in these preceding steps should become familiar with the processes used and their results before concept generation activities begin. (See Chapter 5, Identifying Customer Needs, and Chapter 6, Product Specifications.)

As stated before, the challenge was to "design a better handheld roofing nailer." The scope of the design problem could have been defined more generally (e.g., "fasten roofing materials") or more specifically (e.g., "improve the speed of the existing pneumatic tool concept"). Some of the assumptions in the team's mission statement were:

- The nailer will use nails (as opposed to adhesives, screws, etc.).
- The nailer will be compatible with nail magazines on existing tools.
- The nailer will nail through roofing shingles into wood.
- The nailer will be handheld.

Based on the assumptions, the team had identified the customer needs for a handheld nailer. These included:

- The nailer inserts nails in rapid succession.
- The nailer is lightweight.
- The nailer has no noticeable nailing delay after tripping the tool.

The team gathered supplemental information to clarify and quantify the needs, such as the approximate energy and speed of the nailing. These basic needs were subsequently translated into target product specifications. The target specifications included the following:

- Nail lengths from 25 millimeters to 38 millimeters.
- Maximum nailing energy of 40 joules per nail.
- Nailing forces of up to 2,000 newtons.
- Peak nailing rate of one nail per second.
- Average nailing rate of 12 nails per minute.
- Tool mass less than 4 kilograms.
- Maximum trigger delay of 0.25 second.

Decompose a Complex Problem into Simpler Subproblems

Many design challenges are too complex to solve as a single problem and can be usefully divided into several simpler subproblems. For example, the design of a complex product like a document copier can be thought of as a collection of more focused design problems, including, for example, the design of a document handler, the design of a paper feeder, the design of a printing device, and the design of an image capture device. In some cases, however, the design problem cannot readily be divided into subproblems. For example, the problem of designing a paper clip may be hard to divide into subproblems. As a general rule, we feel that teams should attempt to decompose design problems, but should be aware that such a decomposition may not be very useful for products with extremely simple functions.

Dividing a problem into simpler subproblems is called *problem decomposition*. There are many schemes by which a problem can be decomposed. Here we demonstrate a *functional* decomposition and also list several other approaches that are frequently useful.

EXHIBIT 7-4 Function diagram of a handheld nailer arising from a functional decomposition: (a) overall "black box"; (b) refinement showing subfunctions.

The first step in decomposing a problem functionally is to represent it as a single *black box* operating on material, energy, and signal flows, as shown in Exhibit 7-4(a). Thin solid lines denote the transfer and conversion of energy, thick solid lines signify the movement of material within the system, and dashed lines represent the flows of control and feedback signals within the system. This black box represents the overall function of the product.

The next step in functional decomposition is to divide the single black box into subfunctions to create a more specific description of what the elements of the product might do to implement the overall function of the product. Each subfunction can generally be further divided into even simpler subfunctions. The division process is repeated until the team members agree that each subfunction is simple enough to work with. A good rule of thumb is to create between 3 and 10 subfunctions in the diagram. The end result, shown in Exhibit 7-4(b), is a function diagram containing subfunctions connected by energy, material, and signal flows.

Note that at this stage the goal is to describe the functional elements of the product without implying a specific technological working principle for the product concept. For example, Exhibit 7-4(b) includes the subfunction "isolate nail." This subfunction is expressed in such a way that it does not imply any particular physical solution concept, such as indexing the coil of nails into a slot or breaking a nail sideways off of the stick. The team should consider each subfunction in turn and ask whether it is expressed in a way that does not imply a particular physical solution principle.

There is no single correct way of creating a function diagram and no single correct functional decomposition of a product. A helpful way to create the diagram is to quickly create several drafts and then work to refine them into a single diagram that the team is comfortable with. Some useful techniques for getting started are:

- Create a function diagram of an existing product.
- Create a function diagram based on an arbitrary product concept already generated by the team or based on a known subfunction technology. Be sure to generalize the diagram to the appropriate level of abstraction.
- Follow one of the flows (e.g., material) and determine what operations are required. The details of the other flows can be derived by thinking about their connections to the initial flow.

Note that the function diagram is typically not unique. In particular, subfunctions can often be ordered in different ways to produce different function diagrams. Also note that in some applications the material, energy, and signal flows are difficult to identify. In these cases, a simple list of the subfunctions of the product, without connections between them, is often sufficient.

Functional decomposition is most applicable to technical products, but it can also be applied to simple and apparently nontechnical products. For example, an ice cream scoop has material flow of ice cream being separated, formed, transported, and deposited. These subfunctions could form the basis of a problem decomposition.

Functional decomposition is only one of several possible ways to divide a problem into simpler subproblems. Two other approaches are:

- *Decomposition by sequence of user actions:* For example, the nailer problem might be broken down into three user actions: moving the tool to the gross nailing position, positioning the tool precisely, and triggering the tool. This approach is often useful for products with very simple technical functions involving a lot of user interaction.
- *Decomposition by key customer needs:* For the nailer, this decomposition might include the following subproblems: fires nails in rapid succession, is lightweight, and has a large nail capacity. This approach is often useful for products in which form, and not working principles or technology, is the primary problem. Examples of such products include toothbrushes (assuming the basic brush concept is retained) and storage containers.

Focus Initial Efforts on the Critical Subproblems

The goal of all of these decomposition techniques is to divide a complex problem into simpler problems such that these simpler problems can be tackled in a focused way. Once problem decomposition is complete, the team chooses the subproblems that are most critical to the success of the product and that are most likely to benefit from novel or creative solutions. This approach involves a conscious decision to defer the solution of some of the subproblems. For example, the nailer team chose to focus on the subproblems of storing/ accepting energy, converting the energy to translational energy, and applying the translational energy to the nail. The team felt confident that the nail handling and triggering issues could be solved after the energy storage and conversion issues were addressed. The team also deferred most of the user interaction issues of the tool. The team believed that the choice of a basic working principle for the tool would so constrain the eventual form of the tool that they had to begin with the core technology and then proceed to consider how to embody that technology in an attractive and user-friendly form. Teams can usually agree after a few minutes of discussion on which subproblems should be addressed first and which should be deferred for later consideration.

Step 2: Search Externally

External search is aimed at finding existing solutions to both the overall problem and the subproblems identified during the problem clarification step. While external search is listed as the second step in the concept generation method, this sequential labeling is deceptive; external search occurs continually throughout the development process. Implementing an existing solution is usually quicker and cheaper than developing a new solution. Liberal use of existing solutions allows the team to focus its creative energy on the critical subproblems for which there are no satisfactory prior solutions. Furthermore, a conventional solution to one subproblem can frequently be combined with a novel solution to another subproblem to yield a superior overall design. For this reason external search includes detailed evaluation not only of directly competitive products but also of technologies used in products with related subfunctions.

The external search for solutions is essentially an information-gathering process. Available time and resources can be optimized by using an expand-and-focus strategy: first *expand* the scope of the search by broadly gathering information that might be related to the problem and then *focus* the scope of the search by exploring the promising directions in more detail. Too much of either approach will make the external search inefficient.

There are at least five good ways to gather information from external sources: lead user interviews, expert consultation, patent searches, literature searches, and competitive benchmarking.

Interview Lead Users

While identifying customer needs, the team may have sought out or encountered lead users. *Lead users* are those users of a product who experience needs months or years before the majority of the market and stand to benefit substantially from a product innovation (von Hippel, 1988). Frequently these lead users will have already invented solutions to meet their needs. This is particularly true among highly technical user communities, such as those in the medical or scientific fields. Lead users may be sought out in the market for which the team is developing the new product, or they may be found in markets for products implementing some of the subfunctions of the product.

In the handheld nailer case, the nailer team consulted with the building contractors from the PBS television series *This Old House* to solicit new concepts. These lead users, who are exposed to tools from many manufacturers, made many interesting observations about the weaknesses in existing tools, but in this case did not provide many new product concepts.

Consult Experts

Experts with knowledge of one or more of the subproblems not only can provide solution concepts directly but also can redirect the search in a more fruitful area. Experts may include professionals at firms manufacturing related products, professional consultants, university faculty, and technical representatives of suppliers. These people can be found by calling universities, by calling companies, and by looking up authors of articles. While finding experts can be hard work, it is almost always less time consuming than re-creating existing knowledge.

Most experts are willing to talk on the telephone or meet in person for an hour or so without charge. In general, consultants will expect to be paid for time they spend on a problem beyond an initial meeting or telephone conversation. Suppliers are usually willing to provide several days of effort without direct compensation if they anticipate that someone will use their product as a component in a design. Of course, experts at directly competing firms are in most cases unwilling to provide proprietary information about their product designs. A good habit to develop is to always ask people consulted to suggest others who should be contacted. The best information often comes from pursuing these "second generation" leads.

The nailer design team consulted dozens of experts, including a rocket fuel specialist, electric motor researchers at MIT, and engineers from a vendor of gas springs. Most of this consultation was done on the telephone, although the engineers from the spring vendor made two trips to visit the team, at their company's expense.

Search Patents

Patents are a rich and readily available source of technical information containing detailed drawings and explanations of how many products work. The main disadvantage of patent searches is that concepts found in recent patents are protected (generally for 20 years from the date of the patent application), so there may be a royalty involved in using them; however, patents are also useful to see what concepts are already protected and must be avoided or licensed. Concepts contained in foreign patents without global coverage and in expired patents can be used without payment of royalties. See Chapter 16, Patents and Intellectual Property, for an explanation of patent rights and how to understand patent claims.

The formal indexing scheme for patents is difficult for novices to navigate. Fortunately, several databases contain the actual text of all patents. These text databases can be searched electronically by key words. Key word searches can be conducted efficiently with only modest practice and are remarkably effective in finding patents relevant to a particular product. Copies of U.S. patents including illustrations can be obtained for a nominal fee from the U.S. Patent and Trademark Office and from several suppliers. (See the Web site www.ulrich-eppinger.net for a current list of online patent databases and suppliers of patent documents.)

A U.S. patent search in the area of nailers revealed several interesting concepts. One of the patents described a motor-driven double-flywheel nailer. One of the illustrations from this patent is shown in Exhibit 7-5. The design in this patent uses the accumulation of rotational kinetic energy in a flywheel, which is then suddenly converted into translational energy by a friction clutch. The energy is then delivered to the nail with a single impact of a drive pin.

126 *Chapter 7*

EXHIBIT 7-5   Concept from motor-driven double-flywheel nailer patent (U.S. Patent 4,042,036). The accompanying text describing the patent is nine pages long.

Search Published Literature

Published literature includes journals; conference proceedings; trade magazines; government reports; market, consumer, and product information; and new product announcements. Literature searches are therefore very fertile sources of existing solutions.

Electronic searches are frequently the most efficient way to gather information from published literature. Searching the Internet is often a good first step, although the quality of the results can be hard to assess. More structured databases are available from online sources. Many databases store only abstracts of articles and not the full text and diagrams. A follow-up search for an actual article is often needed for complete information. The two main difficulties in conducting good database searches are determining the key words and limiting the scope of the search. There is a trade-off between the need to use more key words for complete coverage and the need to restrict the number of matches to a manageable number.

Handbooks cataloging technical information can also be very useful references for external search. Examples of such engineering references are *Marks' Standard Handbook of Mechanical Engineering, Perry's Chemical Engineers' Handbook,* and *Mechanisms and Mechanical Devices Sourcebook.*

The nailer team found several useful articles related to the subproblems, including articles on energy storage describing flywheel and battery technologies. In a handbook they found an impact tool mechanism that provided a useful energy conversion concept.

Benchmark Related Products

In the context of concept generation, *benchmarking* is the study of existing products with functionality similar to that of the product under development or to the subproblems on which the team is focused. Benchmarking can reveal existing concepts that have been implemented to solve a particular problem, as well as information on the strengths and weaknesses of the competition.

At this point the team will likely already be familiar with the competitive and closely related products. Products in other markets, but with related functionality, are more difficult to find. One of the most useful sources of this information is the *Thomas Register,* a directory of manufacturers of industrial products organized by product type. Often the hardest part of using the *Thomas Register* is finding out what related products are actually called and how they are cataloged. The *Thomas Register* database can be accessed via the Internet.

For the nailer, the closely related products included a single-shot gunpowder-actuated tool for nailing into concrete, an electrical solenoid-actuated tacker, a pneumatic nailer for factory use, and a palm-held multiblow pneumatic nailer. The products with related functionality (in this case, energy storage and conversion) included air bags and the sodium azide propellant used as an energy source, chemical hand warmers for skiing, air rifles powered by carbon dioxide cartridges, and portable computers and their battery packs. The team obtained and disassembled most of these related products to discover the general concepts on which they were based, as well as other, more detailed information, including, for example, the names of the suppliers of specific components.

External search is an important method of gathering solution concepts. Skill in conducting external searches is therefore a valuable personal and organizational asset. This ability can be developed through careful observation of the world to develop a mental database of technologies and through the development of a network of professional contacts. Even with the aid of personal knowledge and contacts, external search remains "detective work" and is completed most effectively by those who are persistent and resourceful in pursuing leads and opportunities.

Step 3: Search Internally

Internal search is the use of personal and team knowledge and creativity to generate solution concepts. Often called *brainstorming,* and based largely on the creativity methods developed by Osborn in the 1940s, this type of search is *internal* in that all of the ideas to emerge from this step are created from knowledge already in the possession of the team. This activity may be the most open-ended and creative of any task in product development. We find it useful to think of internal search as a process of retrieving a potentially useful piece of information from one's memory and then adapting that information to the problem at hand. This process can be carried out by individuals working in isolation or by a group of people working together.

Five guidelines are useful for improving both individual and group internal search:

1. *Suspend judgment.* In most aspects of daily life, success depends on an ability to quickly evaluate a set of alternatives and take action. For example, none of us would be very productive if deciding what to wear in the morning or what to eat for breakfast involved an extensive period of generating alternatives before making a judgment. Because most decisions in our day-to-day lives have implications of only a few minutes or hours, we are accustomed to making decisions quickly and moving on. Concept generation for product development is fundamentally different. We have to live with the consequences of product concept decisions for years. As a result, suspending evaluation for the days or weeks required to generate a large set of alternatives is critical to success. The imperative to suspend judgment is frequently translated into the rule that during group concept generation sessions no criticism of concepts is allowed. A better approach is for individuals perceiving weaknesses in concepts to channel any judgmental tendencies into suggestions for improvements or alternative concepts.

2. *Generate a lot of ideas.* Most experts believe that the more ideas a team generates, the more likely the team is to explore fully the solution space. Striving for quantity lowers the expectations of quality for any particular idea and therefore may encourage people to share ideas they may otherwise view as not worth mentioning. Further, each idea acts as a stimulus for other ideas, so a large number of ideas has the potential to stimulate even more ideas.

3. *Welcome ideas that may seem infeasible.* Ideas that initially appear infeasible can often be improved, "debugged," or "repaired" by other members of the team. The more infeasible an idea, the more it stretches the boundaries of the solution space and encourages the team to think of the limits of possibility. Therefore, infeasible ideas are quite valuable and their expression should be encouraged.

4. *Make plenty of sketches.* Spatial reasoning about physical objects can be challenging. Text and verbal language are inherently inefficient vehicles for describing physical entities. Whether working as a group or as an individual, abundant sketching materials should be available. Sketch quality is not so critical here; it is the expression of the concept that matters (Yang and Cham, 2007). Moreover, adding key dimensions to concept sketches has been shown to correlate with successful concept development (Yang, 2009).

5. *Build sketch models.* Simple, physical models can quickly be created to express concepts using foam, clay, cardboard, 3-D printing, and other media. Three-dimensional *sketch models* are particularly helpful for problems requiring a deep understanding of form, user interface, and spatial relationships. Research on the timing of sketch models suggests that earlier exploration using simple physical models is linked to better design outcomes (Häggman et al., 2013). Further research found that parallel development of multiple, alternative sketch models, rather than working on a single prototype at a time, is linked to better concept development performance (Neeley et al., 2013).

Both Individual and Group Sessions Can Be Useful

Formal studies of group and individual problem solving suggest that a set of people working alone for a period of time will generate more and better concepts than the same people working together for the same time period (McGrath, 1984). This finding is contrary to the actual practices of the many firms that perform most of their concept generation activities in group sessions. Our observations confirm the formal studies, and we believe that team members should spend at least some of their concept generation time working alone. This is because each person in the group may excel at a different dimension of creativity. That is, some members may be more fluid (many ideas along a single line of thinking), while others are more flexible (many different types of ideas), and others can be more novel (offering fewer but highly divergent ideas). We also believe that group sessions are critical for building consensus, communicating information, and refining concepts. In an ideal setting, each individual on the team would spend several hours working alone and then the group would get together to discuss and improve the concepts generated by individuals.

However, we also know that there is a practical reason for holding group concept generation sessions: it is one way to guarantee that the individuals in the group will devote a certain amount of time to the task. Especially in very intense and demanding work environments, without scheduling a meeting, few people will allocate several hours for concentrated individual effort on generating new concepts. The phone rings, people interrupt, urgent problems and e-mails demand attention. In certain environments, scheduled group sessions may be the only way to guarantee that enough attention is paid to the concept generation activity.

The nailer team used both individual effort and group sessions for internal search. For example, during one particular week each member was assigned one or two subproblems and was expected to develop at least 10 solution concepts. This divided the concept generation work among all members. The group then met to discuss and expand on the individually generated concepts. The more promising concepts were investigated further.

Hints for Generating Solution Concepts

Experienced individuals and teams can usually just sit down and begin generating good concepts for a subproblem. Often these people have developed a set of techniques they use to stimulate their thinking, and these techniques have become a natural part of their problem-solving process. Novice product development professionals may be aided by a set of hints that stimulate new ideas or encourage relationships among ideas. VanGundy (1988), von Oech (1998), and McKim (1980) give dozens of helpful suggestions. Here are some hints we have found to be helpful:

- *Make analogies.* Experienced designers always ask themselves what other devices solve a related problem. Frequently they will ask themselves if there is a natural or biological analogy to the problem. They will think about whether their problem exists at a much larger or smaller dimensional scale than that which they are considering. They will ask what devices do something similar in an unrelated area of application. The nailer team, when posing these questions, realized that construction pile drivers are similar to nailers in some respects. In following up on this idea, they developed the concept of a multiblow tool.

- *Wish and wonder.* Beginning a thought or comment with "I wish we could . . ." or "I wonder what would happen if . . ." helps to stimulate oneself or the group to consider new possibilities. These questions cause reflection on the boundaries of the problem. For example, a member of the nailer team, when confronted with the required length of a rail gun (an electromagnetic device for accelerating a projectile) for driving a nail, said, "I wish the tool could be 1 meter long." Discussion of this comment led to the idea that perhaps a long tool could be used like a cane for nailing decking, allowing users to remain on their feet.

- *Distort ideas.* It is often helpful to modify or rearrange fragments of different solutions to create new ones. Several methods exist to stimulate this type of thinking. For example, the SCAMPER method, derived from Osborn's work, provides stimuli to do this in seven ways that form its acronym: substitute, combine, adapt, modify/magnify/ minimize, put to other uses, eliminate, and reverse/rearrange.

- *Use related stimuli.* Most individuals can think of a new idea when presented with a new stimulus. Related stimuli are those stimuli generated in the context of the problem at hand. For example, one way to use related stimuli is for each individual in a group session to generate a list of ideas (working alone) and then pass the list to his or her neighbor. Upon reflection on someone else's ideas, most people are able to generate new ideas. Other related stimuli include customer needs statements and photographs of the use environment of the product.

- *Use unrelated stimuli.* Occasionally, random or unrelated stimuli can be effective in encouraging new ideas. An example of such a technique, known as *synectics*, is to choose, at random, one of a collection of photographs of objects, and then to think of some way that the randomly generated object might relate to the problem at hand (Gordon, 1961). In a variant of this idea, individuals can be sent out on the streets with a digital camera to capture random images for subsequent use in stimulating new ideas. (This may also serve as a good change of pace for a tired group.)

- *Set quantitative goals.* Generating new ideas can be exhausting. Near the end of a session, individuals and groups may find quantitative goals useful as a motivating force. The nailer team frequently issued individual concept generation assignments with quantitative targets of 10 to 20 concepts.

- *Use the gallery method.* The *gallery method* is a way to display a large number of concepts simultaneously for discussion. Sketches, usually one concept to a sheet, are taped or pinned to the walls of the meeting room. Team members circulate and look at each concept. The creator of the concept may offer explanation, and the group subsequently makes suggestions for improving the concept or spontaneously generates related concepts. This method is a good way to merge individual and group efforts.

In the 1990s, a Russian problem-solving methodology called TRIZ (a Russian acronym for *theory of inventive problem solving*) began to be disseminated in Europe and in the United States. The methodology is primarily useful in identifying physical working principles to solve technical problems. The key idea underlying TRIZ is to identify a contradiction that is implicit in a problem. For example, a contradiction in the nailer problem might be that increasing power (a desirable characteristic) would also tend to increase weight (an undesirable characteristic). One of the TRIZ tools is a matrix of 39 by 39 characteristics with each cell corresponding to a particular conflict between two characteristics. In each cell of the matrix, up to four physical principles are suggested as ways of resolving the corresponding conflict. There are 40 basic principles, including, for example, the *periodic action* principle (i.e., replace a continuous action with a periodic action, like an impulse). Using TRIZ, the nailer team might have arrived at the concept of using repeated smaller impacts to drive the nail. The idea of identifying a conflict in the design problem and then thinking about ways to resolve the conflict appears to be a very useful problem-solving heuristic. This approach can be useful in generating concepts even without adopting the entire TRIZ methodology.

Exhibit 7-6 shows some of the solutions the nailer team generated for the subproblems of (1) storing or accepting energy and (2) delivering translational energy to a nail.

EXHIBIT 7-6
Some of the solutions to the subproblems of (1) storing or accepting energy and (2) delivering translational energy to a nail.

Solutions to Subproblem of Storing or Accepting Energy	Solutions to Subproblem of Applying Translational Energy to Nail
• Self-regulating chemical reaction emitting high-pressure gas	
• Carbide (as for lanterns)	
• Combusting sawdust from job site	Single impact
• Gun powder	
• Sodium azide (air bag explosive)	
• Fuel-air combustion (butane, propane, acetylene, etc.)	
• Compressed air (in tank or from compressor)	
• Carbon dioxide in tank	
• Electric wall outlet and cord	
• High-pressure oil line (hydraulics)	Multiple impacts (tens or hundreds)
• Flywheel with charging (spin-up)	
• Battery pack on tool, belt, or floor	
• Fuel cell	
• Human power: arms or legs	
• Methane from decomposing organic materials	Multiple impacts (hundreds or thousands)
• "Burning" like that of chemical hand warmers	
• Nuclear reactions	
• Cold fusion	
• Solar electric cells	Push
• Solar-steam conversion	
• Steam supply line	
• Wind	
• Geothermal	Twist-push

Step 4: Explore Systematically

As a result of the external and internal search activities, the team will have collected tens or hundreds of concept *fragments*—solutions to the subproblems. Systematic exploration is aimed at navigating the space of possibilities by organizing and synthesizing these solution fragments. The nailer team focused on the energy storage, conversion, and delivery subproblems and had generated dozens of concept fragments for each subproblem. One approach to organizing and synthesizing these fragments would be to consider all of the possible combinations of the fragments associated with each subproblem; however, a little arithmetic reveals the impossibility of this approach. Given the three subproblems on which the team focused and an average of 15 fragments for each subproblem, the team would have to consider 3,375 combinations of fragments ($15 \times 15 \times 15$). This would be

132   *Chapter 7*

EXHIBIT 7-7
A classification
tree for the
nailer energy
source concept
fragments.

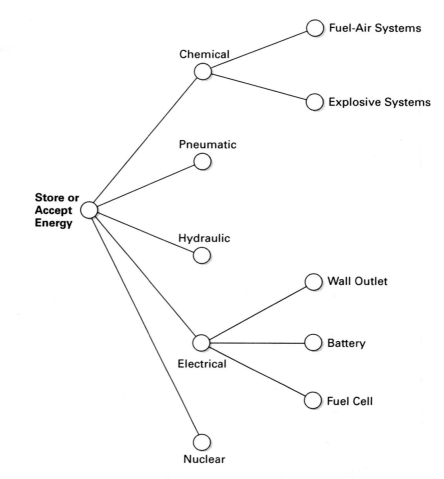

a daunting task for even the most enthusiastic team. Furthermore, the team would quickly discover that many of the combinations do not even make sense. Fortunately, there are two specific tools for managing this complexity and organizing the thinking of the team: the *concept classification tree* and the *concept combination table*. The classification tree helps the team divide the possible solutions into independent categories. The combination table guides the team in selectively considering combinations of fragments.

Concept Classification Tree

The concept classification tree is used to divide the entire space of possible solutions into several distinct classes that will facilitate comparison and pruning. An example of a tree for the nailer example is shown in Exhibit 7-7. The branches of this tree correspond to different energy sources.

The classification tree provides at least four important benefits:

1. *Pruning of less promising branches:* If by studying the classification tree the team is able to identify a solution approach that does not appear to have much merit, then this approach can be pruned and the team can focus its attention on the more promising branches of the tree. Pruning a branch of the tree requires some evaluation and judgment and should therefore be done carefully, but the reality of product development is that there are limited

EXHIBIT 7-8
A new problem decomposition assuming an electrical energy source and the accumulation of energy in the mechanical domain.

resources and that focusing the available resources on the most promising directions is an important success factor. For the nailer team, the nuclear energy source was pruned from consideration. Although the team had identified some very intriguing nuclear devices for use in powering artificial hearts, they felt that these devices would not be economically practical for at least a decade and would probably be hampered by regulatory requirements indefinitely.

2. *Identification of independent approaches to the problem:* Each branch of the tree can be considered a different approach to solving the overall problem. Some of these approaches may be almost completely independent of each other. In these cases, the team can cleanly divide its efforts among two or more individuals or task forces. When two approaches both look promising, this division of effort can reduce the complexity of the concept generation activities. It also may engender some healthy competition among the approaches under consideration. The nailer team found that both the chemical/explosive branch and the electrical branch appeared quite promising. They assigned these two approaches to two different subteams and pursued them independently for several weeks.

3. *Exposure of inappropriate emphasis on certain branches:* Once the tree is constructed, the team is able to reflect quickly on whether the effort applied to each branch has been appropriately allocated. The nailer team recognized that they had applied very little effort to thinking about hydraulic energy sources and conversion technologies. This recognition guided them to focus on this branch of the tree for a few days.

4. *Refinement of the problem decomposition for a particular branch:* Sometimes a problem decomposition can be usefully tailored to a particular approach to the problem. Consider the branch of the tree corresponding to the electrical energy source. Based on additional investigation of the nailing process, the team determined that the instantaneous power delivered during the nailing process was about 10,000 watts for a few milliseconds and so exceeds the power that is available from a wall outlet, a battery, or a fuel cell (of reasonable size, cost, and mass). They concluded, therefore, that energy must be accumulated over a substantial period of the nailing cycle (say 100 milliseconds) and then suddenly released to supply the required instantaneous power to drive the nail. This quick analysis led the team to add a subfunction ("accumulate translational energy") to their function diagram (see Exhibit 7-8). They chose to add the subfunction after the conversion of electrical energy to mechanical energy, but briefly considered the possibility of accumulating the energy in the electrical domain with a capacitor. This kind of refinement of the function diagram is quite common as the team makes more assumptions about the approach and as more information is gathered.

The classification tree in Exhibit 7-7 shows the alternative solutions to the energy source subproblem; however, there are other possible trees. The team might have chosen to use a tree classifying the alternative solutions to the energy delivery subproblem, showing branches for single impact, multiple impacts, or pushing. Trees can be constructed with branches corresponding to the solution fragments of any of the subproblems, but certain classifications are more useful. In general, a subproblem whose solution highly constrains the possible

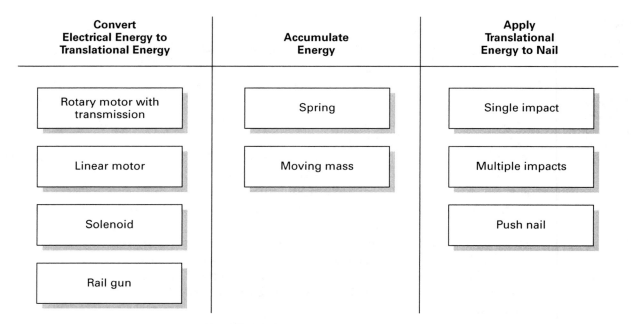

Convert Electrical Energy to Translational Energy	Accumulate Energy	Apply Translational Energy to Nail
Rotary motor with transmission	Spring	Single impact
Linear motor	Moving mass	Multiple impacts
Solenoid		Push nail
Rail gun		

EXHIBIT 7-9   Concept combination table for the handheld nailer.

solutions to the remaining subproblems is a good candidate for a classification tree. For example, the choice of energy source (electrical, nuclear, pneumatic, etc.) constrains whether a motor or a piston-cylinder can be used to convert the energy to translational energy. In contrast, the choice of energy delivery mechanism (single impact, multiple impacts, etc.) does not greatly constrain the solutions to the other subproblems. Reflection on which subproblem is likely to most highly constrain the solutions to the remaining subproblems will usually lead to one or two clear ways to construct the classification tree.

Concept Combination Table

The concept combination table provides a way to consider combinations of solution fragments systematically. Exhibit 7-9 shows an example of a combination table that the nailer team used to consider the combinations of fragments for the electrical branch of the classification tree. The columns in the table correspond to the subproblems identified in Exhibit 7-8. The entries in each column correspond to the solution fragments for each of these subproblems derived from external and internal search. For example, the subproblem of converting electrical energy to translational energy is the heading for the first column. The entries in this column are a rotary motor with a transmission, a linear motor, a solenoid, and a rail gun.

Potential solutions to the overall problem are formed by combining one fragment from each column. For the nailer example, there are 24 possible combinations ($4 \times 2 \times 3$). Choosing a combination of fragments does not lead spontaneously to a solution to the overall problem. The combination of fragments must usually be developed and refined before an integrated solution emerges. This development may not even be possible or may lead to more than one solution, but at a minimum it involves additional creative thought. In some ways, the combination table is simply a way to make forced associations among fragments

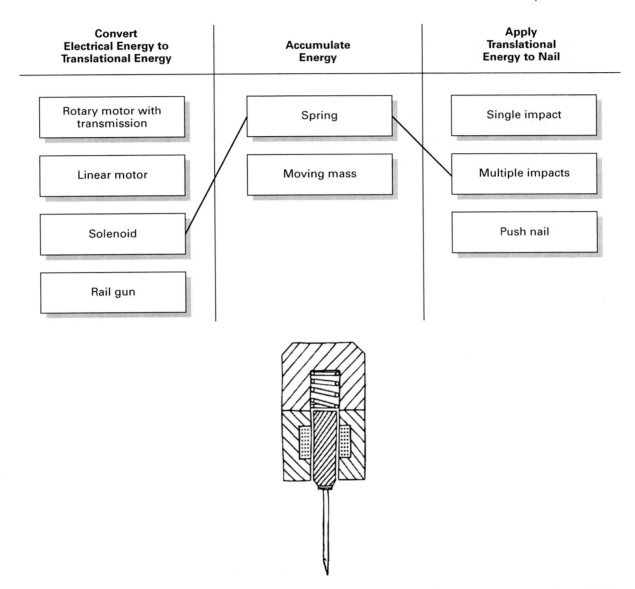

Convert Electrical Energy to Translational Energy	Accumulate Energy	Apply Translational Energy to Nail

EXHIBIT 7-10 In this solution concept, a solenoid compresses a spring and then releases it repeatedly to drive the nail with multiple impacts.

to stimulate further creative thinking; in no way does the mere act of selecting a combination yield a complete solution.

Exhibit 7-10 shows a sketch of a concept arising from the combination of the fragments "solenoid," "spring," and "multiple impacts." Exhibit 7-11 shows some sketches of concepts arising from the combination of the fragments "rotary motor with transmission," "spring," and "single impact." Exhibit 7-12 shows a sketch of a concept arising from the combination of "rotary motor with transmission," "spring," and "multiple impacts." Exhibit 7-13 shows some sketches of concepts arising from the combination of "linear motor," "moving mass," "and single impact."

Convert Electrical Energy to Translational Energy	Accumulate Energy	Apply Translational Energy to Nail
Rotary motor with transmission	Spring	Single impact
Linear motor	Moving mass	Multiple impacts
Solenoid		Push nail
Rail gun		

EXHIBIT 7-11   Multiple solutions arising from the combination of a motor with transmission, a spring, and single impact. The motor winds a spring, accumulating potential energy that is then delivered to the nail in a single blow.

Two guidelines make the concept combination process easier. First, if a fragment can be eliminated as being infeasible before combining it with other fragments, then the number of combinations the team needs to consider is dramatically reduced. For example, if the team could determine that the rail gun would not be feasible under any condition, they could reduce the number of combinations from 24 to 18. Second, the concept combination table should be concentrated on the subproblems that are coupled. Coupled subproblems are those whose solutions can be evaluated only in combination with the solutions to other subproblems. For example, the choice of the specific electrical energy source to be used

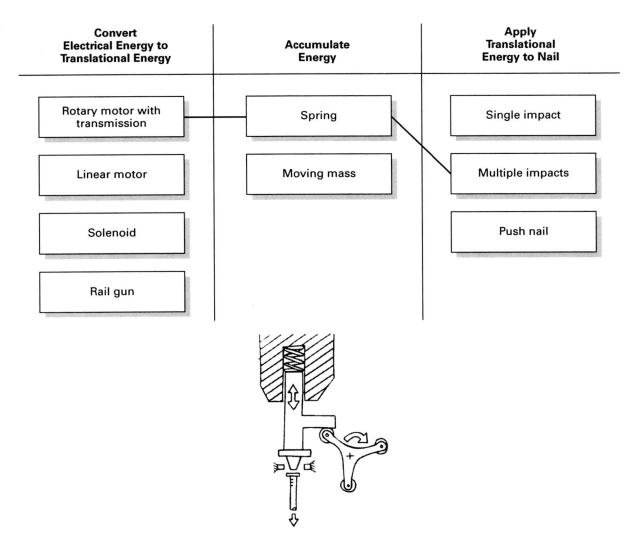

Convert Electrical Energy to Translational Energy	Accumulate Energy	Apply Translational Energy to Nail
Rotary motor with transmission	Spring	Single impact
Linear motor	Moving mass	Multiple impacts
Solenoid		Push nail
Rail gun		

EXHIBIT 7-12   Solution from the combination of a motor with transmission, a spring, and multiple impacts. The motor repeatedly winds and releases the spring, storing and delivering energy over several blows.

(e.g., battery versus wall outlet), although extremely critical, is somewhat independent of the choice of energy conversion (e.g., motor versus solenoid). Therefore, the concept combination table does not need to contain a column for the different types of electrical energy sources. This reduces the number of combinations the team must consider. As a practical matter, concept combination tables lose their usefulness when the number of columns exceeds three or four.

Managing the Exploration Process

The classification tree and combination tables are tools that a team can use somewhat flexibly. They are simple ways to organize thinking and guide the creative energies of the team. Rarely do teams generate only one classification tree and one concept

Convert Electrical Energy to Translational Energy	Accumulate Energy	Apply Translational Energy to Nail
Rotary motor with transmission	Spring	Single impact
Linear motor	Moving mass	Multiple impacts
Solenoid		Push nail
Rail gun		

EXHIBIT 7-13   Solutions from the combination of a linear motor, a moving mass, and single impact. A linear motor accelerates a massive hammer, accumulating kinetic energy that is delivered to the nail in a single blow.

combination table. More typically the team will create several alternative classification trees and several concept combination tables. Interspersed with this exploratory activity may be a refining of the original problem decomposition or the pursuit of additional internal or external search. The exploration step of concept generation usually acts more as a guide for further creative thinking than as the final step in the process.

Recall that at the beginning of the process the team chooses a few subproblems on which to focus attention. Eventually the team must return to address all of the subproblems. This usually occurs after the team has narrowed the range of alternatives for

EXHIBIT 7-14
One of several
refined solution
concepts.

Courtesy of Product Genesis®

the critical subproblems. The nailer team narrowed its alternatives to a few chemical and a few electric concepts and then refined them by working out the user interface, industrial design, and configuration issues. One of the resulting concept descriptions is shown in Exhibit 7-14.

Step 5: Reflect on the Solutions and the Process

Although the reflection step is placed here at the end for convenience in presentation, reflection should in fact be performed throughout the whole process. Questions to ask include:

- Is the team developing confidence that the solution space has been fully explored?
- Are there alternative function diagrams?
- Are there alternative ways to decompose the problem?
- Have external sources been thoroughly pursued?
- Have ideas from everyone been accepted and integrated in the process?

The nailer team members discussed whether they had focused too much attention on the energy storage and conversion issues in the tool while ignoring the user interface and overall configuration. They decided that the energy issues remained at the core of the problem and that their decision to focus on these issues first was justified. They also wondered if they had pursued too many branches of the classification tree. Initially they had pursued electrical, chemical, and pneumatic concepts before ultimately settling on an electric concept. In hindsight, the chemical approach had some obvious safety and customer perception shortcomings (they were exploring the use of explosives as an energy source). They decided that although they liked some aspects of the chemical solution, they should have eliminated it from consideration earlier in the process, allowing more time to pursue some of the more promising branches in greater detail.

The team explored several of these concepts in more detail and built working prototypes of nailers incorporating two fundamentally different directions: (1) a motor winding a spring with energy released in a single blow, and (2) a motor with a rotating mass that repeatedly hit the nail at a rate of about 10 cycles per second until the nail was fully driven. Ultimately, the multiblow tool proved to be the most technically feasible approach and the final product (Exhibit 7-1) was based on this concept.

Summary

A product concept is an approximate description of the technology, working principles, and form of the product. The degree to which a product satisfies customers and can be successfully commercialized depends to a large measure on the quality of the underlying concept.

- The concept generation process begins with a set of customer needs and target specifications and results in a set of product concepts from which the team will make a final selection.

- In most cases, an effective development team will generate hundreds of concepts, of which 5 to 20 will merit serious consideration during the subsequent concept selection activity.

- The concept generation method presented in this chapter consists of five steps:

  1. *Clarify the problem.* Understand the problem and decompose it into simpler sub-problems.
  2. *Search externally.* Gather information from lead users, experts, patents, published literature, and related products.
  3. *Search internally.* Use individual and group methods to retrieve and adapt the knowledge of the team.
  4. *Explore systematically.* Use classification trees and combination tables to organize the thinking of the team and to synthesize solution fragments.
  5. *Reflect on the solutions and the process.* Identify opportunities for improvement in subsequent iterations or future projects.

- Although concept generation is an inherently creative process, teams can benefit from using a structured method. Such an approach allows full exploration of the design space and reduces the chance of oversight in the types of solution concepts considered. It also acts as a map for those team members who are less experienced in design problem solving.

- Despite the linear presentation of the concept generation process in this chapter, the team will likely return to each step of the process several times. Iteration is particularly common when the team is developing a radically new product.

- Professionals who are good at concept generation seem to always be in great demand as team members. Contrary to popular opinion, we believe concept generation is a skill that can be learned and developed.

References and Bibliography

Many current resources are available on the Internet via
www.ulrich-eppinger.net

Pahl, Beitz, Hubka, and Eder were driving forces behind structured design methods in Europe. We adapt many of their ideas for functional decomposition and systematic concept generation.

Hubka, Vladimir, and W. Ernst Eder, *Theory of Technical Systems: A Total Concept Theory for Engineering Design*, Springer-Verlag, New York, 1988.

Pahl, Gerhard, Wolfgang Beitz, Jörg Feldhusen, and Karl-Heinrich Grote, *Engineering Design*, third edition, K. Wallace and L. Blessing, translators, Springer-Verlag, New York, 2007.

Research on creative behavior has shown that people with greater confidence in their own creative problem-solving ability actually do produce more innovative solutions.

Tierney, Pamela, and Steven M. Farmer, "Creative Self-Efficacy: Its Potential Antecedents and Relationship to Creative Performance," *Academy of Management Journal*, Vol. 45, No. 6, 2002, pp. 1137–1148.

McGrath presents studies comparing the relative performance of groups and individuals in generating new ideas.

McGrath, Joseph E., *Groups: Interaction and Performance*, Prentice Hall, Englewood Cliffs, NJ, 1984.

Osborn's research in the mid twentieth-century first codified the principles of brainstorming, from which many creativity methods have since been derived.

Osborn, Alex F., *Applied Imagination: Principles and Procedures of Creative Thinking*, Scribner, New York, 1953.

Numerous authors have explained a wide variety of methods for ideation and problem solving, many of which are directly applicable to product concept generation.

Terwiesch, Christian, and Karl T. Ulrich, *Innovation Tournaments: Creating and Selecting Exceptional Opportunities*, Harvard Business Press, Boston, May 2009.

Treffinger, Donald J., Scott G. Isaksen, and K. Brian Stead-Dorval, *Creative Problem Solving: An Introduction*, Prufrock Press, Waco TX, 2005.

VanGundy, Arthur B., Jr., *Techniques of Structured Problem Solving*, second edition, Van Nostrand Reinhold, New York, 1988.

Both McKim and von Oech present approaches to developing creative thinking skills in individuals and in groups.

McKim, Robert H., *Experiences in Visual Thinking*, second edition, Brooks/Cole Publishing, Monterey, CA, 1980.

von Oech, Roger, *A Whack on the Side of the Head: How You Can Be More Creative*, revised edition, Warner Books, New York, 1998.

Von Hippel reports on his empirical research on the sources of new product concepts. His central argument is that lead users are the innovators in many markets.

von Hippel, Eric, *The Sources of Innovation*, Oxford University Press, New York, 1988.

Yang and her research team have conducted a range of experiments to explore the timing, quality, and types of sketch modeling used in concept development.

Häggman, Anders, Honda, Tomonori, and Maria C. Yang, "The Influence of Timing in Exploratory Prototyping and Other Activities in Design Projects," ASME International Design Engineering Technical Conferences, August 2013.

Neeley, W. Lawrence, Kirsten Lim, April Zhu, and Maria C. Yang, "Building Fast to Think Faster: Exploiting Rapid Prototyping to Accelerate Ideation During Early Stage Design," ASME International Design Engineering Technical Conferences, August 2013.

Yang, Maria C., "Observations on Concept Generation and Sketching in Engineering Design." *Research in Engineering Design*, Vol. 20, No. 1, 2009, pp. 1–11.

Yang, Maria C., and Jorge G. Cham, "An Analysis of Sketching Skill and its Role in Early Stage Engineering Design," *Journal of Mechanical Design*, Vol. 129, No. 5, 2007, pp. 476–482.

Goldenberg and Mazursky have done interesting research on a set of standard "templates" for identifying novel product concepts.

Goldenberg, Jacob, and David Mazursky, *Creativity in Product Innovation*, Cambridge University Press, Cambridge, 2002.

Some specific methods for creative problem solving mentioned in this chapter (SCAMPER, synectics, and TRIZ) are explained in the following references.

Eberle, Bob, *SCAMPER: Games for Imagination Development*, Prufrock Press, Waco TX, 1996.

Gordon, William J. J., *Synectics: The Development of Creative Capacity*, Harper, New York, 1961.

Altshuller, Genrich, *40 Principles: TRIZ Keys to Technical Innovation*, Technical Innovation Center, Worcester, MA, 1998.

Terninko, John, Alla Zusman, and Boris Zlotin, *Systematic Innovation: An Introduction to TRIZ*, St. Lucie Press, Boca Raton, FL, 1998.

Engineering handbooks are handy sources of information on standard technical solutions. Three good handbooks are:

Avallone, Eugene A., Theodore Baumeister III, and Ali Sadegh (eds.), *Marks' Standard Handbook of Mechanical Engineering*, eleventh edition, McGraw-Hill, New York, 2006.

Green, Don W., and Robert H. Perry (eds.), *Perry's Chemical Engineers' Handbook*, eighth edition, McGraw-Hill, New York, 2003.

Sclater, Neil, *Mechanisms and Mechanical Devices Sourcebook*, fifth edition, McGraw-Hill, New York, 2011.

Exercises

1. Decompose the problem of designing a new barbecue grill. Try a functional decomposition as well as a decomposition based on the user interactions with the product.
2. Generate 20 concepts for the subproblem "prevent fraying of end of rope" as part of a system for cutting lengths of nylon rope from a spool.
3. Prepare an external-search plan for the problem of permanently applying serial numbers to plastic products.

Thought Questions

1. What are the prospects for computer support for concept generation activities? Can you think of any computer tools that would be especially helpful in this process?
2. What would be the relative advantages and disadvantages of involving actual customers in the concept generation process?
3. For what types of products would the initial focus of the concept generation activity be on the form and user interface of the product and not on the core technology? Describe specific examples.
4. Could you apply the five-step method to an everyday problem like choosing the food for a picnic?
5. Consider the task of generating new concepts for the problem of dealing with leaves on a lawn. How would a plastic-bag manufacturer's assumptions and problem decomposition differ from those of a manufacturer of lawn tools and equipment and from those of a company responsible for maintaining golf courses around the world? Should the context of the firm dictate the way concept generation is approached?

CHAPTER EIGHT

Concept Selection

Courtesy of Novo Nordisk A/S

EXHIBIT 8-1
One of the existing outpatient syringes.

A medical supply company retained a product design firm to develop a reusable syringe with precise dosage control for outpatient use. One of the products sold by a competitor is shown in Exhibit 8-1. To focus the development effort, the medical supply company identified two major problems with its current product: cost (the existing model was made of stainless steel) and accuracy of dose metering. The company also requested that the product be tailored to the physical capabilities of the elderly, an important segment of the target market. To summarize the needs of its client and of the intended end users, the team established seven criteria on which the choice of a product concept would be based:

- Ease of handling.
- Ease of use.
- Readability of dose settings.
- Dose metering accuracy.
- Durability.
- Ease of manufacture.
- Portability.

The team described the concepts under consideration with the sketches shown in Exhibit 8-3. Although each concept nominally satisfied the key customer needs, the team was faced with choosing the best concept for further design, refinement, and production. The need to select one syringe concept from many raises several questions:

- How can the team choose the best concept, given that the designs are still quite abstract?
- How can a decision be made that is embraced by the whole team?
- How can desirable attributes of otherwise weak concepts be identified and used?
- How can the decision-making process be documented?

This chapter uses the syringe example to present a concept selection methodology addressing these and other issues.

Concept Selection Is an Integral Part of the Product Development Process

Early in the development process the product development team identifies a set of customer needs. By using a variety of methods, the team then generates alternative solution concepts in response to these needs. (See Chapter 5, Identifying Customer Needs, and Chapter 7, Concept Generation, for more detail on these activities.) *Concept selection* is the process of evaluating concepts with respect to customer needs and other criteria, comparing the relative strengths and weaknesses of the concepts, and selecting one or more concepts for further investigation, testing, or development. Exhibit 8-2 illustrates how the concept selection activity is related to the other activities that make up the concept development phase of the product development process. Although this chapter focuses on the selection of an overall product concept at the beginning of the development process, the method we present is also useful later in the development process when the team must select subsystem concepts, components, and production processes.

EXHIBIT 8-2 Concept selection is part of the overall concept development phase.

While many stages of the development process benefit from unbounded creativity and divergent thinking, concept selection is the process of narrowing the set of concept alternatives under consideration. Although concept selection is a convergent process, it is frequently iterative and may not produce a dominant concept immediately. A large set of concepts is initially winnowed down to a smaller set, but these concepts may subsequently be combined and improved to temporarily enlarge the set of concepts under consideration. Through several iterations a dominant concept is finally chosen. Exhibit 8-4 illustrates the successive narrowing and temporary widening of the set of options under consideration during the concept selection activity.

All Teams Use Some Method for Choosing a Concept

Whether or not the concept selection process is explicit, all teams use some method to choose among concepts. (Even those teams generating only one concept are using a method: choosing the first concept they think of.) The methods vary in their effectiveness and include the following:

- *External decision:* Concepts are turned over to the customer, client, or some other external entity for selection.
- *Product champion:* An influential member of the product development team chooses a concept based on personal preference.
- *Intuition:* The concept is chosen by its feel. Explicit criteria or trade-offs are not used. The concept just *seems* better.
- *Multivoting:* Each member of the team votes for several concepts. The concept with the most votes is selected.
- *Web-based survey:* Using an online survey tool, each concept is rated by many people to find the best ones.
- *Pros and cons:* The team lists the strengths and weaknesses of each concept and makes a choice based upon group opinion.
- *Prototype and test:* The organization builds and tests prototypes of each concept, making a selection based upon test data.
- *Decision matrices:* The team rates each concept against prespecified selection criteria, which may be weighted.

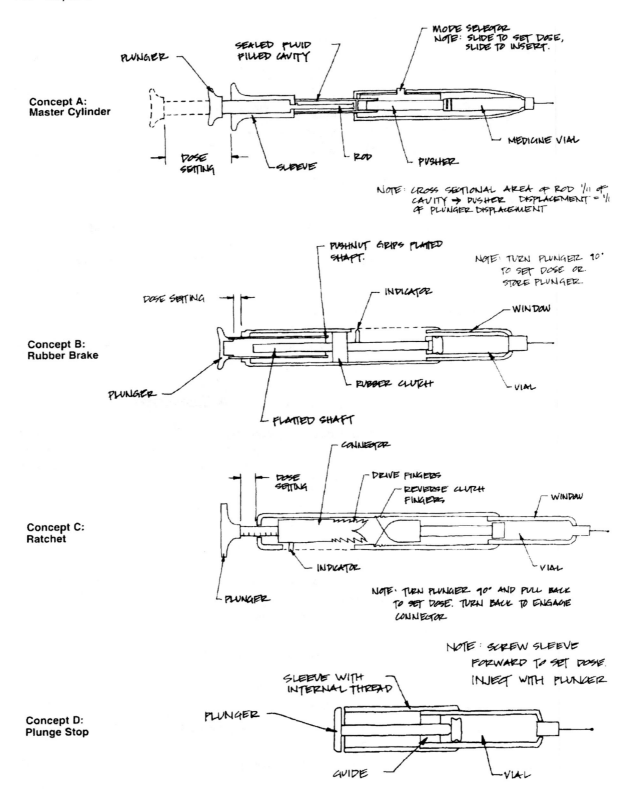

EXHIBIT 8-3 Seven concepts for the outpatient syringe. The product development team generated the seven sketches to describe the basic concepts under consideration.

Concept E:
Swash Ring

Concept F:
Lever Set

Concept G:
Dial Screw

EXHIBIT 8-3   *Continued*

150   *Chapter* 8

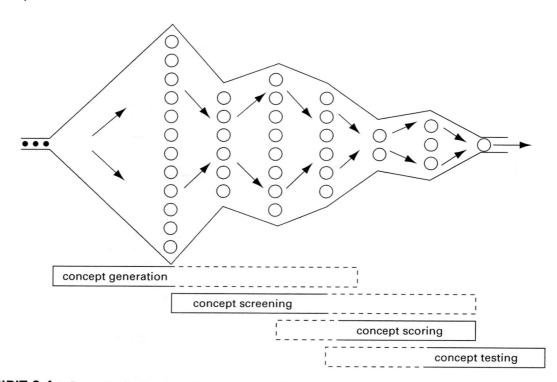

concept generation

concept screening

concept scoring

concept testing

EXHIBIT 8-4   Concept selection is an iterative process closely related to concept generation and testing. The concept screening and scoring methods help the team refine and improve the concepts, leading to one or more promising concepts upon which further testing and development activities will be focused.

The concept selection method in this chapter is built around the use of decision matrices for evaluating each concept with respect to a set of selection criteria.

A Structured Method Offers Several Benefits

All of the front-end activities of product development have tremendous influence on eventual product success. Certainly the response of the market to a product depends critically on the product concept, but many practitioners and researchers also believe that the choice of a product concept dramatically constrains the eventual manufacturing cost of the product. A structured concept selection process helps to maintain objectivity throughout the concept phase of the development process and guides the product development team through a critical, difficult, and sometimes emotional process. Specifically, a structured concept selection method offers the following potential benefits:

- *A customer-focused product:* Because concepts are explicitly evaluated against customer-oriented criteria, the selected concept is likely to be focused on the customer.
- *A competitive design:* By benchmarking concepts with respect to existing designs, designers push the design to match or exceed their competitors' performance along key dimensions.

- *Better product-process coordination:* Explicit evaluation of the product with respect to manufacturing criteria improves the product's manufacturability and helps to match the product with the process capabilities of the firm.

- *Reduced time to product introduction:* A structured method becomes a common language among design engineers, manufacturing engineers, industrial designers, marketers, and project managers, resulting in decreased ambiguity, faster communication, and fewer false starts.

- *Effective group decision making:* Within the development team, organizational philosophy and guidelines, willingness of members to participate, and team member experience may constrain the concept selection process. A structured method encourages decision making based on objective criteria and minimizes the likelihood that arbitrary or personal factors influence the product concept.

- *Documentation of the decision process:* A structured method results in a readily understood archive of the rationale behind concept decisions. This record is useful for assimilating new team members and for quickly assessing the impact of changes in the customer needs or in the available alternatives.

Overview of Methodology

We present a two-stage concept selection methodology, although the first stage may suffice for simple design decisions. The first stage is called *concept screening* and the second stage is called *concept scoring.* Each is supported by a decision matrix that is used by the team to rate, rank, and select the best concept(s). Although the method is structured, we emphasize the role of group insight to improve and combine concepts.

Concept selection is often performed in two stages as a way to manage the complexity of evaluating dozens of product concepts. The application of these two methods is illustrated in Exhibit 8-4. Screening is a quick, approximate evaluation aimed at producing a few viable alternatives. Scoring is a more careful analysis of these relatively few concepts to choose the single concept most likely to lead to product success.

During concept screening, rough initial concepts are evaluated relative to a common reference concept using the *screening matrix.* At this preliminary stage, detailed quantitative comparisons are difficult to obtain and may be misleading, so a coarse comparative rating system is used. After some alternatives are eliminated, the team may choose to move on to concept scoring and conduct more detailed analyses and finer quantitative evaluation of the remaining concepts using the *scoring matrix* as a guide. Throughout the screening and scoring process, several iterations may be performed, with new alternatives arising from the combination of the features of several concepts. Exhibits 8-5 and 8-7 illustrate the screening and scoring matrices, using the selection criteria and concepts from the syringe example.

Both stages, concept screening and concept scoring, follow a six-step process that leads the team through the concept selection activity. The steps are:

1. Prepare the selection matrix.
2. Rate the concepts.
3. Rank the concepts.
4. Combine and improve the concepts.

5. Select one or more concepts.

6. Reflect on the results and the process.

Although we present a well-defined process, the team, not the method, creates the concepts and makes the decisions that determine the quality of the product. Ideally, teams are made up of people from different functional groups within the organization. Each member brings unique views that increase the understanding of the problem and thus facilitate the development of a successful, customer-oriented product. The concept selection method exploits the matrices as visual guides for consensus building among team members. The matrices focus attention on the customer needs and other decision criteria and on the product concepts for explicit evaluation, improvement, and selection.

Concept Screening

Concept screening is based on a method developed by the late Stuart Pugh in the 1980s and is often called *Pugh concept selection* (Pugh, 1990). The purposes of this stage are to narrow the number of concepts quickly and to improve the concepts. Exhibit 8-5 illustrates the screening matrix used during this stage.

Step 1: Prepare the Selection Matrix

To prepare the matrix, the team selects a physical medium appropriate to the problem at hand. Individuals and small groups with a short list of criteria may use matrices on paper similar to Exhibit 8-5 or Appendix A for their selection process. For larger groups a chalkboard or flip chart is desirable to facilitate group discussion.

Selection Criteria	Concepts						
	A Master Cylinder	B Rubber Brake	C Ratchet	D (Reference) Plunge Stop	E Swash Ring	F Lever Set	G Dial Screw
Ease of handling	0	0	−	0	0	−	−
Ease of use	0	−	−	0	0	+	0
Readability of settings	0	0	+	0	+	0	+
Dose metering accuracy	0	0	0	0	−	0	0
Durability	0	0	0	0	0	+	0
Ease of manufacture	+	−	−	0	0	−	0
Portability	+	+	0	0	+	0	0
Sum +'s	2	1	1	0	2	2	1
Sum 0's	5	4	3	7	4	3	5
Sum −'s	0	2	3	0	1	2	1
Net Score	2	−1	−2	0	1	0	0
Rank	1	6	7	3	2	3	3
Continue?	Yes	No	No	Combine	Yes	Combine	Revise

EXHIBIT 8-5   The concept-screening matrix. For the syringe example, the team rated the concepts against the reference concept using a simple code (+ for "better than," 0 for "same as," − for "worse than") to identify some concepts for further consideration. Note that the three concepts ranked "3" all received the same net score.

Next, the inputs (concepts and criteria) are entered on the matrix. Although possibly generated by different individuals, concepts should be presented at the same level of detail for meaningful comparison and unbiased selection. The concepts are best portrayed by both a written description and a graphical representation. A simple one-page sketch of each concept greatly facilitates communication of the key features of the concept. The concepts are entered along the top of the matrix, using graphical or textual labels of some kind.

If the team is considering more than about 12 concepts, the *multivoting* technique may be used to quickly choose the dozen or so concepts to be evaluated with the screening matrix. Multivoting is a technique in which members of the team simultaneously vote for three to five concepts by applying "dots" to the sheets describing their preferred concepts. See Chapter 3, Opportunity Identification, for a description of multivoting applied to a broad set of product opportunities. The concepts with the most dots are chosen for concept screening. It is also possible to use the screening matrix method with a large number of concepts. This is facilitated by a spreadsheet and it is then useful to transpose the rows and columns. (Arrange the concepts in this case in the left column and the criteria along the top.)

The selection criteria are listed along the left-hand side of the screening matrix, as shown in Exhibit 8-5. These criteria are chosen based on the customer needs the team has identified, as well as on the needs of the enterprise, such as low manufacturing cost or minimal risk of product liability. The criteria at this stage are usually expressed at a fairly high level of abstraction and typically include from 5 to 10 dimensions. The selection criteria should be chosen to differentiate among the concepts; however, because each criterion is given equal weight in the concept screening method, the team should be careful not to list many relatively unimportant criteria in the screening matrix. Otherwise, the differences among the concepts relative to the more important criteria will not be clearly reflected in the outcome.

After careful consideration, the team chooses a concept to become the benchmark, or *reference concept,* against which all other concepts are rated. The reference is generally either an industry standard or a straightforward concept with which the team members are very familiar. It can be a commercially available product, a best-in-class benchmark product that the team has studied, an earlier generation of the product, any one of the concepts under consideration, or a combination of subsystems assembled to represent the best features of different products.

Step 2: Rate the Concepts

A relative score of "better than" (+), "same as" (0), or "worse than" (−) is placed in each cell of the matrix to represent how each concept rates in comparison to the reference concept relative to the particular criterion. It is generally advisable to rate every concept on one criterion before moving to the next criterion; however, with a large number of concepts, it is faster to use the opposite approach—to rate each concept completely before moving on to the next concept.

Some people find the coarse nature of the relative ratings difficult to work with; however, at this stage in the design process, each concept is only a general notion of the ultimate product, and more detailed ratings are largely meaningless. In fact, given the imprecision of the concept descriptions at this point, it is very difficult to consistently compare concepts to one another unless one concept (the reference) is consistently used as a basis for comparison.

When available, objective metrics can be used as the basis for rating a concept. For example, a good approximation of assembly cost is the number of parts in a design. Similarly, a good approximation of ease of use is the number of operations required to use the device. Such metrics help to minimize the subjective nature of the rating process. Some objective metrics suitable for concept selection may arise from the process of establishing target specifications for the product. (See Chapter 6, Product Specifications, for a discussion of metrics.) Absent objective metrics, ratings are established by team consensus, although secret ballot or other methods may also be useful. At this point the team may also wish to note which selection criteria need further investigation and analysis.

Step 3: Rank the Concepts

After rating all the concepts, the team sums the number of "better than," "same as," and "worse than" scores and enters the sum for each category in the lower rows of the matrix. From our example in Exhibit 8-5, concept A was rated to have two criteria better than, five the same as, and none worse than the reference concept. Next, a net score can be calculated by subtracting the number of "worse than" ratings from the "better than" ratings.

Once the summation is completed, the team rank-orders the concepts. Obviously, in general those concepts with more pluses and fewer minuses are ranked higher. Often at this point the team can identify one or two criteria that really seem to differentiate the concepts.

Step 4: Combine and Improve the Concepts

Having rated and ranked the concepts, the team should verify that the results make sense and then consider if there are ways to combine and improve certain concepts. Two issues to consider are:

- Is there a generally good concept that is degraded by one bad feature? Can a minor modification improve the overall concept and yet preserve a distinction from the other concepts?

- Are there two concepts that can be combined to preserve the "better than" qualities while annulling the "worse than" qualities?

Combined and improved concepts are then added to the matrix, rated by the team, and ranked along with the original concepts. In our example, the team noticed that concepts D and F could be combined to remove several of the "worse than" ratings to yield a new concept, DF, to be considered in the next round. Concept G was also considered for revision. The team decided that this concept was too bulky, so the excess storage space was removed while retaining the injection technique. These revised concepts are shown in Exhibit 8-6.

Step 5: Select One or More Concepts

Once the team members are satisfied with their understanding of each concept and its relative quality, they decide which concepts are to be selected for further refinement and analysis. Based upon previous steps, the team will likely develop a clear sense of which are the most promising concepts. The number of concepts selected for further review will be limited by team resources (personnel, money, and time). In our example, the team selected concepts A and E to be considered along with the revised concept G+ and the

EXHIBIT 8-6 New and revised concepts for the syringe. During the selection process, the syringe team revised concept G and generated a new concept, DF, arising from the combination of concepts D and F.

new concept DF. Having determined the concepts for further analysis, the team must clarify which issues need to be investigated further before a final selection can be made.

The team must also decide whether another round of concept screening will be performed or whether concept scoring will be applied next. If the screening matrix is not seen to provide sufficient resolution for the next step of evaluation and selection, then the concept-scoring stage with its weighted selection criteria and more detailed rating scheme would be used.

Step 6: Reflect on the Results and the Process

All of the team members should be comfortable with the outcome. If an individual is not in agreement with the decision of the team, then perhaps one or more important criteria are missing from the screening matrix, or perhaps a particular rating is in error, or at least is not clear. An explicit consideration of whether the results make sense to everyone reduces the likelihood of making a mistake and increases the likelihood that the entire team will be solidly committed to the subsequent development activities.

		Concept							
		A (Reference) Master Cylinder		**DF Lever Stop**		**E Swash Ring**		**G+ Dial Screw+**	
Selection Criteria	**Weight**	**Rating**	**Weighted Score**	**Rating**	**Weighted Score**	**Rating**	**Weighted Score**	**Rating**	**Weighted Score**
Ease of handling	5%	**3**	0.15	3	0.15	4	0.2	4	0.2
Ease of use	15%	**3**	0.45	4	0.6	4	0.6	3	0.45
Readability of settings	10%	2	0.2	**3**	0.3	5	0.5	5	0.5
Dose metering accuracy	25%	**3**	0.75	3	0.75	2	0.5	3	0.75
Durability	15%	2	0.3	5	0.75	4	0.6	**3**	0.45
Ease of manufacture	20%	**3**	0.6	3	0.6	2	0.4	2	0.4
Portability	10%	**3**	0.3	3	0.3	3	0.3	3	0.3
	Total Score	2.75		3.45		3.10		3.05	
	Rank	4		1		2		3	
	Continue?	No		Develop		No		No	

EXHIBIT 8-7   The concept-scoring matrix. This method uses a weighted sum of the ratings to determine concept ranking. While concept A serves as the overall reference concept, the separate reference points for each criterion are signified by **bold** rating values.

Concept Scoring

Concept scoring is used when increased resolution will better differentiate among competing concepts. In this stage, the team weighs the relative importance of the selection criteria and focuses on more refined comparisons with respect to each criterion. The concept scores are determined by the weighted sum of the ratings. Exhibit 8-7 illustrates the scoring matrix used in this stage. In describing the concept scoring process, we focus on the differences relative to concept screening.

Step 1: Prepare the Selection Matrix

As in the screening stage, the team prepares a matrix and identifies a reference concept. In most cases a computer spreadsheet is the best format to facilitate ranking and sensitivity analysis. The concepts that have been identified for analysis are entered on the top of the matrix. The concepts have typically been refined to some extent since concept screening and may be expressed in more detail. In conjunction with more detailed concepts, the team may wish to add more detail to the selection criteria. The use of hierarchical relations is a useful way to illuminate the criteria. For the syringe example, suppose the team decided that the criterion "ease of use" did not provide sufficient detail to help distinguish among the remaining concepts. "Ease of use" could be broken down, as shown in Exhibit 8-8, to include "ease of injection," "ease of cleaning," and "ease of loading." The level of criteria detail will depend upon the needs of the team; it may not be necessary to expand the criteria at all. If the team has created a hierarchical list of customer needs, the secondary and tertiary needs are good candidates for more detailed selection criteria.

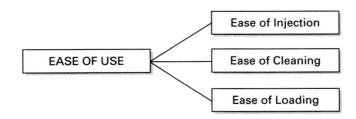

EXHIBIT 8-8   Hierarchical decomposition of selection criteria. In conjunction with more detailed concepts, the team may choose to break down criteria to the level of detail necessary for meaningful comparison.

(See Chapter 5, Identifying Customer Needs, for an explanation of primary, secondary, and tertiary needs, and see Appendixes A and B for examples of hierarchical selection criteria.)

After the criteria are entered, the team adds importance weights to the matrix. Several different schemes can be used to weight the criteria, such as assigning an importance value from 1 to 5, or allocating 100 percentage points among them, as the team has done in Exhibit 8-7. There are marketing techniques for empirically determining weights from customer data, and a thorough process of identifying customer needs may result in such weights (Urban and Hauser, 1993); however, for the purpose of concept selection the weights are often determined subjectively by team consensus.

Step 2: Rate the Concepts

As in the screening stage, it is generally easiest for the team to focus its discussion by rating all of the concepts with respect to one criterion at a time. Because of the need for additional resolution to distinguish among competing concepts, a finer scale is now used. We recommend a scale from 1 to 5:

Relative Performance	Rating
Much worse than reference	1
Worse than reference	2
Same as reference	3
Better than reference	4
Much better than reference	5

Another scale, such as 1 to 9, may certainly be used, but finer scales generally require more time and effort.

A single reference concept can be used for the comparative ratings, as in the screening stage; however, this is not always appropriate. Unless by pure coincidence the reference concept is of average performance relative to all of the criteria, the use of the same reference concept for the evaluation of each criterion will lead to "scale compression" for some of the criteria. For example, if the reference concept happens to be the easiest concept to manufacture, all of the remaining concepts will receive an evaluation of 1, 2, or 3 ("much worse than," "worse than," or "same as") for the ease-of-manufacture criterion, compressing the rating scale from five levels to three levels.

To avoid scale compression, it is possible to use different reference points for the various selection criteria. Reference points may come from several of the concepts under consideration, from comparative benchmarking analysis, from the target values of the product specifications, or other means. It is important that the reference point for each criterion be well understood to facilitate direct one-to-one comparisons. Using multiple reference points does not prevent the team from designating one concept as the overall reference for the purposes of ensuring that the selected concept is competitive relative to this benchmark. Under such conditions the overall reference concept will simply not receive a neutral score.

Exhibit 8-7 shows the scoring matrix for the syringe example. The team believed that the master cylinder concept was not suitable as a reference point for two of the criteria, and other concepts were used as reference points in these cases.

Appendix B illustrates a more detailed scoring matrix for which the team rated the concepts on each criterion with no explicit reference points. These ratings were accomplished by discussing the merits of every concept with respect to one criterion at a time and arranging the scores on a 9-point scale.

Step 3: Rank the Concepts

Once the ratings are entered for each concept, weighted scores are calculated by multiplying the raw scores by the criteria weights. The total score for each concept is the sum of the weighted scores

$$S_j = \sum_{i=1}^{n} r_{ij} w_i$$

where

r_{ij} = raw rating of concept j for the ith criterion
w_i = weighting for ith criterion
n = number of criteria
S_j = total score for concept j

Finally, each concept is given a rank corresponding to its total score, as shown in Exhibit 8-7.

Step 4: Combine and Improve the Concepts

As in the screening stage, the team looks for changes or combinations that improve concepts. Although the formal concept generation process is typically completed before concept selection begins, some of the most creative refinements and improvements occur during the concept selection process as the team realizes the inherent strengths and weaknesses of certain features of the product concepts.

Step 5: Select One or More Concepts

The final selection is not simply a question of choosing the concept that achieves the highest ranking after the first pass through the process. Rather, the team should explore this initial evaluation by conducting a sensitivity analysis. Using a computer spreadsheet, the team can vary weights and ratings to determine their effect on the ranking.

By investigating the sensitivity of the ranking to variations in a particular rating, the team members can assess whether uncertainty about a particular rating has a large impact on their choice. In some cases they may select a lower-scoring concept about which there is little uncertainty instead of a higher-scoring concept that may possibly prove unworkable or less desirable as they learn more about it.

Based on the selection matrix, the team may decide to select the top two or more concepts. These concepts may be further developed, prototyped, and tested to elicit customer feedback. See Chapter 9, Concept Testing, for a discussion of methods to assess customer response to product concepts.

The team may also create two or more scoring matrices with different weightings to yield the concept ranking for various market segments with different customer preferences. It may be that one concept is dominant for several segments. The team should also consider carefully the significance of differences in concept scores. Given the resolution of the scoring system, small differences are generally not significant.

For the syringe example, the team agreed that concept DF was the most promising and would be likely to result in a successful product.

Step 6: Reflect on the Results and the Process

As a final step the team reflects on the selected concept(s) and on the concept selection process. In some ways, this is the "point of no return" for the concept development process, so everyone on the team should feel comfortable that all of the relevant issues have been discussed and that the selected concept(s) have the greatest potential to satisfy customers and be economically successful.

After each stage of concept selection, it is a useful reality check for the team to review each of the concepts that are to be eliminated from further consideration. If the team agrees that any of the dropped concepts is better overall than some of those retained, then the source of this inconsistency should be identified. Perhaps an important criterion is missing, not weighted properly, or inconsistently applied.

The organization can also benefit from reflection on the process itself. Two questions are useful in improving the process for subsequent concept selection activities:

- In what way (if at all) did the concept selection method facilitate team decision making?
- How can the method be modified to improve team performance?

These questions focus the team on the strengths and weaknesses of the methodology in relation to the needs and capabilities of the organization.

Caveats

With experience, users of the concept selection methods will discover several subtleties. Here we discuss some of these subtleties and point out a few areas for caution.

- *Decomposition of concept quality:* The basic theory underlying the concept selection method is that selection criteria—and, by implication, customer needs—can be evaluated independently and that concept quality is the sum of the qualities of the concept relative to each criterion. The quality of some product concepts may not be easily decomposed into a set of independent criteria, or the performance of the concept relative to the different criteria may be difficult to relate to overall concept quality. For example, the overall appeal or performance of a tennis racquet design may arise in a highly complex way from its weight, ease of swinging, shock transmission, and energy absorption. Simply choosing a concept based on the sum of performance relative to each criterion may fail to capture complex relationships among these criteria. Keeney and Raiffa (1993) discuss the problem of multiattribute decision making, including the issue of nonlinear relationships among selection criteria.

- *Subjective criteria:* Some selection criteria, particularly those related to aesthetics, are highly subjective. Choices among alternatives based solely on subjective criteria must be made carefully. In general, the development team's collective judgment is not the best way to evaluate concepts on subjective dimensions. Rather, the team should narrow the alternatives to three or four and then solicit the opinions of representative customers from the target market for the product, perhaps using mock-ups or models to represent the concepts. (See Chapter 9, Concept Testing.)

- *To facilitate improvement of concepts:* While discussing each concept to determine its rating, the team may wish to make note of any outstanding (positive or negative) attributes of the concepts. It is useful to identify any features that could be applied to other concepts, as well as issues that could be addressed to improve the concept. Notes may be placed directly in the cells of the selection matrix. Such notes are particularly useful in step 4, when the team seeks to combine, refine, and improve the concepts before making a selection decision.

- *Where to include cost:* Most of the selection criteria are adaptations of the customer needs; however, "ease of manufacturing" and "manufacturing cost" are not customer needs. The only reason customers care about manufacturing cost is that it establishes the lower bound on sale price. Nevertheless, cost is an extremely important factor in choosing a concept, because it is one of the factors determining the economic success of the product. For this reason, we advocate the inclusion of some measure of cost or ease of manufacturing when evaluating concepts, even though these measures are not true customer needs. Similarly, there may be needs of other stakeholders that were not expressed by actual customers but are important for economic success of the product.

- *Selecting elements of aggregate concepts:* Some product concepts are really aggregations of several simpler concepts. If all of the concepts under consideration include choices from a set of simpler elements, then the simple elements can be evaluated first and in an independent fashion before the more complex concepts are evaluated. This sort of decomposition may follow partly from the structure used in concept generation. For example, if all of the syringes in our example could be used with all of several different needle types, then the selection of a needle concept could be conducted independently of the selection of an overall syringe concept.

- *Applying concept selection throughout the development process:* Although throughout this chapter we have emphasized the application of the method to the selection of a basic product concept, concept selection is used again and again at many levels of detail in the design and development process. For example, in the syringe example, concept selection could be used at the very beginning of the development project to decide between a single-use or multiple-use approach. Once the basic approach had been determined, concept selection could be used to choose the basic product concept, as illustrated in this chapter. Finally, concept selection could be used at the most detailed level of design for resolving decisions such as the choice of colors or materials.

Summary

Concept selection is the process of evaluating concepts with respect to customer needs and other criteria, comparing the relative strengths and weaknesses of the concepts, and selecting one or more concepts for further investigation or development.

- All teams use some method, implicit or explicit, for selecting concepts. Decision techniques employed for selecting concepts range from intuitive approaches to structured methods.
- Successful design is facilitated by structured concept selection. We recommend a two-stage process: concept screening and concept scoring.
- Concept screening uses a reference concept to evaluate concept variants against selection criteria. Concept scoring may use different reference points for each criterion.
- Concept screening uses a coarse comparison system to narrow the range of concepts under consideration.
- Concept scoring uses weighted selection criteria and a finer rating scale. Concept scoring may be skipped if concept screening produces a dominant concept.
- Both screening and scoring use a matrix as the basis of a six-step selection process. The six steps are:
  1. Prepare the selection matrix.
  2. Rate the concepts.
  3. Rank the concepts.
  4. Combine and improve the concepts.
  5. Select one or more concepts.
  6. Reflect on the results and the process.
- Concept selection is applied not only during concept development but throughout the subsequent design and development process.
- Concept selection is a group process that facilitates the selection of a winning concept, helps build team consensus, and creates a record of the decision-making process.

References and Bibliography

Many current resources are available on the Internet via
www.ulrich-eppinger.net

The concept selection methodology is a decision-making process. Souder outlines other decision techniques.

Souder, William E., *Management Decision Methods for Managers of Engineering and Research,* Van Nostrand Reinhold, New York, 1980.

For a more formal treatment of multiattribute decision making, illustrated with a set of eclectic and interesting case studies, see Keeney and Raiffa.

Keeney, Ralph L., and Howard Raiffa, *Decisions with Multiple Objectives: Preferences and Value Trade-Offs,* Cambridge University Press, New York, 1993.

Pahl and Beitz's influential engineering design textbook contains an excellent set of systematic methods. The book outlines two concept selection methods similar to concept scoring.

Pahl, Gerhard, Wolfgang Beitz, Jörg Feldhusen, and Karl-Heinrich Grote, *Engineering Design: A Systematic Approach,* third edition, K. Wallace and L. Blessing, translators, Springer-Verlag, New York, 2007.

Weighting alternatives for selection is not a new idea. The following is one of the earlier references for using selection matrices with weights.

Alger, J.R., and C.V. Hays, *Creative Synthesis in Design,* Prentice Hall, Englewood Cliffs, NJ, 1964.

The concept-screening method is based upon the concept selection process presented by Stuart Pugh. Pugh was known to criticize more quantitative methods, such as the concept-scoring method presented in this chapter. He cautioned that numbers can be misleading and can reduce the focus on creativity required to develop better concepts.

Pugh, Stuart, *Total Design,* Addison-Wesley, Reading, MA, 1990.

Concept scoring is similar to a method often called the Kepner-Tregoe method. It is described, along with other techniques for problem identification and solution, in their text.

Kepner, Charles H., and Benjamin B. Tregoe, *The Rational Manager,* McGraw-Hill, New York, 1965.

Urban and Hauser describe techniques for determining the relative importance of different product attributes.

Urban, Glen L., and John R. Hauser, *Design and Marketing of New Products,* second edition, Prentice Hall, Englewood Cliffs, NJ, 1993.

Otto and Wood present a method to include certainty bounds with the ratings given to concepts in concept scoring. These can be combined to derive an estimate of the error in selecting the highest-scoring concept and to compute a confidence interval for the results.

Otto, Kevin N., and Kristin L. Wood, "Estimating Errors in Concept Selection," *ASME Design Engineering Technical Conferences,* Vol. DE-83, 1995, pp. 397–412.

Exercises

1. How can the concept selection methods be used to benchmark or evaluate existing products? Perform such an evaluation for five automobiles you might consider purchasing.
2. Propose a set of selection criteria for the choice of a battery technology for use in a portable computer.
3. Perform concept screening for the four pencil holder concepts shown below. Assume the pencil holders are for a member of a product development team who is continually moving from site to site.
4. Repeat Exercise 3, but use concept scoring.

Zip Pouch   Screw Cap   Clam Shell   Slider

Thought Questions

1. How might you use the concept selection method to decide whether to offer a single product to the marketplace or to offer several different product options?

2. How might you use the method to determine which product features should be standard and which should be optional or add-ons?

3. Can you imagine an interactive computer tool that would allow a large group (say, 20 or more people) to participate in the concept selection process? How might such a tool work?

4. What could cause a situation in which a development team uses the concept selection method to agree on a concept that then results in commercial failure?

Appendix A

Concept-Screening Matrix Example

This matrix was created and used by a development team designing a collar to hold weights onto a barbell.

Selection Criteria	Handcuff	Master Lock	Velcro Belt	Rubber Belt	Alligator Clip	4-Part Latch (REF)	Torsional Spring	Screw Type	Wing Nut	Clothespin	Hose Clamp	C-Clamp	Spring-Loaded Bar	Magnetic Plates	Threaded Bar
Functionality															
Lightweight	+	0	+	+	+	0	+	−	−	+	0	0	+	+	0
Fits different bars	+	0	+	+	+	0	0	0	0	+	0	+	0	−	0
Weights secured laterally	0	0	−	−	0	0	0	−	+	−	0	0	−	0	+
Convenience															
Tighten from end/side	0	0	0	0	0	0	−	−	−	0	−	0	+	+	−
Does not roll	0	0	0	0	0	0	0	0	0	0	0	0	0	0	0
Change weights without removing collar	0	0	0	0	0	0	0	0	0	0	0	0	+	+	0
Convenience of placement when changing weights	0	0	+	+	0	0	−	−	−	0	−	0	+	+	−
Ergonomics															
Secure/release (one motion)	+	0	−	−	+	0	−	−	−	0	−	−	+	−	−
Low force to secure/release	0	0	0	0	−	0	−	0	0	0	0	0	+	−	0
RH/LH usage	0	0	0	0	0	0	0	−	−	0	−	−	0	0	−
Not slippery when wet	0	0	+	+	0	0	0	0	0	0	0	0	+	+	0
Use with one hand	+	0	0	0	+	0	0	0	0	0	0	0	+	+	0
Durability															
Longevity	−	−	−	−	0	0	0	+	0	0	+	+	−	−	+
Other															
Cost of raw materials	0	0	+	+	0	0	0	0	−	+	0	0	−	−	−
Manufacturability	0	−	+	+	0	0	0	+	0	+	+	0	−	−	−
Uses existing weight bars	0	0	0	0	0	0	0	0	0	0	0	0	−	0	−
Sum +'s	4	0	6	6	4	0	1	2	1	4	2	2	8	6	2
Sum 0's	11	14	7	7	11	16	11	8	8	11	10	12	3	4	7
Sum −'s	1	2	3	3	1	0	4	6	7	1	4	2	5	6	7
Net Score	3	−2	3	3	3	0	−3	−4	−6	3	−2	0	3	0	−5
Rank	1	10	1	1	1	7	12	13	15	1	10	7	1	7	15

Appendix B

Concept-Scoring Matrix Example

A development team generated this matrix while selecting a new concept for a spillproof beverage holder to be used on boats. Note that in this case the team chose not to define a single concept as the reference for all of the selection criteria.

Selection Criteria	Weight	Concept A Rating	Concept A Weighted Score	Concept C Rating	Concept C Weighted Score	Concept F Rating	Concept F Weighted Score	Concept I Rating	Concept I Weighted Score	Concept J Rating	Concept J Weighted Score	Concept K Rating	Concept K Weighted Score	Concept O Rating	Concept O Weighted Score
Flexible Use	20														
Use in different locations	15	7	105	7	105	8	120	6	90	6	90	5	75	7	105
Holds different beverages	5	5	25	5	25	3	15	4	20	5	25	3	15	3	15
Maintains Drink Condition	15														
Retains temperature of drink	13	5	65	5	65	5	65	1	13	5	65	5	65	5	65
Prevents water from getting in	2	5	10	7	14	5	10	5	10	5	10	5	10	5	10
Survives Boating Environment	5														
Doesn't break when dropped	1	6	6	6	6	9	9	7	7	5	5	9	9	6	6
Resists corrosion from sea spray	2	7	14	7	14	8	16	8	16	5	10	9	18	7	14
Floats when it falls in water	2	5	10	6	12	8	16	4	8	5	10	8	16	7	14
Keeps Drink Container Stable	20														
Prevents spilling	7	3	21	4	28	3	21	5	35	5	35	3	21	3	21
Prevents bouncing in waves	6	7	42	8	48	7	42	5	30	5	30	7	42	7	42
Will not slide during pitch/roll	7	5	35	5	35	5	35	5	35	5	35	5	35	5	35
Requires Little Maintenance	5														
Easily stored when not in use	1	7	7	6	6	8	8	9	9	4	4	8	8	7	7
Easy to maintain a clean appearance	2	6	12	6	12	3	6	4	8	5	10	5	10	6	12
Allows liquid to drain out bottom	2	5	10	5	10	5	10	5	10	5	10	5	10	5	10
Easy to Use	15														
Usable with one hand	5	7	35	7	35	7	35	6	30	5	25	7	35	7	35
Easy/comfortable to grip	5	8	40	8	40	6	30	5	25	5	25	6	30	8	40
Easy to exchange beverage containers	2	5	10	5	10	5	10	8	16	5	10	5	10	5	10
Works reliably	3	3	9	3	9	3	9	3	9	4	12	4	12	3	9
Attractive in Environment	10														
Doesn't damage boat surface	5	8	40	8	40	8	40	8	40	8	40	6	30	8	40
Attractive to look at	5	7	35	8	40	3	15	4	20	5	25	5	25	8	40
Manufacturing Ease	10														
Low-cost materials	4	5	20	4	16	7	28	8	32	4	16	8	32	6	24
Low complexity of parts	3	4	12	3	9	7	21	4	12	3	9	8	24	5	15
Low number of assembly steps	3	5	15	5	15	8	24	3	9	3	9	8	24	6	18
Total Score			578		594		585		484		510		556		587
Rank			4		1		3		7		6		5		2

CHAPTER THIRTEEN

Design for Manufacturing

Courtesy of General Motors Corp.

EXHIBIT 13-1   The General Motors 3.8-liter V6 engine.

256   *Chapter* 13

General Motors Powertrain Division manufactures about 3,500 3.8-liter V6 engines every day (Exhibit 13-1). Facing such high production volumes, the company had a strong interest in reducing the cost of the engine while simultaneously enhancing its quality. A team was formed to improve one of the most expensive subassemblies in the engine: the air intake manifold. (The intake manifold's primary function is to route air from the throttle to the intake valves at the cylinders.) The original and redesigned intake manifold assemblies are shown in Exhibit 13-2. This chapter presents a method of design for manufacturing using the GM V6 intake manifold as an example.

EXHIBIT 13-2
The original and redesigned air intake manifolds. The body of the original manifold (top) is made of cast aluminum. The redesigned manifold (bottom) is made of molded thermoplastic composite.

Photos by Stuart Cohen

Design for Manufacturing Defined

Customer needs and product specifications are useful for guiding the concept phase of product development; however, during the later development activities teams often have difficulty linking needs and specifications to the specific design issues they face. For this reason, many teams practice "design for X" (DFX) methodologies, where X may correspond to one of dozens of quality criteria such as reliability, robustness, serviceability, environmental impact, or manufacturability. The most common of these methodologies is *design for manufacturing* (DFM), which is of universal importance because it directly addresses manufacturing costs.

This chapter is primarily about DFM, but it is also intended to illustrate, by example, these general principles, which apply to methodologies for achieving any of the Xs in DFX:

- Detail-design decisions can have substantial impact on product quality and cost.
- Development teams face multiple, and often conflicting, goals.
- It is important to have metrics with which to compare alternative designs.
- Dramatic improvements often require substantial creative efforts early in the process.
- A well-defined method assists the decision-making process.

Manufacturing cost is a key determinant of the economic success of a product. In simple terms, economic success depends on the profit margin earned on each sale of the product and on how many units of the product the firm can sell. Profit margin is the difference between the manufacturer's selling price and the cost of making the product. The number of units sold and the sales price are to a large degree determined by the overall quality of the product. Economically successful design is therefore about ensuring high product quality while minimizing manufacturing cost. DFM is one method for achieving this goal; effective DFM practice leads to low manufacturing costs without sacrificing product quality. (See Chapter 18, Product Development Economics, for a more detailed discussion of models relating manufacturing costs to economic success.)

DFM Requires a Cross-Functional Team

Design for manufacturing is one of the most integrative practices involved in product development. DFM utilizes information of several types, including (1) sketches, drawings, product specifications, and design alternatives; (2) a detailed understanding of production and assembly processes; and (3) estimates of manufacturing costs, production volumes, and ramp-up timing. DFM therefore requires the contributions of most members of the development team as well as outside experts. DFM efforts commonly draw upon expertise from manufacturing engineers, cost accountants, and production personnel, in addition to product designers. Many companies use structured, team-based workshops to facilitate the integration and sharing of views required for DFM.

DFM Is Performed throughout the Development Process

DFM begins during the concept development phase, when the product's functions and specifications are being determined. When choosing a product concept, cost is almost always one of the criteria on which the decision is made—even though cost estimates at this phase are highly subjective and approximate. When product specifications are finalized, the team makes trade-offs between desired performance characteristics. For example, weight reduction may increase manufacturing costs. At this point, the team may have an approximate bill of materials (a list of parts) with estimates of costs. During the system-level design phase of development, the team makes decisions about how to break up the product into individual components, based in large measure on the expected cost and manufacturing complexity implications. Accurate cost estimates finally become available during the detail-design phase of development, when many more decisions are driven by manufacturing concerns.

Overview of the DFM Process

Our DFM method is illustrated in Exhibit 13-3. It consists of five steps plus iteration:

1. Estimate the manufacturing costs.
2. Reduce the costs of components.
3. Reduce the costs of assembly.
4. Reduce the costs of supporting production.
5. Consider the impact of DFM decisions on other factors.

As shown in Exhibit 13-3, the DFM method begins with the estimation of the manufacturing cost of the proposed design. This helps the team to determine at a general level which aspects of the design—components, assembly, or support—are most costly. The team then directs its attention to the appropriate areas in the subsequent steps. This process is iterative. It is not unusual to recompute the manufacturing cost estimate and to improve the design of the product dozens of times before agreeing that it is good enough. As long as the product design is improving, these DFM iterations may continue even until pilot production begins. At some point, the design is frozen (or "released"), and any further modifications are considered formal "engineering changes" or become part of the next generation of the product.

In the next section, we use the original GM V6 intake manifold as an example and explain how manufacturing costs are determined. Then, recognizing that accurate cost estimates are difficult (if not impossible) to obtain, we present several useful methods for reducing the costs of components, assembly, and production support. We use the redesigned intake manifold and other products as examples to illustrate these DFM principles. Finally, we discuss the results achieved through DFM and some of the broader implications of DFM decisions.

Step 1: Estimate the Manufacturing Costs

Exhibit 13-4 shows a simple input-output model of a manufacturing system. The inputs include raw materials, purchased components, employees' efforts, energy, and equipment. The outputs include finished goods and waste. Manufacturing cost is the sum of all of the expenditures for the inputs of the system and for disposal of the wastes produced by the system. As the metric of cost for a product, firms generally use *unit manufacturing cost,* which is computed by dividing the total manufacturing costs for some period (usually a quarter or a year) by the number of units of the product manufactured during that period. This simple concept is complicated in practice by several issues:

EXHIBIT 13-3

The design for manufacturing (DFM) method.

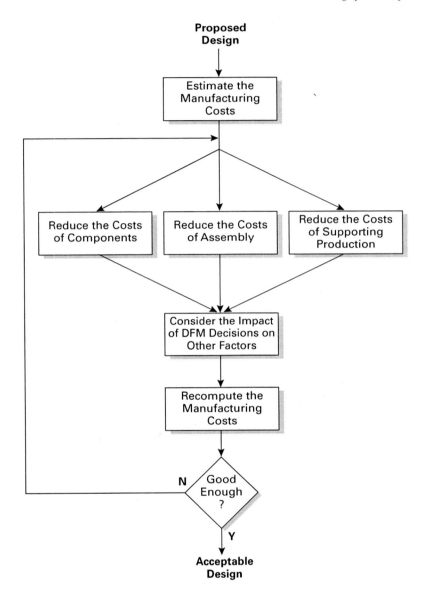

- What are the boundaries of the manufacturing system? Should the field service operations be included? What about product development activities?
- How do we "charge" the product for the use of expensive general-purpose equipment that lasts for many years?
- How are costs allocated among more than one product line in large, multiproduct manufacturing systems?

These are issues around which much of the field of managerial accounting is built, and we do not treat them in depth here. Nevertheless, we will be mindful of these complications as we discuss cost and DFM in this chapter.

EXHIBIT 13-4
A simple
input-output
model of a
manufacturing
system.

Exhibit 13-5 shows one way of categorizing the elements of manufacturing cost. Under this scheme, the unit manufacturing cost of a product consists of costs in three categories:

1. *Component costs:* The *components* of a product (also simply called parts of the product) may include *standard parts* purchased from suppliers. Examples of standard components include motors, switches, electronic chips, and screws. Other components are *custom parts,* made according to the manufacturer's design from raw materials, such as sheet steel, plastic pellets, or aluminum bars. Some custom components are made in the manufacturer's own plant, while others may be produced by suppliers according to the manufacturer's design specifications.

2. *Assembly costs:* Discrete goods are generally assembled from parts. The process of assembling almost always incurs labor costs and may also incur costs for equipment and tooling.

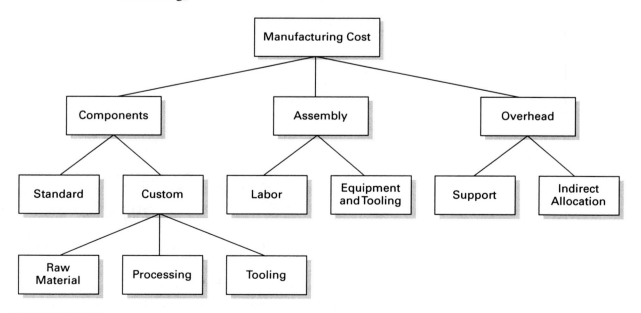

EXHIBIT 13-5   Elements of the manufacturing cost of a product.

3. *Overhead costs:* Overhead is the category used to encompass all of the other costs. We find it useful to distinguish between two types of overhead: *support costs* and other *indirect allocations.* Support costs are the costs associated with materials handling, quality assurance, purchasing, shipping, receiving, facilities, and equipment/tooling maintenance (among others). These are the support systems required to manufacture the product, and these costs do greatly depend upon the product design. Nevertheless, because these costs are often shared by more than one product line, they are lumped together in the category of overhead. Indirect allocations are the costs of manufacturing that cannot be directly linked to a particular product but that must be paid for to be in business. For example, the salary of the security guard and the cost of maintenance to the building and grounds are indirect costs because these activities are shared among several different products and are difficult to allocate directly to a specific product. Because indirect costs are not specifically linked to the design of the product, they are not relevant to DFM, even though they do contribute to the cost of the product.

Transportation Costs

The model of manufacturing cost in Exhibit 13-5 does not include any costs for transporting finished goods through the distribution system. Manufacturing often occurs at a location a great distance from the eventual customer. Although the DFM method presented here does not explicitly include transportation expense, estimating those costs is relatively easy. For instance, most goods are transported overseas using standard shipping containers, which hold about 70 cubic meters of cargo. In most cases, these containers are shipped from one location to another at a fixed cost. Currently the cost of shipping a container between Asia and the United States is roughly $6,000 (USD), resulting in a shipping cost rate of 86 USD/m^3. Rates for air freight and trucking, although based on a combination of weight and volume, are also readily available. Based on these rates, the product design team can easily include transportation costs in its analysis, and doing so may be warranted when the team faces design decisions involving the physical volume or weight of the product.

Fixed Costs versus Variable Costs

Another way to divide manufacturing costs is between *fixed costs* and *variable costs.* Fixed costs are those that are incurred in a predetermined amount, regardless of how many units of the product are manufactured. Purchasing the injection mold required for the new intake manifold is an example of a fixed cost. Whether 1,000 or 1 million units are produced, the fixed cost of the mold is incurred and does not change. Another example is the cost of setting up the factory work area for the intake manifold assembly line. This cost is also fixed, regardless of how many units are produced. Despite the terminology, however, no cost is truly fixed. If we quadruple the production quantity, we may have to build another production line. Conversely, we may be able to consolidate two assembly cells if we cannot use all the capacity due to dramatically lower production quantities. When considering a cost as fixed, ranges of production quantities and the assumed time horizon should be specified.

Variable costs are those incurred in direct proportion to the number of units produced. For example, the cost of raw materials is directly proportional to how many intake manifolds are produced, and therefore to how many 3.8-liter V6 engines are made. Assembly labor is sometimes considered a variable cost as well because many firms can adjust the staffing of assembly operations by shifting workers to other areas on short notice.

The Bill of Materials

Because manufacturing cost estimation is fundamental to DFM, it is useful to keep this information well organized. Exhibit 13-6 shows an information system for recording manufacturing cost estimates. It basically consists of a bill of materials (BOM) augmented with cost information. The BOM (usually pronounced bomb) is a list of each individual component in the product. Frequently the BOM is created using an indented format in which the assembly "tree structure" is illustrated by the indentation of components and subassembly names.

The columns of the BOM show the cost estimates broken down into fixed and variable costs. The variable costs may include materials, machine time, and labor. Fixed costs consist of tooling and other nonrecurring expenses (NRE) such as specialized equipment and one-time setup costs. The tooling lifetime is used to compute the unit fixed cost (unless the tool's expected lifetime exceeds the product's lifetime volume, in which case the lower product volume is used). To compute total cost, overhead is added according to the firm's accepted cost accounting scheme. Note that additional fixed costs, such as depreciation of capital equipment used for several products, are often also included in the overhead charge.

Component	Purchased Materials	Processing (Machine + Labor)	Assembly (Labor)	Total Unit Variable Cost	Tooling and Other NRE, K$	Tooling Lifetime, K units	Total Unit Fixed Cost	Total Cost
Manifold machined casting	12.83	5.23		18.06	1960	500+	0.50	18.56
EGR return pipe	1.30		0.15	1.45				1.45
PCV assembly								
Valve	1.35		0.14	1.49				1.49
Gasket	0.05		0.13	0.18				0.18
Cover	0.76		0.13	0.89				0.89
Screws (3)	0.06		0.15	0.21				0.21
Vacuum source block assembly								
Block	0.95		0.13	1.08				1.08
Gasket	0.03		0.05	0.08				0.08
Screw	0.02		0.09	0.11				0.11
Total Direct Costs	17.35	5.23	0.95	23.53	1960		0.50	24.03
Overhead Charges	2.60	9.42	1.71				0.75	14.48
Total Cost								**38.51**

EXHIBIT 13-6   Indented bill of materials showing cost estimates for the original intake manifold and related components. The EGR (exhaust gas recirculation), PCV (positive crankcase ventilation), and vacuum block components are included here to facilitate comparison with the redesigned manifold assembly.

Estimating the Costs of Standard Components

The costs of standard components are estimated by either (1) comparing each part to a substantially similar part the firm is already producing or purchasing in comparable volumes or (2) soliciting price quotes from vendors or suppliers. The costs of minor components (e.g., bolts, springs, and inserts) are usually obtained from the firm's experience with similar components, while the costs of major components are usually obtained from vendor quotes.

In obtaining price quotes, the estimated production quantities are extremely important. For example, the unit price on a purchase of a dozen screws or inserts may be 10 times higher than the unit prices paid by GM when purchasing 100,000 of these parts every month. If the anticipated production quantities are high enough, an application engineer or sales engineer is usually quite willing to work with the development team to specify a component properly. For internally fabricated standard components, if the required quantities are high, there may not be available production capacity, necessitating the purchase of additional equipment or the use of outside suppliers.

Some suppliers will design and fabricate a custom variation to a standard component if production quantities are high enough. For example, small electric motors, such as those found in powered hand tools, are often designed and built specifically for the product application. If the production quantities are high enough (say, 100,000 per year in this case), these custom motors are quite economical ($1 to $5 per unit, depending on the performance characteristics). For the intake manifold, the volumes are sufficiently high that custom studs, bushings, and other parts may not cost much more than standard components; however, as we discuss later, introducing new parts can add substantial cost and complexity to the production system and field service operations, which increases the support costs.

Vendors for most standard components can be found online, often by simply using a search engine. Some more specialized Web-based platforms are emerging for facilitating the search for manufacturers and vendors. Some vendors will provide online quotation tools via their own Web sites. Others will just provide contact information. When requesting cost information, make sure to inform vendors that the information is for estimation purposes only; otherwise, they may claim they do not have enough information to determine exact prices.

Estimating the Costs of Custom Components

Custom components, which are parts designed especially for the product, are made by the manufacturer or by a supplier. Most custom components are produced using the same types of production processes as standard components (e.g., injection molding, stamping, machining); however, custom parts are typically special-purpose parts, useful only in a particular manufacturer's products.

When the custom component is a single part, we estimate its cost by adding up the costs of raw materials, processing, and tooling. In cases where the custom component is actually an assembly of several parts, then we consider it a "product" in and of itself; to arrive at the cost of this "product" we estimate the cost of each subcomponent and then add assembly and overhead costs (these costs are described later). For the purposes of this explanation, we assume the component is a single part.

The raw materials costs can be estimated by computing the mass of the part, allowing for some scrap (e.g., 5 percent to 50 percent for an injection molded part, and 25 percent

EXHIBIT 13-7
Cost estimate for the original intake manifold. Note that the processing costs for casting and machining reflect the costs for a complete casting line and several machining stations.

Variable Cost		
Materials	5.7 kg aluminum at $2.25/kg	$12.83
Processing (casting)	150 units/hr at $530/hr	3.53
Processing (machining)	200 units/hr at $340/hr	1.70
Fixed Cost		
Tooling for casting	$160,000/tool at 500K units/tool (lifetime)	0.32
Machine tools and fixtures	$1,800,000/line at 10M units (lifetime)	0.18
Total Direct Cost		**$18.56**
Overhead charges		$12.09
Total Unit Cost		**$30.65**

to 100 percent for a sheet metal part), and multiplying by the cost (per unit mass) of the raw material. A table of raw material costs is given in Appendix A (Exhibit 13-17).

Processing costs include costs for the operator(s) of the processing machinery as well as the cost of using the equipment itself. Most standard processing equipment costs between $25 per hour (a simple stamping press) and $75 per hour (a medium-sized, computer-controlled milling machine) to operate, including depreciation, maintenance, utilities, and labor costs. Estimating the processing time generally requires experience with the type of equipment to be used; however, it is useful to understand the range of typical costs for common production processes. For this purpose, tables of approximate processing times and costs are given in Appendix B for a variety of stampings, castings, injection moldings, and machined parts.

Tooling costs are incurred for the design and fabrication of the cutters, molds, dies, or fixtures required to use certain machinery to fabricate parts. For example, an injection molding machine requires a custom injection mold for every different type of part it produces. These molds generally range in cost from $10,000 to $500,000. Approximate tooling costs are also given for the parts listed in Appendix B. The unit tooling cost is simply the cost of the tooling divided by the number of units to be made over the life of the tool. A high-quality injection mold or stamping die can usually be used for a few million parts.

The cost of the original intake manifold's machined casting is estimated as shown in Exhibit 13-7. Note that the estimate reveals that the cost is dominated by the expense of the aluminum material. We will see that the redesign using a composite material not only reduced the material costs but also eliminated machining and allowed many features to be formed into the molded body.

Estimating the Cost of Assembly

Products made of more than one part require assembly. For products made in quantities of less than several hundred thousand units per year, this assembly is almost always performed manually. One exception to this generalization is the assembly of electronic circuit boards, which is now almost always done automatically, even at relatively low volumes.

Manual assembly costs can be estimated by summing the estimated time of each assembly operation and multiplying by a labor rate. Assembly operations require from about 4 seconds to about 60 seconds each, depending upon the size of the parts, the

EXHIBIT 13-8
Assembly cost estimation for the PCV valve assembly of the redesigned intake manifold.

Component	Quantity	Handling Time	Insertion Time	Total Time
Valve	1	1.50	1.50	3.00
O-rings	2	2.25	4.00	12.50
Spring	1	2.25	6.00	8.25
Cover	1	1.95	6.00	7.95
Total Time (seconds)				**31.70**
Assembly Cost at $45/hour				**$0.40**

Source: Manual assembly tables in Boothroyd, Geoffrey, and Peter Dewhurst, Product Design for Assembly, Boothroyd Dewhurst, Inc., Wakefield, RI, 1989

difficulty of the operation, and the production quantities. At high volumes, workers can specialize in a particular set of operations, and special fixtures and tools can assist the assembly. Appendix C contains a table of approximate times for manual assembly of various products, which is helpful in estimating the range of times required for assembly operations. A popular method for estimating assembly times has been developed over the past 35 years by Boothroyd Dewhurst, Inc., and is now available as a software tool. This system involves a tabular information system for keeping track of the estimated assembly times for each part. The system is supported by a comprehensive database of standard handling and insertion times for a wide range of situations. Special software is also available for estimating the assembly cost of electronic circuit boards.

Assembly labor can cost from less than $1 per hour in low-wage countries to more than $40 per hour in some industrialized nations. In the United States, assembly labor is likely to cost between $15 and $30 per hour. (Each firm has different assembly labor cost structures, and some industries, such as the automobile and aircraft industries, have substantially higher cost structures.) These figures include an allowance for benefits and other worker-related expenses and are meant to reflect the true cost to the firm of assembly labor.

Consider the redesigned intake manifold. The assembly cost of the PCV (positive crankcase ventilation) valve assembly is estimated as shown in Exhibit 13-8.

Estimating the Overhead Costs

Accurately estimating overhead costs for a new product is difficult, and the industry practices are not very satisfying. Nevertheless, we will describe the standard industry practice here and identify some of its problems. Applying the overhead estimation schemes used by most firms is simple. Estimating the actual overhead costs incurred by the firm due to a particular product is not. The indirect costs of supporting production are very difficult to track and assign to particular product lines. The future costs of supporting production are even more difficult to predict for a new product.

Most firms assign overhead charges by using *overhead rates* (also called burden rates). Overhead rates are typically applied to one or two *cost drivers*. Cost drivers are parameters of the product that are directly measurable. Overhead charges are added to direct costs in proportion to the drivers. Common cost drivers are the cost of any purchased materials, the cost of assembly labor, and the number of hours of equipment time the product consumes. For example, the overhead rate for purchased materials might be 10 percent and the overhead rate for assembly labor might be 80 percent. (Of course, purchased components already have the vendor's overhead included in the price; we only add the purchasing overhead.) Under these conditions, a product containing $100 of purchased components and $10 of assembly labor would incur $18 of overhead costs

(10 percent of $100 plus 80 percent of $10). Some typical overhead structures are given in Appendix D for different types of products and firms.

The problem with this scheme is that it implies that overhead costs are directly proportional to the cost drivers. A thought experiment reveals that this cannot always be so: Most firms use "cost of purchased materials" as one cost driver, yet why would any of their overhead costs actually change if a vendor of a $50 component raises its price to $60? The answer is that they would not change at all. Overhead rates are used as a convenient way to account for overhead costs, but this scheme can yield inaccurate estimates of the true costs experienced by the manufacturer to support production.

This problem is partially addressed by activity-based costing (ABC) methods (Kaplan, 1990). Under the ABC approach, a firm utilizes more and different cost drivers and allocates all indirect costs to the associated cost drivers where they fit best. As a result, the firm may have overhead rates applied to various dimensions of product complexity (such as the number of different machining operations required or the number of different components or suppliers needed), in addition to overhead on tooling, materials, machine time, and direct labor. For the purposes of estimating manufacturing costs, the use of more cost drivers not only allows more accurate overhead cost estimates to be made but also provides important insights for reducing overhead costs by focusing attention on the cost drivers.

Step 2: Reduce the Costs of Components

For most highly engineered discrete goods the cost of purchased components will be the most significant element of the manufacturing cost. This section presents several strategies for minimizing these costs. Many of these strategies can be followed even without the benefit of accurate cost estimates. In this case, these strategies become *design rules,* or rules of thumb, to guide DFM cost reduction decisions.

Understand the Process Constraints and Cost Drivers

Some component parts may be costly simply because the designers did not understand the capabilities, cost drivers, and constraints of the production process. For example, a designer may specify a small internal corner radius on a machined part without realizing that physically creating such a feature requires an expensive electro-discharge machining (EDM) operation. A designer may specify dimensions with excessively tight tolerances, without understanding the difficulty of achieving such accuracy in production. Sometimes these costly part features are not even necessary for the component's intended function; they arise out of lack of knowledge. It is often possible to redesign the part to achieve the same performance while avoiding costly manufacturing steps; however, to do this the design engineer needs to know what types of operations are difficult in production and what drives their costs.

In some cases, the constraints of a process can be concisely communicated to designers in the form of design rules. For example, the capabilities of an automatic laser cutting machine for sheet metal can be concisely communicated in terms of allowable material types, material thicknesses, maximum part dimensions, minimum slot widths, and cutting accuracy. When this is possible, part designers can avoid exceeding the normal capabilities of a process and thereby avoid incurring unusually high costs.

For some processes, the cost of producing a part is a simple mathematical function of some attributes of the part, which would be the cost drivers for the process. For example,

EXHIBIT 13-9
Cost estimate
for the
redesigned
intake manifold
(two moldings).

Variable Cost		
Materials (manifold housing)	1.4 kg glass-filled nylon at $2.75/kg	$ 3.85
Materials (intake runner insert)	0.3 kg glass-filled nylon at $2.75/kg	0.83
Molding (manifold housing)	80 units/hr at $125/hr	1.56
Molding (intake runner insert)	100 units/hr at $110/hr	1.10
Fixed Cost		
Mold tooling (manifold housing)	$350,000/tool at 1.5M units/tool	$ 0.23
Mold tooling (intake runner insert)	$150,000/tool at 1.5M units/tool	0.10
Total Direct Cost		**$ 7.67**
Overhead charges		**$ 5.99**
Total Unit Cost		**$13.66**

a welding process could have a cost directly proportional to two attributes of the product: (1) the number of welds and (2) the total length of welds the machine creates.

For processes whose capabilities are not easily described, the best strategy is to work closely with the people who deeply understand the part production process. These manufacturing experts will generally have plenty of ideas about how to redesign components to reduce production costs.

Redesign Components to Eliminate Processing Steps

Careful scrutiny of the proposed design may lead to suggestions for redesign that can result in simplification of the production process. Reducing the number of steps in the part fabrication process generally results in reduced costs as well. Some process steps may simply not be necessary. For example, aluminum parts may not need to be painted, especially if they will not be visible to the user of the product. In some cases, several steps may be eliminated through substitution of an alternative process step. A common example of this strategy is "net-shape" fabrication. A net-shape process is one that produces a part with the final intended geometry in a single manufacturing step. Typical examples include molding, casting, forging, and extrusion. Frequently designers are able to use one of the net-shape processes to create a part that is very close to the final requirement (near net shape) and may demand only minor additional processing (e.g., drilling and tapping a hole, cutting to length).

The original intake manifold required an expensive casting, followed by several machining operations. The redesigned manifold is molded in two parts to net shape. The cost estimate for these two moldings is shown in Exhibit 13-9. (Compare with Exhibit 13-7.)

Choose the Appropriate Economic Scale for the Part Process

The manufacturing cost of a product usually drops as the production volume increases. This phenomenon is labeled *economies of scale*. Economies of scale for a fabricated component occur for two basic reasons: (1) fixed costs are divided among more units and (2) variable costs become lower because the firm can justify the use of larger and more efficient processes and equipment. For example, consider an injection-molded plastic part. The part may require a mold that costs $50,000. If the firm produces 50,000 units of the part over the product's lifetime, each part will have to assume $1 of the cost of the mold. If, however, 100,000 units are produced, each part will assume only $0.50 of the

268 *Chapter* 13

**EXHIBIT
13-10**

Total cost of
a hypothetical
part as a
function of
the number of
units produced
for injection
molding versus
machining.

cost of the mold. As production volumes increase further, the firm may be able to justify a four-cavity mold, for which each cycle of the molding machine produces four parts instead of one. As shown in Exhibit 13-9, the tooling costs for the redesigned intake manifold are quite high; however, spread over the life of the tool, the unit fixed cost is small.

Processes can be thought of as incurring fixed and variable costs. Fixed costs are incurred once per part type regardless of how many parts are produced. Variable costs are incurred each time a part is made. Processes with inherently low fixed costs and high variable costs, such as machining, are appropriate when few parts will be made, while processes with inherently high fixed costs and low variable costs, such as injection molding, are appropriate when many parts will be made. This concept is illustrated by the graph in Exhibit 13-10. As shown in the exhibit, if production volume is expected to be below 1,000 units, machining would be more economical; otherwise, injection molding would incur lower total costs.

Standardize Components and Processes

The principle of economies of scale also applies to the selection of components and processes. As the production volume of a component increases, the unit cost of the component decreases. Quality and performance often increase as well with increasing production quantities because the producer of the component can invest in learning and improvement of the component's design and its production process. For a given expected product volume, the benefits of substantially higher component volumes can be achieved through the use of standard components.

Standard components are those common to more than one product. This standardization may occur within the product line of a single firm or may occur, via an outside supplier, across the product lines of several firms. For example, the use of the 3.8-liter V6 engine in several GM cars is an example of *internal standardization.* The use of a common 10-millimeter socket head cap screw across several auto manufacturers is an example of *external standardization.* In either case, all other things being equal, the component unit cost is lower than if the component were used in only a single product.

**EXHIBIT
13-11**

An example of
standardization
within a model.
Wheels of the
Ford Explorer
are the same on
the right and left
sides of the car.

Courtesy of Ford Motor Co.

The redesigned intake manifold is used on all of GM's 3.8-liter V6 engines, even though each particular vehicle application requires different EGR (exhaust gas recirculation) return and vacuum hose routings. To accommodate this, the new intake manifold has two standard interfaces, a vacuum port and an EGR port. For each vehicle model, a custom vacuum block and EGR adapter are used. This allows the major component, the intake manifold, to be standardized internally, rather than using a different manifold for each vehicle.

Components may also be standardized within the same model. For example, most auto manufacturers use the same type of wheel on the right and left side of their cars, even though this causes directional "spokes" to have different orientations on different sides (Exhibit 13-11).

Adhere to "Black Box" Component Procurement

A component cost reduction strategy used effectively in the Japanese auto industry is called *black box* supplier design. Under this approach, the team provides a supplier with only a black box description of the component—a description of what the component has to do, not how to achieve it (Clark and Fujimoto, 1991). This kind of specification leaves the vendor with the widest possible latitude to design or select the component for minimum cost. An additional advantage of this approach is that it relieves the internal team of the responsibility to engineer and design the component. Successful black box development efforts require careful system-level design and extremely clear definitions of the functions, interfaces, and interactions of each component. (See Chapter 10, Product Architecture.)

For the redesigned intake manifold, the PCV valve assembly was designed by GM's AC Rochester Division, which supplies the component. The supplier was given system-level specifications and complete responsibility for the performance of this subsystem.

Step 3: Reduce the Costs of Assembly

Design for assembly (DFA) is a fairly well-established subset of DFM that involves minimizing the cost of assembly. For most products, assembly contributes a relatively small fraction of the total cost. Nevertheless, focusing attention on assembly costs yields strong indirect benefits. Often as a result of emphasis on DFA, the overall parts count, manufacturing complexity, and support costs are all reduced along with the assembly cost. In this section, we present a few principles useful to guide DFA decisions.

Keeping Score

Boothroyd and Dewhurst (1989) advocate maintaining an ongoing estimate of the cost of assembly. In addition to this absolute score, they propose the concept of *assembly efficiency*. This is measured as an index that is the ratio of the *theoretical minimum assembly time* to an estimate of the actual assembly time for the product. This concept is useful in developing an intuition for what drives the cost of assembly. The expression for the *DFA index* is

$$\text{DFA index} = \frac{(\text{Theoretical minimum number of parts}) \times (3 \text{ seconds})}{\text{Estimated total assembly time}}$$

To determine the theoretical minimum number of parts, ask the following three questions of each part in the proposed assembly. Only parts satisfying one or more of these conditions must "theoretically" be separate.

1. Does the part need to move relative to the rest of the assembly? Small motions that can be accomplished using compliance (e.g., elastic hinges or springs) do not count.
2. Must the part be made of a different material from the rest of the assembly for fundamental physical reasons?
3. Does the part have to be separated from the assembly for assembly access, replacement, or repair?

The "3 seconds" in the numerator reflects the theoretical minimum time required to handle and insert a part that is perfectly suited for assembly. One can think of this as the average time (sustainable over a whole work shift) required to assemble a small part that is easy to grasp, requires no particular orientation, and demands no special insertion effort; such an operation is as fast as placing a ball into a circular hole with adequate clearance.

Integrate Parts

If a part does not qualify as one of those theoretically necessary, then it is a candidate for physical integration with one or more other parts. The resulting multifunctional component is often very complex as a result of the integration of several different geometric features that would otherwise be separate parts. Nevertheless, molded or stamped parts can often incorporate additional features at little or no added cost. Exhibit 13-12 shows the throttle-body end of the redesigned intake manifold. Integrated into this component are the attachments for the EGR return and the vacuum source block. These attachments use a molded "push in and turn" geometry, eliminating the need for several threaded fasteners.

Part integration provides several benefits:

- Integrated parts do not have to be assembled. In effect, the "assembly" of the geometric features of the part is accomplished by the part fabrication process.

EXHIBIT 13-12
Integration of several features into a single component. The EGR return and vacuum source ports are molded into the redesigned intake manifold.

Photo by Stuart Cohen

- Integrated parts are often less expensive to fabricate than are the separate parts they replace. For molded, stamped, and cast parts, this cost savings occurs because a single complex mold or die is usually less expensive than two or more less complex molds or dies and because there is usually less processing time and scrap for the single, integrated part.
- Integrated parts allow the relationships among critical geometric features to be controlled by the part fabrication process (e.g., molding) rather than by an assembly process. This usually means that these dimensions can be more precisely controlled.

Note, however, that part integration is not always a wise strategy and may be in conflict with other sound approaches to minimizing costs. For example, the main intake manifold assembly on the old design was a single cast piece, requiring extensive machining. The team replaced this part with two less-expensive, injection-molded pieces. This is an example of disintegrating parts in order to achieve benefits in the piece-part production costs.

Maximize Ease of Assembly

Two products with an identical number of parts may nevertheless differ in required assembly time by a factor of two or three. This is because the actual time to grasp, orient, and insert a part depends on the part geometry and the required trajectory of the part insertion. The ideal characteristics of a part for an assembly are (adapted from Boothroyd and Dewhurst, 1989):[1]

- *Part is inserted from the top of the assembly.* This attribute of a part and assembly is called *z-axis assembly.* By using z-axis assembly for all parts, the assembly never has to be inverted, gravity helps to stabilize the partial assembly, and the assembly worker can generally see the assembly location.

[1] Adapted from Boothroyd, Geoffrey, and Peter Dewhurst, Product Design for Assembly, Boothroyd Dewhurst, Inc., Wakefield, RI, 1989.

- *Part is self-aligning.* Parts that require fine positioning in order to be assembled require slow, precise movements on the part of the assembly worker. Parts and assembly sites can be designed to be self-aligning so that fine motor control is not required of the worker. The most common self-alignment feature is the *chamfer.* A chamfer can be implemented as a tapered lead on the end of a peg, or a conical widening at the opening of a hole.

- *Part does not need to be oriented.* Parts requiring correct orientation, such as a screw, require more assembly time than parts requiring no orientation, such as a sphere. In the worst case, a part must be oriented correctly in three dimensions. For example, the following parts are listed in order of increasing requirements for orientation: sphere, cylinder, capped cylinder, capped and keyed cylinder.

- *Part requires only one hand for assembly.* This characteristic relates primarily to the size of the part and the effort required to manipulate the part. All other things being equal, parts requiring one hand to assemble require less time than parts requiring two hands, which in turn require less effort than parts requiring a crane or lift to assemble.

- *Part requires no tools.* Assembly operations requiring tools, such as attaching snap rings, springs, or cotter pins, generally require more time than those that do not.

- *Part is assembled in a single, linear motion.* Pushing in a pin requires less time than driving a screw. For this reason, numerous fasteners are commercially available that require only a single, linear motion for insertion.

- *Part is secured immediately upon insertion.* Some parts require a subsequent securing operation, such as tightening, curing, or the addition of another part. Until the part is secured, the assembly may be unstable, requiring extra care, fixtures, or slower assembly.

Consider Customer Assembly

Customers may tolerate completing some of the product assembly themselves, especially if doing so provides other benefits, such as making the purchase and handling of the packaged product easier; however, designing a product such that it can be easily and properly assembled by the most inept customers, many of whom will ignore directions, is a substantial challenge in itself.

Step 4: Reduce the Costs of Supporting Production

In working to minimize the costs of components and the costs of assembly, the team may also achieve reductions in the demands placed on the production support functions. For example, a reduction in the number of parts reduces the demands on inventory management. A reduction in assembly content reduces the number of workers required for production and therefore reduces the cost of supervision and human resource management. Standardized components reduce the demands on engineering support and quality control. There are, in addition, some direct actions the team can take to reduce the costs of supporting production.

It is important to remember that manufacturing cost estimates are often insensitive to many of the factors that actually drive overhead charges. (Recall the discussion of overhead cost estimation earlier.) Nevertheless, the goal of the design team in this respect

Drivers of Complexity	Rev. 1	Rev. 2
Number of new parts introduced to the manufacturing system	6	5
Number of new vendors introduced to the manufacturing system	3	2
Number of custom parts introduced to the manufacturing system	2	3
Number of new "major tools" (e.g., molds and dies) introduced to the manufacturing system	2	2
Number of new production processes introduced to the manufacturing system	0	0
Total	**13**	**12**

EXHIBIT 13-13   Scorecard of manufacturing complexity.

should be to reduce the actual costs of production support even if overhead cost estimates do not change.

Minimize Systemic Complexity

An extremely simple manufacturing system would utilize a single process to transform a single raw material into a single part—perhaps a system extruding a single diameter of plastic rod from plastic pellets. Unfortunately, few such systems exist. Complexity arises from variety in the inputs, outputs, and transforming processes. Many real manufacturing systems involve hundreds of suppliers, thousands of different parts, hundreds of people, dozens of types of products, and dozens of types of production processes. Each variant of suppliers, parts, people, products, and processes introduces complexity to the system. These variants must usually be tracked, monitored, managed, inspected, handled, and inventoried at tremendous cost to the enterprise. Much of this complexity is driven by the design of the product and can therefore be minimized through smart design decisions.

Exhibit 13-13 shows a simple "scorecard" of manufacturing complexity useful for reminding designers of how the product design drives the complexity of the manufacturing system. The team establishes a score for the initial design and then uses changes in the score as a measure of success in reducing complexity. Note that the drivers given in the scorecard shown are generic categories. In practice, the team develops this list (and may prioritize it with weightings) based on the realities and constraints of the firm's production environment. Firms that use activity-based costing usually know quite well their primary drivers of complexity, as these are the cost drivers they use in allocating overhead. As a simple substitute for an accurate support cost model, such a scorecard allows the team to make informed decisions without formally estimating the indirect costs of production.

Error Proofing

An important aspect of DFM is to anticipate the possible failure modes of the production system and to take appropriate corrective actions early in the development process. This strategy is known as *error proofing*. One type of failure mode arises from having slightly different parts that can be easily confused. Examples of slightly different parts are screws differing only in the pitch of the threads (e.g., 4 × .70 mm and 4 × .75 mm screws) or in the direction of turning (left- and right-handed threads), parts that are mirror images of each other, and parts differing only in material composition.

We recommend either that these subtle differences be eliminated or that slight differences be exaggerated. Exhibit 13-14 shows an example of exaggerating subtle differences between parts: the left and right versions of the reel lock on a videocassette, which are

274   *Chapter* 13

**EXHIBIT
13-14**
Left and right
reel locks inside
a videocassette
(top center).
The two nearly
identical parts
are color
coded to avoid
confusion.

Photo by Stuart Cohen

mirror images of each other, are molded in two different colors. Color coding allows the parts to be identified easily and differentiated in materials handling and assembly.

Step 5: Consider the Impact of DFM Decisions on Other Factors

Minimizing manufacturing cost is not the only objective of the product development process. The economic success of a product also depends on the quality of the product, the timeliness of product introduction, and the cost of developing the product. There may also be situations in which the economic success of a project is compromised in order to maximize the economic success of the entire enterprise. In contemplating a DFM decision, these issues should be considered explicitly.

The Impact of DFM on Development Time

Development time can be precious. For an automobile development project, time may be worth as much as several hundred thousand dollars per day. For this reason, DFM decisions must be evaluated for their impact on development time as well as for their impact on manufacturing cost. While saving $1 in cost on each manifold would be worth perhaps $1 million in annual cost savings, it would almost certainly not be worth causing a six-month delay in an automobile program.

The relationship between DFM and development time is complex. Here, we note a few aspects of the relationship. The application of some of the DFA guidelines may result in very complex parts. These parts may be so complex that their design or the procurement of their tooling becomes the activity that determines the duration of the overall development effort (Ulrich et al., 1993). The cost benefits of the DFM decision may not be worth the delay in project duration. This is particularly true for products competing in dynamic markets.

The Impact of DFM on Development Cost

Development cost closely mirrors development time; therefore, the same caution about the relationship between part complexity and development time applies to development cost. In general, however, teams that aggressively pursue low manufacturing costs as an integral part of the development process seem to be able to develop products in about the same time and with about the same budget as teams that do not. Part of this phenomenon certainly arises from the correlation between good project management practices and the application of sound DFM methods.

The Impact of DFM on Product Quality

Before proceeding with a DFM decision, the team should evaluate the impact of the decision on product quality. Under ideal circumstances, actions to decrease manufacturing cost would also improve product quality. For example, the new GM manifold resulted in cost reduction, weight reduction, and improved engine performance. It is not uncommon for DFM efforts focused primarily on manufacturing cost reduction to also result in improved serviceability, ease of disassembly, and recycling; however, in some cases actions to decrease manufacturing cost can have adverse effects on product quality (such as reliability or robustness), so it is advisable for the team to keep in mind the many dimensions of quality that are important for the product.

The Impact of DFM on External Factors

Design decisions may have implications beyond the responsibilities of a single development team. In economic terms, these implications may be viewed as externalities. Two such externalities are component reuse and life cycle costs.

- *Component reuse:* Taking time and money to create a low-cost component may be of value to other teams designing similar products. In general, this value is not explicitly accounted for in manufacturing cost estimates. The team may choose to take an action that is actually more costly for their product because of the positive cost implications for other projects.

- *Life cycle costs:* Throughout their life cycles, certain products may incur some company or societal costs that are not (or are rarely) accounted for in the manufacturing cost. For example, products may contain toxic materials requiring special handling in disposal. Products may incur service and warranty costs. Although these costs may not appear in the manufacturing cost analysis, they should be considered before adopting a DFM decision. Chapter 12, Design for Environment, provides a detailed method of addressing life cycle costs.

Results

Design-for-manufacturing practices have been put into place in thousands of firms. Today DFM is an essential part of almost every product development effort. No longer can designers "throw the design over the wall" to production engineers. As a result of this emphasis on improved design quality, some manufacturers claim to have reduced production costs of products by up to 50 percent. In fact, comparing current new product designs with earlier generations, one can usually identify fewer parts in the new product, as well as new materials, more integrated and custom parts, higher-volume standard parts and subassemblies, and simpler assembly procedures.

A sketch of the redesigned intake manifold is shown in Exhibit 13-15. This DFM effort achieved impressive results. Exhibit 13-16 shows the cost estimate for the redesigned

276 *Chapter* 13

EXHIBIT 13-15
The redesigned intake manifold.

Courtesy of General Motors Corp.

Component	Purchased Materials	Processing (Machine + Labor)	Assembly (Labor)	Total Unit Variable Cost	Tooling and Other NRE, K$	Tooling Lifetime, K units	Total Unit Fixed Cost	Total Cost
Manifold housing	3.85	1.56		5.41	350	1500	0.23	5.65
Intake runner insert	0.83	1.10	0.13	2.05	150	1500	0.10	2.15
Steel inserts (16)	0.32		1.00	1.32				1.32
EGR adapter	1.70		0.13	1.83				1.83
PCV valve								
Valve	0.85		0.04	0.89				0.89
O-rings(2)	0.02		0.16	0.18				0.18
Spring	0.08		0.10	0.18				0.18
Cover	0.02		0.10	0.12				0.12
Vacuum source block	0.04		0.06	0.10				0.10
Total Direct Costs	7.71	2.66	1.71	12.08	500		0.33	12.41
Overhead Charges	1.16	4.79	3.08				0.50	9.52
Total Cost								**21.93**

EXHIBIT 13-16 Cost estimate for the redesigned intake manifold.

intake manifold. (Compare with Exhibit 13-6.) The improvements over the previous design include:

- Unit cost savings of 45 percent.
- Mass savings of 66 percent (3.3 kilograms).
- Simplified assembly and service procedures.
- Improved emissions performance due to routing of EGR into the manifold.
- Improved engine performance due to reduced air induction temperatures.
- Reduced shipping costs due to lighter components.
- Increased standardization across vehicle programs.

For this product, the manufacturing cost savings alone amount to several million dollars annually. The other benefits listed earlier are also significant, although somewhat more difficult to quantify.

Summary

Design for manufacturing (DFM) is aimed at reducing manufacturing costs while simultaneously improving (or at least not inappropriately compromising) product quality, development time, and development cost.

- DFM begins with the concept development phase and system-level design phase; in these phases important decisions must be made with the manufacturing cost implications in mind.
- DFM utilizes estimates of manufacturing cost to guide and prioritize cost reduction efforts. Cost estimation requires expertise with the relevant production processes. Suppliers and manufacturing experts must be involved in this process.
- Because accurate cost estimation is very difficult, much of DFM practice involves making informed decisions in the absence of detailed cost data.
- Component costs are reduced by understanding what drives these costs. Solutions may involve novel component design concepts or the incremental improvement of existing designs through simplification and standardization.
- Assembly costs can be reduced by following well-established design-for-assembly (DFA) guidelines. Components can be redesigned to simplify assembly operations, or components can be eliminated entirely by integration of their functions into other components.
- Reduction of manufacturing support costs begins with an understanding of the drivers of complexity in the production process. Design decisions have a large impact on the costs of supporting production. Choices should be made with these effects in mind, even though overhead cost estimates are often insensitive to such changes.
- DFM is an integrative method taking place throughout the development process and requiring inputs from across the development team.
- DFM decisions can affect product development lead time, product development cost, and product quality. Trade-offs will frequently be necessary between manufacturing cost and these equally important broader issues.

References and Bibliography

Many current resources are available on the Internet via
www.ulrich-eppinger.net

Two articles describe the needs, methods, and success of DFM in the 1980s.

Dean, James W., Jr., and Gerald I. Susman, "Organizing for Manufacturable Design," *Harvard Business Review,* January–February 1989, pp. 28–36.

Whitney, Daniel E., "Manufacturing by Design," *Harvard Business Review,* July–August 1988, pp. 83–91.

There are numerous documented examples of DFM success. One classic example is the story of the IBM Proprinter, described by Dewhurst and Boothroyd.

Dewhurst, Peter, and Geoffrey Boothroyd, "Design for Assembly in Action," *Assembly Engineering,* January 1987.

There are many references available to aid in component design, materials choice, manufacturing process selection, and understanding of process capabilities. Here are several sources that offer specific guidelines for hundreds of applications, materials, and processes.

Bolz, Roger W., *Production Processes: The Productivity Handbook,* fifth edition, Industrial Press, New York, 1981.

Bralla, James G. (ed.), *Design for Manufacturability Handbook,* McGraw-Hill, New York, 1999.

Cubberly, William H., and Ramon Bakerjian, *Tool and Manufacturing Engineers Handbook,* Society of Manufacturing Engineers, Dearborn, MI, 1989.

Farag, Mahmoud M., *Materials and Process Selection for Engineering Design,* second edition, CRC Press, Boca Raton, FL, 2008.

Poli, Corrado, *Engineering Design and Design for Manufacturing: A Structured Approach,* Butterworth-Heinemann, 2001.

Thompson, Rob, *Manufacturing Processes for Design Professionals,* Thames & Hudson, London, 2008.

Trucks, H. E., *Designing for Economical Production,* second edition, Society of Manufacturing Engineers, Dearborn, MI, 1987.

Gupta et al. provide a review of state-of-the-art manufacturability analysis methods and related DFM research.

Gupta, Satyandra K., et al., "Automated Manufacturability Analysis: A Survey," *Research in Engineering Design,* Vol. 9, No. 3, 1997, pp. 168–190.

The most popular method for DFA is by Boothroyd and Dewhurst. Software is also available to aid in estimating costs for both manual and automatic assembly, as well as a wide range of component costs.

Boothroyd, Geoffrey, and Peter Dewhurst, *Product Design for Assembly,* Boothroyd Dewhurst, Inc., Wakefield, RI, 1989.

Boothroyd, Geoffrey, Peter Dewhurst, and Winston A. Knight, *Product Design for Manufacture and Assembly,* third edition, CRC Press, Boca Raton, FL, 2011.

Detailed research on automated assembly has resulted in guidelines for designing products suited for assembly automation.

Boothroyd, Geoffrey, *Assembly Automation and Product Design,* second edition, CRC Press, Boca Raton, FL, 2005.

Nevins, James L., and Daniel E. Whitney, *Concurrent Design of Products and Processes,* McGraw-Hill, New York, 1989.

Whitney, Daniel E., *Mechanical Assemblies: Their Design, Manufacture, and Role inProduct Development,* Oxford University Press, New York, 2004.

Kaplan and others describe the development of activity-based costing systems, which provide insight into a firm's cost drivers and facilitate more accurate cost estimation.

Kaplan, Robert S. (ed.), *Measures for Manufacturing Excellence,* Harvard Business School Press, Boston, 1990.

Clark and Fujimoto conducted a comprehensive study of product development in the world automobile industry. They provide an interesting analysis and discussion of the concept of black box component design.

Clark, Kim B., and Takahiro Fujimoto, *Product Development Performance: Strategy, Organization, and Management in the World Auto Industry,* Harvard Business School Press, Boston, 1991.

Ulrich et al. describe the trade-off between development time and manufacturing cost. They also describe an effort to model support costs in some detail.

Ulrich, Karl, Scott Pearson, David Sartorius, and Mark Jakiela, "Including the Value of Time in Design-for-Manufacturing Decision Making," *Management Science,* Vol. 39, No. 4, April 1993, pp. 429–447.

Ulrich and Pearson present a method for studying products, their costs, and some of the many detail design decisions resulting in the artifacts we see.

Ulrich, Karl T., and Scott Pearson, "Assessing the Importance of Design through Product Archaeology," *Management Science,* Vol. 44, No. 3, March 1998, pp. 352–369.

Exercises

1. Estimate the production cost for a simple product you may have purchased. Try costing a product with fewer than 10 components, such as a kitchen accessory, a pen, a jackknife, or a baby's toy. Remember that one reasonable upper bound for your estimate, including overhead, is the wholesale price (between 50 percent and 70 percent of retail).

2. Suggest some potential cost-reducing modifications you could make to improve the product costed earlier. Compute the DFA index before and after these changes.

3. List 10 reasons why reducing the number of parts in a product might reduce production costs. Also list some reasons why costs might increase.

280 *Chapter* 13

Thought Questions

1. Consider the following 10 "design rules" for electromechanical products. Do these seem like reasonable guidelines? Under what circumstances could one rule conflict with another one? How should such a trade-off be settled?
   a. Minimize parts count.
   b. Use modular assembly.
   c. Stack assemblies.
   d. Eliminate adjustments.
   e. Eliminate cables.
   f. Use self-fastening parts.
   g. Use self-locating parts.
   h. Eliminate reorientation.
   i. Facilitate parts handling.
   j. Specify standard parts.

2. Is it practical to design a product with 100 percent assembly efficiency (DFA index = 1.0)? What conditions would have to be met? Can you think of any products with very high (greater than 75 percent) assembly efficiency?

3. Is it possible to determine what a product really costs once it is put into production? If so, how might you do this?

4. Can you propose a set of metrics that would be useful for the team to predict changes in the actual costs of supporting production? To be effective, these metrics must be sensitive to changes in the design that affect indirect costs experienced by the firm. What are some of the barriers to the introduction of such techniques in practice?

Appendix A

Materials Costs

**EXHIBIT
13-17**
Range of costs
for common
engineering
materials. Price
ranges shown
correspond to
various grades
and forms of
each material,
purchased in
bulk quantities
(2015 prices).

Source: Adapted from
David G. Ullman, *The
Mechanical Design
Process,* third edition,
McGraw-Hill, New
York, 2003

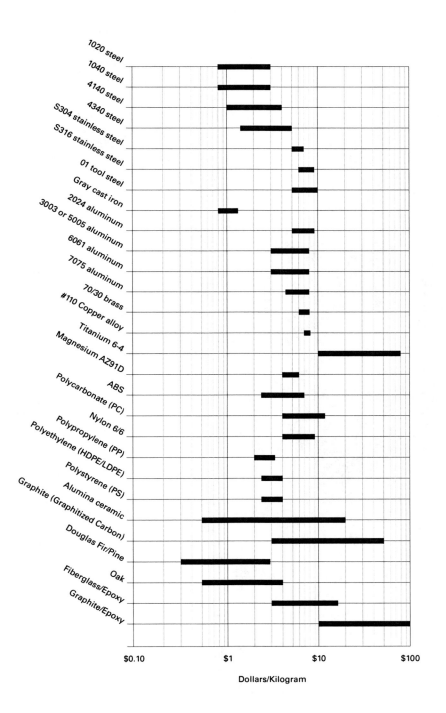

Dollars/Kilogram

282 *Chapter* 13

Appendix B

Component Manufacturing Costs

The exhibits in this appendix show example components and their cost data for computer-numerical control (CNC) machining (Exhibit 13-18), injection molding (Exhibit 13-19), progressive die stamping (Exhibit 13-20), and sand casting and investment casting (Exhibit 13-21). The purpose of these examples is to show, in general terms, what typical operations cost and how the cost structure of each process is affected by part complexity.

	Fixed Costs		Variable Costs		Volume	Total Unit Cost
a.	Setup:	0.75 hr. at $60/hr.	Material:	$9 ea. stock: 1.11 kg of 6061 aluminum	1	$75.00
	Tooling:	programming: 0.25 hr. at $60/hr.	Processing:	6 min./unit at $60/hr.	10	$21.00
					100	$15.50
b.	Setup:	1.75 hr. at $60/hr.	Material:	$16 ea. stock: 1.96 kg of 6061 aluminum	1	$386.00
	Tooling:	programming: 1.0 hr. at $60/hr. Fixtures: $150	Processing:	55 min./unit at $60/hr.	10	$102.50
					100	$74.15
c.	Setup:	5.5 hr. at $60/hr.	Material:	$25 ea. stock: 4.60 kg of ultra-high molecular weight polyethylene	1	$646.00
	Tooling:	programming: 2.0 hr. at $60/hr.	Processing:	2.85 hr./unit at $60/hr.	10	$241.00
					100	$200.50
d.	Setup:	2.0 hr. at $60/hr.	Material:	$12 ea. stock: 1.50 kg of 6061 aluminum	1	$612.00
	Tooling:	programming: 2.0 hr. at $60/hr.	Processing:	6 hr./unit at $60/hr.	10	$396.00
					100	$374.40

Source: Photos by Stuart Cohen. Examples and data courtesy of Ramco, Inc.

Notes: 1. Programming time is a one-time expense and is included here in tooling costs.
  2. Material prices assume low volumes and include cutting charges.
  3. Processing costs include overhead charges.

EXHIBIT 13-18 CNC machining example components and cost data.

	Fixed Costs	Variable Costs	Volume	Total Unit Cost
	Setup:	Material: $0.075 ea. 45 g of linear low density polyethylene (LLDPF)	10K	$1.915
			100K	$0.295
	Tooling: $18K 8 cavities/mold no actions	Processing: 1000 pcs/hr. on an 1800 KN press at $40/hr.	1M	$0.133
	Setup:	Material: $0.244 ea. 10 g of steel-filled polycarbonate (PC)	10K	$1.507
			100K	$0.607
	Tooling: $10K 1 cavity/mold no actions	Processing: 160 pcs/hr. on a 900 KN press at $42/hr.	1M	$0.517
	Setup:	Material: $0.15 ea. 22 g of modified polyphenylene oxide (PPO)	10K	$2.125
			100K	$0.505
	Tooling: $18K 2 cavities/mold no actions 3 retracting pins	Processing: 240 pcs/hr. on an 800 KN press at $42/hr.	1M	$0.343
	Setup:	Material: $2.58 ea. 227 g of polycarbonate (PC) with 8 brass inserts	10K	$11.085
			100K	$3.885
	Tooling: $80K 1 cavity/mold 1 action 4 retracting pins	Processing: 95 pcs/hr. on a 2700 KN press at $48/hr.	1M	$3.165

Source: Photos by Stuart Cohen. Examples and data courtesy of Lee Plastics, Inc., and Digital Equipment Corporation

Notes: 1. Setup costs (only a few hours in each case) are negligible for high-volume injection molding.
2. Processing costs include overhead charges.

EXHIBIT 13-19   Injection molding example components and cost data.

284   *Chapter* 13

	Fixed Costs		Variable Costs		Volume	Total Unit Cost
a.	Setup:		Material: $0.040 ea. 2.2g 70/30 Brass		100K	$0.281
					1M	$0.083
	Tooling:	$22K	Processing: 3000 pcs/hr. on a 550 KN press at $63/hr.		10M	$0.063
b.	Setup:		Material: $0.032 ea. 3.5 g 304 SST		100K	$0.775
					1M	$0.136
	Tooling:	$71K	Processing: 4300 pcs/hr. on a 550 KN press at $140/hr.		10M	$0.072
c.	Setup:		Material: $0.128 ea. 19.2 g 102 copper		100K	$0.248
					1M	$0.149
	Tooling:	$11K	Processing: 4800 pcs/hr. on a 650 KN press at $50/hr.		10M	$0.140
d.	Setup:		Material: $0.28 ea. 341 g galvanized steel		100K	$2.516
					1M	$0.761
	Tooling:	$195K	Processing: 700 pcs/hr. on a 1000 KN press at $200/hr.		10M	$0.585

Source: Photos by Stuart Cohen. Examples and data courtesy of Brainin Advance Industries and other sources

Notes: 1. Setup costs (only a few hours in each case) are negligible for high-volume stamping.
2. Material weights represent the finished stampings. Material costs include scrap.
3. Hourly processing costs are not only driven by press size, but also can include ancillary processing equipment, such as in-die tapping.
4. Processing costs include overhead charges.

EXHIBIT 13-20   Volume progressive die stamping example components and cost data.

	Fixed Costs	Variable Costs	Volume	Total Unit Cost
a.	Setup:	Material: $0.53 ea. 570 g of gray cast iron	10	$180.91
			100	$18.91
	Tooling: $1.8K 8 impressions/pattern no core	Processing: 120 pcs/hr. at $46/hr.	1000	$2.71
b.	Setup:	Material: $2.42 ea. 2,600 g of gray cast iron	10	$243.95
			100	$27.95
	Tooling: $2.4K 2 impressions/pattern 1 core	Processing: 30 pcs/hr. at $46/hr.	1000	$6.35

	Fixed Costs	Variable Costs	Volume	Total Unit Cost
c.	Setup:	Material: $0.713 ea. 260 g of yellow brass	10	$163.21
			100	$28.21
	Tooling: $1.5K no cores	Processing: 4 pcs/hr. at $50/hr.	1000	$14.71
d.	Setup:	Material: $0.395 ea. 180 g of 712 aluminum	10	$750.40
			100	$120.40
	Tooling: $7K 3 cores	Processing: 1 pc/hr. at $50/hr.	1000	$57.40

Source: Photos by Stuart Cohen. Examples and data courtesy of Cumberland Foundry Co., Inc. (sand casting), and Castronics, Inc. (investment casting)

Notes: 1. Setup is not generally charged in costing.
2. Processing costs include overhead charges.

EXHIBIT 13-21 Sand casting (top) and investment casting (bottom) example components and cost data.

Terminology

The following terminology applies to all of the tables in this appendix:

- *Setup* is the work required to prepare the equipment for a production run. Setup costs are charged for each run.
- *Tooling costs* are incurred in advance of the first production run, and tooling can usually be reused for later production runs; however, in very high-volume production runs, tooling wears out and therefore is a recurring expense. Tooling costs may be spread over the entire production volume or may be charged separately. CNC programming time is generally also a one-time expense, like a tooling cost.
- *Material types* are listed for each part. Material weights and costs include processing scrap and waste.
- *Processing costs* vary with the type of manufacturing equipment used and include charges for both machine time and labor.

While fixed costs (setup and tooling) are sometimes billed separately from material and processing costs, for these examples, fixed costs are spread over the production volume shown. Unit costs are calculated as

$$\text{Total unit cost} = \frac{\text{Setup costs} + \text{Tooling costs}}{\text{Volume}} + \text{Variable costs}$$

The cost rates given include overhead charges, so these data are representative of custom components purchased from suppliers.

Description of Processes

CNC machining includes computer-controlled milling and turning processes. CNC machines are highly flexible due to automatic tool-changing mechanisms, multiple work axes, and programmable computer control. To produce a particular part, a machinist must first program the cutting tool trajectories and tool selections into the machine's computer. Also, fixtures or other tooling may be utilized to produce multiple parts more efficiently. Once the program is written and fixtures are made, subsequent production runs can be set up much more quickly.

Injection molding is the process of forcing hot melted plastic under high pressure into a mold, where it cools and solidifies. When the part is sufficiently cool, the mold is opened, the part is ejected, the mold closes, and the cycle begins again. Mold complexity depends highly on the part geometry; undercuts (features that would prevent the part from ejecting out of the mold) are achieved using mold "actions" or "retracting pins."

Progressive die stamping is the process of passing a sheet or strip of metal through a set of dies to cut and/or form it to a desired size and shape. While some stampings require only cutting, formed stampings are made by bending and stretching the metal beyond its yield point, thereby causing permanent deformation.

Sand castings are created by forming a sand mold from master patterns (tooling in the shape of the final part). Special binders are mixed with the sand to allow the sand to retain shape when packed around the pattern to create a single-use mold. Internal cavities in a casting can be created using additional sand cores inside the outer mold. Molten metal is then poured into the mold where the metal cools and solidifies. Once cool, the sand is broken off to reveal the metal casting. Sand castings generally require subsequent machining operations to create finished components.

Investment castings are made by first creating a temporary wax pattern, using master tooling. The wax pattern is then dipped or immersed in plaster or ceramic slurry, which is allowed to solidify. The form is then heated, melting out the wax and leaving behind only the thin shell as a mold. Molten metal is then poured into the mold, where it cools and solidifies. When the metal is cool, the mold is broken off to reveal the metal part.

Detailed process descriptions for the aforementioned and numerous other processes, as well as more detailed cost estimating techniques, can be found in the reference books listed for this chapter.

288   *Chapter* 13

Appendix C

Assembly Costs

Product	Part Data		Assembly Times (Seconds)	
	No. of Parts	16	Total	125.7
	No. of Unique Parts	12	Slowest Part	9.7
	No. of Fasteners	0	Fastest Part	2.9
	No. of Parts	34	Total	186.5
	No. of Unique Parts	25	Slowest Part	10.7
	No. of Fasteners	5	Fastest Part	2.6
	No. of Parts	49	Total	266.0
	No. of Unique Parts	43	Slowest Part	14.0
	No. of Fasteners	5	Fastest Part	3.5
	No. of Parts	56/17*	Total	277.0/138.0*
	No. of Unique Parts	44/12*	Slowest Part	8.0/8.0*
	No. of Fasteners	0/0*	Fastest Part	0.75/3.0*

Source: Photos by Stuart Cohen. Data obtained by using Boothroyd Dewhurst Inc. DFA software

*Data for the mouse are given as: total components (including electronic)/mechanical components only.

Notes: 1. This table gives manual assembly times, which can be converted to assembly costs using applicable labor rates.

2. Assembly times shown include times for individual part handling and insertion, as well as other operations such as subassembly handling and insertion, reorientations, and heat riveting.

EXHIBIT 13-22   Assembly data for common products. Obtained using Boothroyd Dewhurst, Inc., DFA Software.

Component	Time (Seconds)			Component	Time (Seconds)		
	Min	Max	Avg		Min	Max	Avg
Screw	7.5	13.1	10.3	Pin	3.1	10.1	6.6
Snap-fit	3.5	8.0	5.9	Spring	2.6	14.0	8.3

Source: Manual assembly tables in Boothroyd, Geoffrey, and Peter Dewhurst, Product Design for Assembly, Boothroyd Dewhurst, Inc., Wakefield, RI, 1989

EXHIBIT 13-23 Typical handling and insertion times for common components.

Appendix D

Cost Structures

Type of Firm	Cost Calculation
Electromechanical products manufacturer (Traditional cost structure)	Cost = (113%) × (Materials cost) + (360%) × (Direct labor cost)
Precision valve manufacturer (Activity-based cost structure)	Cost = (108%) × [(Direct labor cost) + (Setup labor cost) + (160%) × (Materials cost) + ($27.80) × (Machine hours) + ($2,000.00) × (Number of shipments)]
Heavy equipment component manufacturer (Activity-based cost structure)	Cost = (110%) × (Materials cost) + (109%) × [(211%) × (Direct labor cost) + ($16.71) × (Machine hours) + ($33.76) × (Setup hours) + ($114.27) × (Number of production orders) + ($19.42) × (Number of material handling loads) + ($487.00) × (Number of new parts added to the system)]

Sources, top to bottom: Unpublished company source; Harvard Business School cases: Destin Brass Products Co., 9-190-089, and John Deere Component Works, 9-187-107

Notes: 1. This table shows total costs per customer order.
    2. Materials costs include costs of raw materials and purchased components.

EXHIBIT 13-24 Typical cost structures for manufacturing firms.

CHAPTER FOURTEEN

Prototyping

Courtesy of iRobot Corp.

EXHIBIT 14-1   PackBot mobile robot by iRobot.

Courtesy of iRobot Corp.

EXHIBIT 14-2   The PackBot ready for deployment in a military search operation.

The iRobot PackBot line of tactical mobile robots was designed by iRobot Corporation to assist law enforcement and military personnel to conduct operations in dangerous environments. For example, PackBot robots were used to help search for survivors in the wreckage of the World Trade Center in September 2001 and were the first robots to enter the damaged Fukushima nuclear power plant after the 2011 earthquake and tsunami. They have assisted military operations around the world, and they are used in highly dangerous situations by police for bomb disposal and by workers for detection of hazardous materials. The mobile chassis of the PackBot accepts a wide range of payloads, including a robotic arm that can be fitted with a gripper, video camera, lighting, acoustic sensors, chemical and radiation detectors, or specialized equipment such as that needed for disarming bombs. Exhibit 14-1 shows the PackBot configured with a robotic arm, camera, gripper, and fiber-optic communications tether. Exhibit 14-2 shows the PackBot ready for use in the field.

The PackBot may be carried by military troops, thrown through a window, or dropped off a fire truck into a wide range of challenging and unpredictable situations. In developing the PackBot, the product development team at iRobot utilized various forms of prototypes throughout the product development process. Prototypes not only helped develop a successful product quickly, but also helped ensure the reliability of the PackBot in the field.

This chapter defines *prototype,* explains why prototypes are built, and then presents several principles of prototyping practice. The chapter also describes a method for planning prototypes before they are built. The PackBot is used as an illustrative example throughout.

Understanding Prototypes

Although dictionaries define *prototype* as a noun only, in product development practice the word is used as a noun, a verb, and an adjective. For example:

- Industrial designers produce *prototypes* of their concepts.
- Engineers *prototype* a design.
- Software developers write *prototype* programs.

We define *prototype* as "an approximation of the product along one or more dimensions of interest." Under this definition, any entity exhibiting at least one aspect of the product that is of interest to the development team can be viewed as a prototype. This definition deviates from standard usage in that it includes such diverse forms of prototypes as concept sketches, mathematical models, simulations, test components, and fully functional preproduction versions of the product. *Prototyping* is the process of developing such an approximation of the product.

Types of Prototypes

Prototypes can be usefully classified along two dimensions. The first dimension is the degree to which a prototype is *physical* as opposed to *analytical*. Physical prototypes are tangible artifacts created to approximate the product. Aspects of the product of interest to the development team are actually built into an artifact for testing and experimentation. Examples of physical prototypes include models that look and feel like the product, proof-of-concept prototypes used to test an idea quickly, and experimental hardware used to validate the functionality of a product. Exhibit 14-3 shows three forms of physical prototypes used for diverse purposes. Analytical prototypes represent the product in a nontangible, usually mathematical or visual, manner. Interesting aspects of the product are analyzed, rather than built. Examples of analytical prototypes include computer simulations, systems of equations encoded within a spreadsheet, and computer models of three-dimensional geometry. Exhibit 14-4 shows three forms of analytical prototypes used for diverse purposes.

The second dimension is the degree to which a prototype is *comprehensive* as opposed to *focused*. Comprehensive prototypes implement most, if not all, of the attributes of a product. A comprehensive prototype corresponds closely to the everyday use of the word *prototype*, in that it is a full-scale, fully operational version of the product. An example of a comprehensive prototype is one given to customers in order to identify any remaining design flaws before committing to production. In contrast to comprehensive prototypes, focused prototypes implement one, or a few, of the attributes of a product. Examples of focused prototypes include foam models to explore the form of a product and hand-built circuit boards to investigate the electronic performance of a product design. A common practice is to use two or more focused prototypes together to investigate the overall performance of a product. One of these prototypes is often a "looks-like" prototype, and the other is a "works-like" prototype. By building two separate focused prototypes, the team may be able to answer its questions much earlier than if it had to create one integrated, comprehensive prototype.

Exhibit 14-5 displays a plot with axes corresponding to these two dimensions. Several different prototypes from the PackBot example are shown on this plot. Note that focused

294 *Chapter* 14

EXHIBIT 14-3
Examples
of physical
prototypes in
the PackBot
project.
(a) Looks-
like model
for customer
communication
and approval,
(b) wheel
prototype under
load during
creep testing,
(c) sand test of
the complete
system.

Courtesy of iRobot
Corp.

(a)

(b)

(c)

EXHIBIT 14-4
Examples
of analytical
prototypes of
the PackBot.
(a) 3D CAD
rendering
created for
a customer
proposal,
(b) finite-
element analysis
of wheel spoke
geometry,
(c) dynamic
simulation
model.

Courtesy of iRobot
Corp.

(a)

(b)

(c)

296   *Chapter* 14

EXHIBIT 14-5   Types of prototypes. Prototypes can be classified according to the degree to which they are physical and the degree to which they implement all of the attributes of the product.

prototypes can be either physical or analytical, but that for tangible manufactured products, fully comprehensive prototypes must generally be physical. Prototypes sometimes contain a combination of analytical and physical elements. For example, control hardware including the user interface for the PackBot could be linked to a software simulation of the PackBot dynamic motion. Some analytical prototypes can be viewed as being more "physical" than others. For example, a video animation of the PackBot's dynamic balance based on simulation of the physical interactions of its components is, in one sense, more physical than a set of equations approximating the overall balance of the same mechanism.

What Are Prototypes Used For?

Within a product development project, prototypes are used for four purposes: learning, communication, integration, and milestones.

Learning   Prototypes are often used to answer two types of questions: "Will it work?" and "How well does it meet the customer needs?" When used to answer such questions, prototypes serve as learning tools. In developing the wheels for the PackBot, the team built focused-physical prototypes of the novel spiral spoke geometry of the wheels. The wheels were mounted to a weighted platform and dropped at various heights to test the shock absorption properties and the strength of the wheels. Exhibit 14-6 shows several of the wheel prototypes and one of the impact tests. Also in development of the wheel design, mathematical models of the spokes were analyzed to estimate the stiffness and strength of the wheels. This is an example of a focused-analytical prototype used as a learning tool.

Courtesy of iRobot Corp.

EXHIBIT 14-6   PackBot wheel prototypes (top) and impact testing (bottom).

Communication   Prototypes enrich communication with top management, vendors, partners, extended team members, customers, and investors. This is particularly true of physical prototypes: a visual, tactile, three-dimensional representation of a product is much easier to understand than a verbal description or even a sketch of the product. When developing new payload capabilities for the PackBot, communication among engineers, managers, suppliers, and customers is enhanced through the use of "look and feel" prototypes. New customers often fail to appreciate the small size of the "crush zone" into which the PackBot payload must fit; however, a physical model clearly illustrates this space constraint. The rough physical prototype shown in Exhibit 14-3(a) was used to communicate to early customers the physical size of the PackBot and the range of mobility of its camera support arm. This model was constructed from components using stereolithography rapid prototyping technology, assembled, and painted to represent the actual size and appearance of the product.

Integration   Prototypes are used to ensure that components and subsystems of the product work together as expected. Comprehensive physical prototypes are most effective as integration tools in product development projects because they require the assembly and physical interconnection of all the parts and subassemblies that make up a product. In doing so, the prototype forces coordination between different members of the product development team. If the combination of any of the components of the product interferes with the overall function of the product, the problem may be detected through physical integration in a comprehensive prototype. Common names for these comprehensive physical prototypes are *testbed, alpha, beta,* or *preproduction prototypes.* Two such prototypes of the PackBot are shown in Exhibit 14-7. In the alpha prototype, the radios are visible in the center of the robot. In the beta prototype, the radios were integrated into the body for protection from damage. Extensive testing of the alpha prototype helped identify several improvements to the track system, which was redesigned before the beta prototype was built. Further testing of the beta prototype included a wide range of field conditions, such as mud, sand, and water testing.

Prototypes also help integrate the perspectives of the different functions represented on a product development team (Leonard-Barton, 1991). A simple physical model of the form of a product can be used as the medium through which the marketing, design, and manufacturing functions agree on a basic design decision.

Many software development processes use prototypes to integrate the activities of dozens of software developers. Microsoft, for example, employs a "daily build," in which a new version of the product is compiled at the end of every day. Software developers "check in" their code by a fixed time of day (e.g., 5:00 p.m.) and a team compiles the code to create a new prototype version of the software. The most recent version of the software is then tested and used by everyone on the team, in a practice Microsoft calls "eating your own dog food." This practice of creating daily comprehensive prototypes ensures that the efforts of the developers are always synchronized and integrated. Any conflicts are detected immediately and the team can never diverge more than one day from a working version of the product (Cusumano, 1997).

Milestones Particularly in the later stages of product development, prototypes are used to demonstrate that the product has achieved a desired level of functionality. Milestone prototypes provide tangible goals, demonstrate progress, and serve to enforce the schedule. Senior management (and sometimes the customer) often requires a prototype that demonstrates certain functions before allowing the project to proceed. For example, in many government procurements, a prototype must pass a "qualification test" and later

Courtesy of iRobot Corp.

EXHIBIT 14-7 Alpha (left) and beta (right) prototypes of the PackBot.

	Learning	Communication	Integration	Milestones
Focused analytical	●	○	○	○
Focused physical	●	●	○	○
Comprehensive physical	●	●	●	●

EXHIBIT 14-8   Appropriateness of different types of prototypes for different purposes (● = more appropriate, ○ = less appropriate). Note that fully comprehensive analytical prototypes are rarely possible for physical products.

a "first-article test" before a contractor can proceed with production. A major milestone for the PackBot development was a test conducted by the U.S. Army. During this test the PackBot prototype was thrown out of a moving vehicle and controlled by a soldier with minimal training in an unknown environment. There could be no failures of the PackBot system and its user interface in order to pass this test.

While all types of prototypes are used for all four of these purposes, some types of prototypes are more appropriate than others for some purposes. A summary of the relative appropriateness of different types of prototypes for different purposes is shown in Exhibit 14-8.

Principles of Prototyping

Several principles are useful in guiding decisions about prototypes during product development. These principles inform decisions about what type of prototype to build and about how to incorporate prototypes into the development project plan.

Analytical Prototypes Are Generally More Flexible Than Physical Prototypes

Because an analytical prototype is a mathematical approximation of the product, it will generally contain parameters that can be varied in order to represent a range of design alternatives. In most cases, changing a parameter in an analytical prototype is easier than changing an attribute of a physical prototype. For example, consider an analytical prototype of the PackBot drivetrain that includes a set of equations representing the electric motor. One of the parameters in the mathematical model of the motor is the stall torque. Varying this parameter and then solving the equations is much easier than changing an actual motor in a physical prototype. In most cases, the analytical prototype not only is easier to change than a physical prototype but also allows larger changes than could be made in a physical prototype. For this reason, an analytical prototype frequently precedes a physical prototype. The analytical prototype is used to narrow the range of feasible parameters, and then the physical prototype is used to fine-tune or confirm the design. See Chapter 15, Robust Design, for a detailed example of the use of an analytical prototype to explore several design parameters.

Physical Prototypes Are Required to Detect Unanticipated Phenomena

A physical prototype often exhibits unanticipated phenomena completely unrelated to the original objective of the prototype. One reason for these surprises is that all of the laws of physics are operating when the team experiments with physical prototypes. Physical prototypes intended to investigate purely geometric issues will also have thermal and optical properties. Some of the incidental properties of physical prototypes are irrelevant to the final product and act as annoyances during testing; however, some of these incidental properties of physical prototypes will also manifest themselves in the final product. In these cases, a physical prototype can serve as a tool for detecting unanticipated detrimental phenomena that may arise in the final product. For example, in a pull test of various PackBot gripper finger coatings, the team discovered that some of the coatings with good grip characteristics had poor durability. Analytical prototypes, in contrast, can never reveal phenomena that are not part of the underlying analytical model on which the prototype is based. For this reason at least one physical prototype is almost always built in a product development effort.

A Prototype May Reduce the Risk of Costly Iterations

Exhibit 14-9 illustrates the role of risk and iteration in product development. In many situations, the outcome of a test may dictate whether a development task will have to be

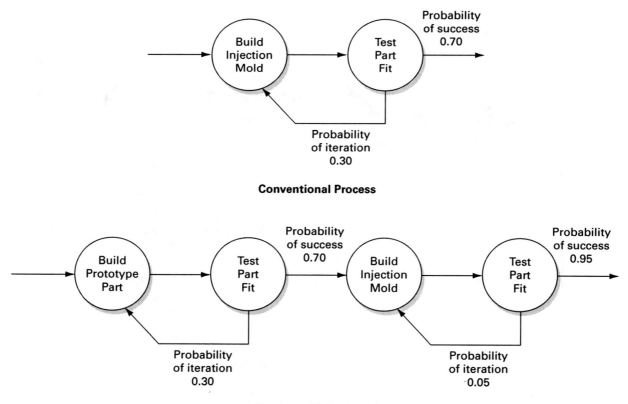

EXHIBIT 14-9   A prototype may reduce the risk of costly iteration. Taking time to build and test a prototype may allow the development team to detect a problem that would otherwise not have been detected until after a costly development activity, such as building an injection mold.

repeated. For example, if a molded part fits poorly with its mating parts, the mold tooling may have to be rebuilt. In Exhibit 14-9, a 30 percent risk of returning to the mold-building activity after testing part fit is represented with an arrow labeled with a probability of 0.30. If building and testing a prototype substantially increases the likelihood that the subsequent activities will proceed without iteration (e.g., from 70 percent to 95 percent, as indicated in Exhibit 14-9), the prototype phase may be justified.

The anticipated benefits of a prototype in reducing risk must be weighed against the time and money required to build and evaluate the prototype. This is particularly important for comprehensive prototypes. Products that are high in risk or uncertainty, because of the high costs of failure, new technology, or the revolutionary nature of the product, will benefit from such prototypes. On the other hand, products for which failure costs are low and the technology is well known do not derive as much risk-reduction benefit from prototyping. Most products fall between these extremes. Exhibit 14-10 represents the range of situations that can be encountered in different types of development projects.

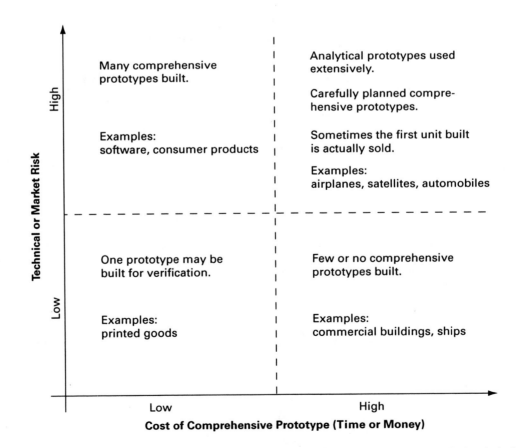

EXHIBIT 14-10   The use of comprehensive prototypes depends on the relative level of technical or market risk and the cost of building a comprehensive prototype.

302 *Chapter* 14

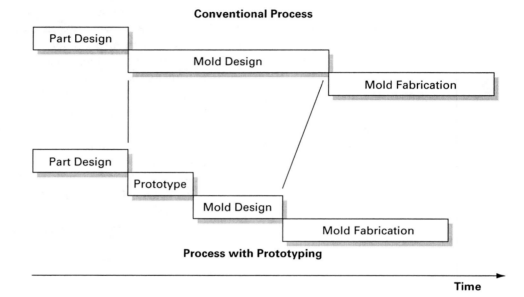

EXHIBIT 14-11 Role of a prototype in expediting another step. Taking time to build a prototype may enable more rapid completion of a subsequent step.

A Prototype May Expedite Other Development Steps

Sometimes the addition of a short prototyping phase may allow a subsequent activity to be completed more quickly than if the prototype were not built. If the required additional time for the prototype phase is less than the savings in duration of the subsequent activity, then this strategy is appropriate. One of the most common occurrences of this situation is in mold design, as illustrated in Exhibit 14-11. The existence of a physical model of a geometrically complex part allows the mold designer to more quickly visualize and design the mold tooling.

EXHIBIT 14-12 Use of a prototype to remove a task from the critical path.

A Prototype May Restructure Task Dependencies

The top part of Exhibit 14-12 illustrates a set of tasks that are completed sequentially. It may be possible to complete some of the tasks concurrently by building a prototype. For example, a software test may depend on the existence of a physical circuit. Rather than waiting for the production version of the printed circuit board to use in the test, the team may be able to rapidly fabricate a prototype (e.g., a hand-built board) and use it for the test while the production of the printed circuit board proceeds.

Prototyping Technologies

Hundreds of different production technologies are used to create prototypes, particularly physical prototypes. Two technologies have emerged as particularly important in the past 20 years: three-dimensional computer modeling (3D CAD) and free-form fabrication (3D printing).

3D CAD Modeling and Analysis

Since the 1990s, the dominant mode of representing designs has shifted dramatically from drawings, often created using a computer, to *3D computer-aided design models,* known as 3D CAD models. 3D CAD models represent designs as collections of 3D solid entities, each usually constructed from geometric primitives, such as cylinders, blocks, and holes.

The advantages of 3D CAD modeling include the ability to easily visualize the three-dimensional form of the design; the ability to create photo-realistic images for assessment of product appearance; the ability to automatically compute physical properties such as mass and volume; and the efficiency arising from the creation of one and only one canonical description of the design, from which other, more focused descriptions, such as cross-sectional views and fabrication drawings, can be created. Through the use of *computer-aided engineering* (CAE) tools, 3D CAD models have begun to serve as analytical prototypes. In some settings this can eliminate one or more physical prototypes. When 3D CAD models are used to carefully plan the final, integrated assembly of the product and to detect geometric interference among parts, this may indeed eliminate the need for a full-scale prototype. For example, in the development of the Boeing 777 and 787 jets, the development teams were able to avoid building full-scale wooden prototype models of the planes, which had historically been used to detect geometric interferences among structural elements and the components of various other systems, such as hydraulic lines. Using a 3D CAD model of an entire product in this manner is known, depending on the industry setting, as a *digital mock-up*, *digital prototype*, or *virtual prototype*.

3D CAD models are also the underlying representation for many types of computer-based analyses. Forms of CAE include finite-element analysis of thermal flow or stress distribution, virtual crash testing of automobiles, kinematic and dynamic motion of complex mechanisms, all of which have become more sophisticated every year. In the PackBot development, engineers conducted finite-element analysis of structural integrity to understand impact stresses at various drop and crash angles. Exhibit 14-13 shows one such analytical result, based on a 3D CAD model of the PackBot. Engineers also computed heat flows and thermal dissipation performance using finite-element analysis based on 3D CAD models.

304 *Chapter* 14

EXHIBIT 14-13   Finite-element analysis of the PackBot side plate based on a 3D CAD model. The image shows the stress distribution upon side impact at the rear wheel.

3D Printing

In 1984, the first commercial free-form fabrication system was introduced by 3D Systems. This technology, called *stereolithography,* and dozens of competing technologies that followed it, create physical objects directly from 3D CAD models, and can be thought of as "3D printing." This collection of technologies is often called *rapid prototyping.* Most of the technologies work by constructing an object, one cross-sectional layer at a time, by depositing a material or by using a laser to selectively solidify a liquid or powder. The resulting parts are most often made from plastics, but other materials are available, including wax, paper, ceramics, and metals. In some cases the parts are used directly for visualization or in working prototypes; however, the parts are often used as patterns to make molds or patterns from which parts with particular material properties can then be molded or cast.

Three-dimensional printing technologies enable realistic 3D prototypes to be created earlier and less expensively than was possible before. When used appropriately, these prototypes can reduce product development time and/or improve the resulting product quality. In addition to enabling the rapid construction of working prototypes, these technologies can be used to embody product concepts quickly and inexpensively, increasing the ease with which concepts can be communicated to other team members, senior managers, development partners, or potential customers. For example, the PackBot prototype shown in Exhibit 14-3(a) was made of components fabricated using stereolithography in only four days.

Planning for Prototypes

A potential pitfall in product development is what Clausing called the "hardware swamp" (Clausing, 1994).[1] The swamp is caused by misguided prototyping efforts; that is, the building and debugging of prototypes (physical or analytical) that do not substantially contribute to the goals of the overall product development project. One way to avoid the swamp is to carefully define each prototype before embarking on an effort to build and test it. This section presents a four-step method for planning each prototype during a product development project. The method applies to all types of prototypes: focused, comprehensive, physical, and analytical. A template for recording the information generated from the method is given in Exhibit 14-14. We use the PackBot wheel prototype and impact test shown in Exhibit 14-6 as an example to illustrate the method.

Step 1: Define the Purpose of the Prototype

Recall the four purposes of prototypes: learning, communication, integration, and milestones. In defining the purpose of a prototype, the team lists its specific learning and communication needs. Team members also list any integration needs and whether or not the prototype is intended to be one of the major milestones of the overall product development project.

For the wheel prototypes, the purpose was to determine the shock absorption characteristics and robustness of the wheels using various geometry and materials. While these learning prototypes were primarily focused on performance, the team was also considering the manufacturing cost of the materials, some of which were not moldable and must be machined.

Name of Prototype	PackBot Wheel Geometry/Impact Test
Purpose(s)	• Select final wheel spoke geometry and materials based on strength and shock absorption characteristics. • Confirm that wheels absorb shock to withstand impact and protect the PackBot and its payload.
Level of Approximation	• Correct wheel spoke geometry, materials, and platform load.
Experimental Plan	• Build 12 test wheels using six different materials, each with two spoke shapes. • Mount the wheels to the test fixture. • Conduct impact tests at a range of drop heights.
Schedule	1 August select wheel designs and materials 7 August complete design of test fixture 14 August wheels and test fixture constructed 15 August assembly completed 23 August testing completed 25 August analysis of test results completed

Courtesy of iRobot Corp.

EXHIBIT 14-14   Planning template for the PackBot wheel geometry/impact test prototypes.

[1]Clausing, Don, *Total Quality Development*, ASME Press, New York, 1994.

Step 2: Establish the Level of Approximation of the Prototype

Planning a prototype requires definition of the degree to which the final product is to be approximated. The team should consider whether a physical prototype is necessary or whether an analytical prototype would best meet its needs. In most cases, the best prototype is the simplest prototype that will serve the purposes established in step 1. In some cases, an earlier model serves as a testbed and may be modified for the purposes of the prototype. In other cases, an existing prototype or a prototype being built for another purpose can be utilized.

For the wheel prototype, the team decided that materials and geometry of the wheel were critical attributes related to impact performance, so the prototype needed to be constructed carefully with these attributes in mind; however, other aspects of the wheel could be ignored, including the production method (molding versus machining), the attachment to the drive system and the track belt, and the color and overall appearance of the wheel. A member of the team had previously explored an analytical model of the wheel spoke bending performance and felt that the physical prototype was necessary to verify her analysis. She had discovered that there was a basic trade-off between shock absorption, which required more flexible spokes, and strength of the wheel, which required larger spokes. The team used the analytical prototype to determine the wheel spoke dimensions that would be investigated with the physical prototype.

Step 3: Outline an Experimental Plan

In most cases, the use of a prototype in product development can be thought of as an experiment. Good experimental practice helps ensure the extraction of maximum value from the prototyping effort. The experimental plan includes the identification of the variables of the experiment (if any), the test protocol, an indication of what measurements will be performed, and a plan for analyzing the resulting data. When many variables must be explored, efficient experiment design greatly facilitates this process. Chapter 15, Robust Design, discusses design of experiments in detail.

For the wheel prototype tests, the team decided to vary only the materials and web geometry of the spokes. Based on the analytical models, two spoke shapes were selected for testing. Six different materials were also chosen, for a total of 12 test designs. The team designed a weighted platform to which each wheel could be mounted and a test apparatus for dropping the platform at various heights. They decided to instrument the platform to measure the acceleration forces transmitted through the wheels to the PackBot upon impact. After each test, they inspected the wheel for damage in the form of cracks or plastic deformation before increasing the test height. These test results would not only be used to choose the best spoke geometry and material, but also to improve the analytical model for future use, which may eliminate further physical prototyping of modified wheel designs.

Step 4: Create a Schedule for Procurement, Construction, and Testing

Because the building and testing of a prototype can be considered a subproject within the overall development project, the team benefits from a schedule for the prototyping activity. Three dates are particularly important in defining a prototyping effort. First, the team defines when the parts will be ready to assemble. (This is sometimes called the "bucket of parts" date.) Second, the team defines the date when the prototype will first be tested. (This is sometimes called the "smoke test" date, because it is the date the team will first apply power and "look for smoke" in products with electrical systems.) Third, the team defines the date when it expects to have completed testing and produced the final results.

For the wheel prototypes, no assembly was involved, so when parts were available the prototypes could be assembled and tested rather quickly. The team planned for eight days of testing and two days of analysis.

Planning Milestone Prototypes

The previously metioned method for planning a prototype applies to all prototypes, including those as simple as the wheel geometry and those as complex as the beta prototype of the entire PackBot. Nevertheless, the comprehensive prototypes a team uses as development milestones benefit from additional planning. This planning activity typically occurs in conjunction with the overall product development planning activity at the end of the concept development phase. In fact, planning the milestone dates is an integral part of establishing an overall product development project plan. (See Chapter 19, Managing Projects.)

All other things being equal, the team would prefer to build as few milestone prototypes as possible because designing, building, and testing comprehensive prototypes consumes a great deal of time and money. However, in reality, few highly engineered products are developed with fewer than two milestone prototypes, and many efforts require four or more.

As a base case, the team should consider using alpha, beta, and preproduction prototypes as milestones. The team should then consider whether any of these milestones can be eliminated or whether in fact additional prototypes are necessary.

Alpha prototypes are typically used to assess whether the product works as intended. The parts in alpha prototypes are usually similar in material and geometry to the parts that will be used in the production version of the product, but they are usually made with prototype production processes. For example, plastic parts in an alpha prototype may be machined or rubber molded instead of injection molded as they would be in production.

Beta prototypes are typically used to assess reliability and to identify remaining bugs in the product. These prototypes are often given to customers for testing in the intended use environment. The parts in beta prototypes are usually made with actual production processes or supplied by the intended component suppliers, but the product is usually not assembled with the intended final assembly facility or tooling. For example, the plastic parts in a beta prototype might be molded with the production injection molds but would probably be assembled by a technician in a prototype shop rather than by production workers or automated equipment.

Preproduction prototypes are the first products produced by the entire production process. At this point the production process is not yet operating at full capacity but is making limited quantities of the product. These prototypes are used to verify production process capability, are subjected to further testing, and are often supplied to preferred customers. Preproduction prototypes are sometimes called *pilot-production prototypes*.

The most common deviations from the standard prototyping plan are to eliminate one of the standard prototypes or to add additional early prototypes. Eliminating a prototype (usually the alpha) may be possible if the product is very similar to other products the firm has already developed and produced, or if the product is extremely simple. Additional early prototypes are common in situations where the product embodies a new concept or technology. These early prototypes are sometimes called *experimental* or *engineering prototypes*. They usually do not look like the final product, and many of the parts of the prototype are not designed with the intention of eventually being produced in quantity.

Once preliminary decisions have been made about the number of prototypes, their characteristics, and the time required to assemble and test them, the team can place these milestones on the overall time line of the project. When the team attempts to schedule these milestones, the feasibility of the overall product development schedule can be assessed. Frequently a team will discover, when working backward from the target date for the product launch, that the assembly and test of one milestone prototype overlaps or is perilously close to the design and fabrication of the next milestone prototype. If this overlapping happens in practice, it is the worst manifestation of the "hardware swamp." When prototyping phases overlap, there is little transfer of learning from one prototype to the next, and the team should consider omitting one or more of the prototypes to allow the remaining prototypes to be spread out more in time. During project planning, overlapping prototyping phases can be avoided by beginning the project sooner, delaying product launch, eliminating a milestone prototype, or devising a way to accelerate the development activities preceding each prototype. (See Chapter 19, Managing Projects, for some techniques for achieving this acceleration.)

Summary

Product development almost always requires the building and testing of prototypes. A prototype is an approximation of the product on one or more dimensions of interest.

- Prototypes can be usefully classified along two dimensions: (1) the degree to which they are physical as opposed to analytical and (2) the degree to which they are comprehensive as opposed to focused.
- Prototypes are used for learning, communication, integration, and milestones. While all types of prototypes can be used for all of these purposes, physical prototypes are usually best for communication, and comprehensive prototypes are best for integration and milestones.
- Several principles are useful in guiding decisions about prototypes during product development:
  - Analytical prototypes are generally more flexible than physical prototypes.
  - Physical prototypes are required to detect unanticipated phenomena.
  - A prototype may reduce the risk of costly iterations.
  - A prototype may expedite other development steps.
  - A prototype may restructure task dependencies.
- 3D CAD modeling and 3D printing technologies have reduced the relative cost and time required to create and analyze prototypes.

- A four-step method for planning a prototype is:
  1. Define the purpose of the prototype.
  2. Establish the level of approximation of the prototype.
  3. Outline an experimental plan.
  4. Create a schedule for procurement, construction, and testing.
- Milestone prototypes are defined in the product development project plan. The number of such prototypes and their timing is one of the key elements of the overall development plan.

References and Bibliography

Many current resources are available on the Internet via
www.ulrich-eppinger.net

Clausing describes some of the pitfalls in prototyping, including the "hardware swamp."
Clausing, Don, *Total Quality Development,* ASME Press, New York, 1994.

Leonard-Barton describes how prototypes are used for the integration of different product development functions.
Leonard-Barton, Dorothy, "Inanimate Integrators: A Block of Wood Speaks," *Design Management Journal,* Vol. 2, No. 3, Summer 1991, pp. 61–67.

Cusumano describes Microsoft's use of the "daily build" in its software development process. The daily build is an extreme example of using comprehensive prototypes to force integration.
Cusumano, Michael A., "How Microsoft Makes Large Teams Work Like Small Teams," *Sloan Management Review,* Fall 1997, pp. 9–20.

Lipson and Kurman summarize the methods used for 3D printing and speculate on the impact this technology may have on society.
Lipson, Hod, and Melba Kurman, *Fabricated: The New World of 3D Printing*, John Wiley & Sons, Indianapolis, IN, 2013.

Schrage presents a view of product development centered around the role of prototyping and simulation in the innovation process.
Schrage, Michael, *Serious Play: How the World's Best Companies Simulate to Innovate,* Harvard Business School Press, Boston, 2000.

Thomke explains the relationship between effective prototyping methods and successful innovation. He argues that new technologies are changing the economics of experimentation, leading to greater product development process performance.
Thomke, Stefan H., *Experimentation Matters: Unlocking the Potential of New Technologies for Innovation,* Harvard Business School Press, Boston, 2003.

Kelley and Littman's presentation of IDEO's highly successful product development process includes a description of how IDEO uses prototypes to solve problems (learning), to engage customers (communication), and to move projects forward through an iterative process (milestones).
Kelley, Tom, with Jonathan Littman, *The Art of Innovation: Lessons in Innovation from IDEO, America's Leading Design Firm,* Doubleday, New York, 2001.

Two books written for general audiences contain very interesting accounts of prototyping. Sabbagh's book on the development of the Boeing 777 contains riveting accounts of brake system tests and wing strength tests, among others. Walton's book on the development of the 1996 Ford Taurus contains fascinating descriptions of prototyping and testing in the automobile industry. Particularly engaging is the description of testing heaters in northern Minnesota in midwinter, using development engineers as subjects.

Sabbagh, Karl, *Twenty-First-Century Jet: The Making and Marketing of the Boeing 777,* Scribner, New York, 1996.

Walton, Mary, *Car: A Drama of the American Workplace,* Norton, New York, 1997.

Wall, Ulrich, and Flowers provide a formal definition of the quality of a prototype in terms of its fidelity to the production version of a product. They use this definition to evaluate the prototyping technologies available for plastic parts.

Wall, Matthew B., Karl T. Ulrich, and Woodie C. Flowers, "Evaluating Prototyping Technologies for Product Design," *Research in Engineering Design,* Vol. 3, 1992, pp. 163–177.

Wheelwright and Clark describe the use of prototypes as a managerial tool for major product development programs. Their discussion of periodic prototyping cycles is particularly interesting.

Wheelwright, Stephen C., and Kim B. Clark, *Revolutionizing Product Development: Quantum Leaps in Speed, Efficiency, and Quality,* The Free Press, New York, 1992.

Exercises

1. A furniture manufacturer is considering a line of seating products to be fabricated by cutting and bending a recycled plastic material available in large sheets. Create a prototype of at least one possible chair design by cutting and bending a sheet of paper or cardboard. (You may wish to design the chair with a sketch first, or just start working with the sheet directly.) What can you learn about the chair design from your prototype? What can't you learn about the chair design from such a prototype?

2. Position the chair prototype described in Exercise 1 on the plot in Exhibit 14-5. For which of the four major purposes would a product development team use such a prototype?

3. Devise a prototyping plan (similar to that in Exhibit 14-14) for investigating the comfort of different types of handles for kitchen knives.

4. Position the prototypes shown in Exhibits 14-3, 14-4, 14-6, 14-7, and 14-13 on the plot in Exhibit 14-5. Briefly explain your reasoning for each placement.

Thought Questions

1. Many product development teams separate the "looks-like" prototype from the "works-like" prototype. They do this because integrating both function and form is difficult in the early phases of development. What are the strengths and weaknesses of this approach? For what types of products might this approach be dangerous?

2. Today there are several 3D printing technologies able to create physical parts directly from 3D CAD files (e.g., stereolithography and selective laser sintering). How might a team use such rapid prototyping technologies during the concept development phase of the product development process? Might these technologies facilitate identifying customer needs, establishing specifications, generating product concepts, selecting product concepts, and/or testing product concepts?

3. Some companies have reportedly abandoned the practice of doing a customer test with the early prototypes of their products, preferring instead to go directly and quickly to market in order to observe the actual customer response. For what types of products and markets might this practice make sense?

4. Is a drawing a physical or an analytical prototype?

5. Microsoft uses frequent comprehensive prototypes in its development of software. In fact, in some projects there is a "daily build," in which a new version of the product is integrated and compiled *every day*. Is this approach only viable for software products, or could it be used for physical products as well? What might be the costs and benefits of such an approach for physical products?

CHAPTER FIFTEEN

Robust Design

Courtesy of Ford Motor Co.

EXHIBIT 15-1
Rear seat belt experiment. This experiment was run on a simulation model to explore many design parameters and noise conditions.

Ford Motor Company safety engineers were working with a supplier to better understand the performance of rear seat belts. In any conventional seat belt system with lap and shoulder belts, if the lap portion of the belt rides upward, the passenger may slide beneath it, potentially resulting in abdominal injury. This phenomenon, called "submarining," is related to a large number of factors, including the nature of the collision, the design of the vehicle, the properties of the seats and seat belts, and other conditions. Based on experimentation, simulation, and analysis, Ford engineers hoped to determine which of the many factors were most critical to passenger safety and to avoiding submarining. The image shown in Exhibit 15-1 depicts the model used in Ford's simulation analysis.

This chapter presents a method for designing and conducting experiments to improve the performance of products even in the presence of uncontrollable variations. This method is known as robust design.

What Is Robust Design?

We define a *robust* product (or process) as one that performs as intended even under nonideal conditions such as manufacturing process variations or a range of operating situations. We use the term *noise* to describe uncontrolled variations that may affect performance, and we say that a quality product should be robust to noise factors.

Robust design is the product development activity of improving the desired performance of the product while minimizing the effects of noise. In robust design we use experiments and data analysis to identify robust setpoints for the design parameters we can control. A *robust setpoint* is a combination of design parameter values for which the product performance is as desired under a range of operating conditions and manufacturing variations.

Conceptually, robust design is simple to understand. For a given performance target (safely restraining rear-seat passengers, for example), there may be many combinations of parameter values that will yield the desired result; however, some of these combinations are more sensitive to uncontrollable variation than others. Because the product will likely operate in the presence of various noise factors, we would like to choose the combination of parameter values that is least sensitive to uncontrollable variation. The robust design process uses an experimental approach to finding these robust setpoints.

To understand the concept of robust setpoints, consider two hypothetical factors affecting some measure of seat belt performance, as shown in Exhibit 15-2. Assume that factor A has a linear effect, f_A, on performance and factor B has a nonlinear effect, f_B. Further consider that we can choose setpoints for each factor: A1 or A2 for factor A, and B1 or B2 for factor B. Assuming that the effects of f_A and f_B are additive, a combination of A1 and B2 will provide approximately the same level of overall performance as a combination of A2 and B1. Manufacturing variations will be present at any chosen setpoint, so that the actual value may not be exactly as specified. By choosing the value of B1 for factor B, where the sensitivity of the response to factor B is relatively small, unintended variation in factor B has a relatively small influence on overall product performance; therefore, the choice of B1 and A2 is a more robust combination of setpoints than the combination of B2 and A1.

The robust design process can be used at several stages of the product development process. As with most product development issues, the earlier that robustness can be considered in the product development process, the better the robustness results can be. Robust design experiments can be used within the concept development phase as a way

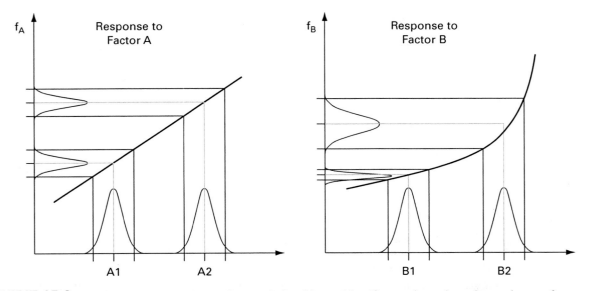

EXHIBIT 15-2   Robust design exploits nonlinear relationships to identify setpoints where the product performance is less sensitive to variations. In this example, the chosen value for the factor A setpoint does not affect robustness, whereas that of factor B does. Choosing B1 minimizes the effect of variation in factor B on overall performance.

to refine the specifications and set realistic performance targets. While it is beneficial to consider product robustness as early as the concept stage, experiments for robust design are used most frequently during the detail-design phase as a way to ensure the desired product performance under a variety of conditions. In detail design, the robust design activity is also known as *parameter design,* as this is a matter of choosing the right setpoints for the design parameters under our control. These include the product's materials, dimensions, tolerances, manufacturing processes, and operating instructions.

For many engineering design problems, equations based on fundamental physical principles can be solved for robust parameter choices; however, engineers generally cannot fully model the kinds of uncertainties, variations, and noise factors that arise under real conditions. Furthermore, the ability to develop accurate mathematical models is limited for many engineering problems. For example, consider the difficulty of accurately modeling the seat belt submarining problem under a wide variety of conditions. In such situations, empirical investigation through designed experiments is necessary. Such experiments can be used to directly support decision making and can also be used to improve the accuracy of mathematical models.

In the case of the seat belt design problem, Ford's engineers wished to test a range of seat belt design parameters and collision conditions; however, crash testing is very expensive, so Ford worked with its seat belt supplier to develop a simulation model, which was calibrated using experimental crash data. Considering the hundreds of possible design parameter combinations, collision conditions, and other factors of interest, the engineers chose to explore the simulation model using a carefully planned experiment. Although simulation requires a great deal of computational effort, the simulation model still allowed Ford engineers to run dozens of experiments under a wide variety of conditions, which would not have been possible using physical crash testing.

For the Ford seat belt design team, the goals of this designed experiment were to learn:

- What combination of seat, seat belt, and attachment parameters minimizes rear-seat passenger submarining during a crash.
- How submarining is affected by uncontrollable conditions. What combination of design parameters is most robust to such noise factors?

Design of Experiments

The approach to robust design presented in this chapter is based on a method called *design of experiments* (DOE). In this method, the team identifies the parameters that can be controlled and the noise factors it wishes to investigate. The team then designs, conducts, and analyzes experiments to help determine the parameter setpoints to achieve robust performance.

In Japan during the 1950s and 1960s, Dr. Genichi Taguchi developed techniques to apply DOE to improve the quality of products and manufacturing processes. Beginning with the quality movement of the 1980s, Taguchi's approach to experimental design started to have an impact on engineering practice in the United States, particularly at Ford Motor Company, Xerox Corporation, AT&T Bell Laboratories, and through the American Supplier Institute (which was created by Ford).

Taguchi receives credit for promoting several key ideas of experimental design for the development of robust products and processes. These contributions include introducing noise factors into experiments to observe these effects and the use of a *signal-to-noise ratio* metric including both the desired performance (signal) and the undesired effects (noise). While statisticians had been showing engineers how to run experiments for decades, it was not until Taguchi's methods were widely explained to the U.S. manufacturing industry during the 1990s that experiments became commonly utilized to achieve robust design.

DOE is not a substitute for technical knowledge of the system under investigation. In fact, the team should use its understanding of the product and how it operates to choose the right parameters to investigate by experiment. The experimental results can be used in conjunction with technical knowledge of the system in order to make the best choices of parameter setpoints. Furthermore, the experimental results can be used to build better mathematical models of the product's function. In this way, experimentation complements technical knowledge. For example, Ford engineers have basic mathematical models of seat belt performance as a function of passenger sizes and collision types. These models allow Ford to size the mechanical elements and to determine the belt attachment geometry. Based on empirical and simulation data, Ford's analytical models and seat belt design guidelines gain precision over time, reducing the need for time-consuming empirical and simulation studies. Eventually, this technical knowledge may improve to the point where only confirming tests of new seat belt configurations are required.

Basic experimental design and analysis for product development can be successfully planned and executed by the development team; however, the field of DOE has many advanced methods to address a number of complicating factors and yield more useful experimental results. Development teams thus can benefit from consulting with a statistician or DOE expert who can assist in designing the experiment and choosing the best analytical approach.

The Robust Design Process

To develop a robust product through DOE, we suggest this seven-step process:

1. Identify control factors, noise factors, and performance metrics.
2. Formulate an objective function.
3. Develop the experimental plan.
4. Run the experiment.
5. Conduct the analysis.
6. Select and confirm factor setpoints.
7. Reflect and repeat.

Step 1: Identify Control Factors, Noise Factors, and Performance Metrics

The robust design procedure begins with identification of three lists: control factors, noise factors, and performance metrics for the experiment:

- *Control factors:* These are the design variables to be varied in a controlled manner during the experiment, in order to explore the product's performance under the many combinations of parameter setpoints. Experiments are generally run at two or three discrete levels (setpoint values) of each factor. These parameters are called control factors because they are among the variables that can be specified for production and/or operation of the product. For example, the webbing stiffness and coefficient of friction are control factors of interest for the experiment.

- *Noise factors:* Noise factors are variables that cannot be explicitly controlled during the manufacturing and operation of the product. Noise factors may include manufacturing variances, changes in materials properties, multiple user scenarios or operating conditions, and even deterioration or misuse of the product. If through special techniques the team can control the noise factors during the experiment (but not in production or operation), then variance can deliberately be induced during the experiment to assess its impact. Otherwise, the team simply lets the noise take place during the experiment, analyzes the results in the presence of typical variation, and seeks to minimize the effects of this variation. For seat belts to be used with a range of seats, the shape of the seat and the seat fabric must be considered noise factors. The goal is to design a seat belt system that works well regardless of the values of these factors.

- *Performance metrics:* These are the product specifications of interest in the experiment. Usually the experiment is analyzed with one or two key product specifications as the performance metrics in order to find control factor setpoints to optimize this performance. These metrics may be derived directly from key specifications where robustness is of critical concern. (See Chapter 6, Product Specifications.) For example, how far the passenger's back or buttocks move forward during the collision would be possible performance metrics for the seat belt experiment.

For the seat belt design problem, the team held a meeting to list the control factors, noise factors, and performance metrics. As Taguchi teaches, they placed these lists into a single graphic, called a *parameter diagram* (or *p-diagram*), as shown in Exhibit 15-3.

EXHIBIT 15-3

Parameter diagram used to design the seat belt experiment. Bold text indicates the performance metric used and the control factors and noise factors chosen for exploration.

After listing the various factors, the team must decide which ones will be explored by experiment. When a large number of parameters are suspected of potentially affecting performance, the selection of critical variables can be substantially narrowed by using analytical models and/or by running a *screening experiment* with two levels for each of many factors. Then a finer experiment is run with two or more levels of the few parameters believed to affect performance.

Ford engineers considered the lists shown in Exhibit 15-3. They chose to focus the experiment on exploration of seven seat belt parameters, holding constant the geometric locations of the three attachment points. They decided to use "back angle at peak" as the output metric, the angle that the passenger's back makes with respect to vertical at the moment of maximum restraint. Back angle is a smaller-is-better performance metric, measured in radians.

A primary concern in this experiment was the effect of three particular noise factors: seat shape, fabric type, and severity of collision. Through preliminary analysis, the team found the best and worst combinations of these noise conditions with respect to the submarining effect. These three noise factors were thereby combined into two extreme noise conditions for the purposes of the experiment. This approach, known as *compounded noise,* can be helpful when many noise factors must be considered. (See Testing Noise Factors in step 3.)

Step 2: Formulate an Objective Function

The experiment's performance metric(s) must be transformed into an *objective function* that relates to the desired robust performance. Several objective functions are useful in robust design for different types of performance concerns. They can be formulated either as functions to be maximized or minimized, and they include:

- *Maximizing:* This type of function is used for performance dimensions where larger values are better, such as maximum deceleration before belt slippage. Common forms of this objective function η are $\eta = \mu$ or $\eta = \mu^2$, where μ is the mean of the experimental observations under a given test condition.

- *Minimizing:* This type of function is used for performance dimensions where smaller values are better, such as back angle at peak deceleration. Common forms of this objective function are $\eta = \mu$ or $\eta = \sigma^2$, where σ^2 is the variance of the experimental observations under a given test condition. Alternatively, such minimization objectives can be formulated as functions to be maximized, such as $\eta = 1/\mu$ or $\eta = 1/\sigma^2$.

- *Target value:* This type of function is used for performance dimensions where values closest to a desired setpoint or target are best, such as amount of belt slackening before restraint. A common maximizing form of this objective function is $\eta = 1/(\mu - t)^2$, where t is the target value.

- *Signal-to-noise ratio:* This type of function is used particularly to measure robustness. Taguchi formulates this metric as a ratio with the desired response in the numerator and the variance in the response as the denominator. Generally the mean value of the desired response, such as the mean back angle at peak, is not difficult to adjust by changing control factors. In the denominator, we place the variance of this response (the noise response), which is to be minimized, such as the variance in back angle resulting from noise conditions. In practice, reducing variance is more difficult than changing the mean. By computing this ratio, we can highlight robust factor settings for which the noise response is relatively low as compared to the signal response. A common maximizing form of this objective function is $\eta = 10 \log (\mu^2/\sigma^2)$.

The Ford statistician consulting with the team suggested two objective functions: the average back angle at peak and the range of the back angle at peak (the difference between the maximum and minimum back angle at peak at the two noise conditions to be tested). Both of these are objectives to be minimized. Together these two metrics would provide deeper insight into the behavior of the system than either one alone.

Step 3: Develop the Experimental Plan

Statisticians have developed many types of efficient experimental plans. These plans lay out how to vary the *factor levels* (values of the control factors and possibly also some of the noise factors) in a series of experiments in order to explore the system's behavior. Some DOE plans are more efficient for characterizing certain types of systems, while others provide more complete analysis.

Experimental Designs

A critical concern in designing experiments is the cost of setting up and running the experimental trials. In situations where this cost is low, running a large number of trials and using an experimental design with resolution high enough to explore more factors, factor combinations, and interactions may be feasible. On the other hand, when the cost of experimentation is high, efficient DOE plans can be used that simultaneously change several factors at once. Some of the most popular experimental designs are listed later and depicted in Exhibit 15-4. Each one has important uses.

- *Full factorial:* This design involves the systematic exploration of every combination of levels of each factor. This allows the team to identify all of the multifactor interaction

Full-Factorial Matrix

EFG	A1								A2							
	B1				B2				B1				B2			
	C1		C2		C1		C2		C1		C2		C1		C2	
	D1	D2	D1	D2	D1	D2	D1	D2	D1	D2	D1	D2	D1	D2	D1	D2
E1 F1 G1	x	x	x	x	x	x	x	x	x	x	x	x	x	x	x	x
E1 F1 G2	x	x	x	x	x	x	x	x	x	x	x	x	x	x	x	x
E1 F2 G1	x	x	x	x	x	x	x	x	x	x	x	x	x	x	x	x
E1 F2 G2	x	x	x	x	x	x	x	x	x	x	x	x	x	x	x	x
E2 F1 G1	x	x	x	x	x	x	x	x	x	x	x	x	x	x	x	x
E2 F1 G2	x	x	x	x	x	x	x	x	x	x	x	x	x	x	x	x
E2 F2 G1	x	x	x	x	x	x	x	x	x	x	x	x	x	x	x	x
E2 F2 G2	x	x	x	x	x	x	x	x	x	x	x	x	x	x	x	x

1/2 Fractional Factorial Matrix

EFG	A1								A2							
	B1				B2				B1				B2			
	C1		C2		C1		C2		C1		C2		C1		C2	
	D1	D2	D1	D2	D1	D2	D1	D2	D1	D2	D1	D2	D1	D2	D1	D2
E1 F1 G1	x			x		x	x			x	x		x			x
E1 F1 G2		x	x		x			x	x			x		x	x	
E1 F2 G1		x	x		x			x	x			x		x	x	
E1 F2 G2	x			x		x	x			x	x		x			x
E2 F1 G1		x	x		x			x	x			x		x	x	
E2 F1 G2	x			x		x	x			x	x		x			x
E2 F2 G1	x			x		x	x			x	x		x			x
E2 F2 G2		x	x		x			x	x			x		x	x	

1/4 Fractional Factorial Matrix

EFG	A1								A2							
	B1				B2				B1				B2			
	C1		C2		C1		C2		C1		C2		C1		C2	
	D1	D2	D1	D2	D1	D2	D1	D2	D1	D2	D1	D2	D1	D2	D1	D2
E1 F1 G1	x			x		x	x			x	x		x			x
E1 F1 G2																
E1 F2 G1																
E1 F2 G2	x			x		x	x			x	x		x			x
E2 F1 G1																
E2 F1 G2	x			x		x	x			x	x		x			x
E2 F2 G1	x			x		x	x			x	x		x			x
E2 F2 G2																

1/8 Fractional Factorial Matrix

EFG	A1								A2							
	B1				B2				B1				B2			
	C1		C2		C1		C2		C1		C2		C1		C2	
	D1	D2	D1	D2	D1	D2	D1	D2	D1	D2	D1	D2	D1	D2	D1	D2
E1 F1 G1	x								x							
E1 F1 G2						x								x		
E1 F2 G1				x								x				
E1 F2 G2							x								x	
E2 F1 G1								x								x
E2 F1 G2			x								x					
E2 F2 G1					x								x			
E2 F2 G2		x								x						

L8 Orthogonal Array (1/16 Fractional Factorial Matrix)

EFG	A1								A2							
	B1				B2				B1				B2			
	C1		C2		C1		C2		C1		C2		C1		C2	
	D1	D2	D1	D2	D1	D2	D1	D2	D1	D2	D1	D2	D1	D2	D1	D2
E1 F1 G1	x															
E1 F1 G2														x		
E1 F2 G1												x				
E1 F2 G2							x									
E2 F1 G1								x								
E2 F1 G2											x					
E2 F2 G1													x			
E2 F2 G2		x														

One Factor at a Time

EFG	A1								A2							
	B1				B2				B1				B2			
	C1		C2		C1		C2		C1		C2		C1		C2	
	D1	D2	D1	D2	D1	D2	D1	D2	D1	D2	D1	D2	D1	D2	D1	D2
E1 F1 G1	x	x	x		x				x							
E1 F1 G2	x															
E1 F2 G1	x															
E1 F2 G2																
E2 F1 G1	x															
E2 F1 G2																
E2 F2 G1																
E2 F2 G2																

Source: Based on Fractional factorial layouts adapted from Ross, Phillip J., Taguchi Techniques for Quality Engineering, McGraw-Hill, New York, 1996

EXHIBIT 15-4   Several alternative experimental plans for seven factors (A, B, C, D, E, F, and G) at two levels each. The full-factorial experiment contains $2^7 = 128$ trials, while the L8 orthogonal array design contains only 8 trials, denoted by the $\times$ marks in the matrices. The L8 orthogonal array plan is the one used for the seat belt experiment and is shown in conventional row/column format in Exhibit 15-5.

effects, in addition to the primary (main) effect of each factor on performance. This type of experiment is generally practical only for a small number of factors and levels and when experiments are inexpensive (as with fast software-based simulations or very flexible hardware). For an investigation of k factors at n levels each, the number of trials in the full-factorial experiment is n^k. Full factorial experimentation is typically infeasible for an experiment with greater than four to five factors.

- *Fractional factorial:* This design uses only a small fraction of the combinations used earlier. In exchange for this efficiency, the ability to compute the magnitudes of all the interaction effects is sacrificed. Instead, the interactions are confounded with other interactions or with some of the main factor effects. Note that the fractional factorial layout still maintains *balance* within the experimental plan. This means that for the several trials at any given factor level, each of the other factors is tested at every level the same number of times.

- *Orthogonal array:* This design is the smallest fractional factorial plan that still allows the team to identify the main effects of each factor; however, these main effects are confounded with many interaction effects. Nevertheless, orthogonal array layouts are widely utilized in technical investigations because they are extremely efficient. Taguchi popularized the orthogonal array DOE approach, even though statisticians had developed such plans several decades earlier and the roots of these designs can be traced back many centuries. Orthogonal array plans are named according to the number of rows (experiments) in the array: L4, L8, L9, L27, and so on. The appendix to this chapter shows several orthogonal array experimental plans.

- *One factor at a time:* This is an unbalanced experimental plan because each trial is conducted with all but one of the factors at nominal levels (and the first trial having all the factors at the nominal level). This is generally considered to be an ineffective way to explore the factor space, even though the number of trials is small, $1 + k\,(n - 1)$; however, for parameter optimization in systems with significant interactions, an adaptive version of the one-at-a-time experimental plan has been shown to be generally more efficient than orthogonal array plans (Frey et al., 2003).

The Ford team chose to use the L8 orthogonal array experiment design because this plan would be an efficient way to explore seven factors at two levels each. Subsequent rounds of experimentation could later be used to explore additional levels of key parameters as well as interaction effects if necessary. The orthogonal array experimental plan is shown in Exhibit 15-5.

Testing Noise Factors

Several methods are used to explore the effects of noise factors in experiments. If some noise factors can be controlled for the purpose of the experiment, then it may be possible to directly assess the effect of these noise factors. If the noise factors cannot be controlled during the experiment, we allow the noise to vary naturally and simply assess the product's performance in the presence of noise. Some common ways to test noise factors are:

- Assign additional columns in the orthogonal array or fractional factorial layout to the noise factors, essentially treating the noise as another variable. This allows the effects of the noise factors to be determined along with the control factors.

322 *Chapter* 15

EXHIBIT 15-5
Factor assignments and the L8 orthogonal array experiment design used for the seat belt experiment. This DOE plan tests seven factors at two levels each. Each row was replicated twice, under the two compounded noise conditions, yielding 16 test data points for analysis.

Factor	Description
A	**Belt webbing stiffness:** Compliance characteristic of the webbing measured in a tensile load machine
B	**Belt webbing friction:** Coefficient of friction, which is a function of the belt weave and surface coating
C	**Lap belt force limiter:** Allows controlled release of the seat belt at a certain force level
D	**Upper anchorage stiffness:** Compliance characteristic of the structure to which the upper anchorage (D-loop) is mounted
E	**Buckle cable stiffness:** Compliance characteristic of the cables by which the buckle is attached to the vehicle body
F	**Front seatback bolster:** Profile and stiffness of seatback where the knees may contact
G	**Tongue friction:** Coefficient of friction for the bearing area of the tongue, which slides along the webbing

	A	B	C	D	E	F	G	N–	N+
1	1	1	1	1	1	1	1		
2	1	1	1	2	2	2	2		
3	1	2	2	1	1	2	2		
4	1	2	2	2	2	1	1		
5	2	1	2	1	2	1	2		
6	2	1	2	2	1	2	1		
7	2	2	1	1	2	2	1		
8	2	2	1	2	1	1	2		

- Use an *outer array* for the noise factors. This method tests several combinations of the noise factors for each row in the main (inner) array. An example of this approach is shown in the appendix, where the outer array consists of an L4 design, testing combinations of three noise factors by replicating each row four times.

- Run replicates of each row, allowing the noise to vary in a natural, uncontrolled manner throughout the experiment, resulting in measurable variance in performance for each row. With this approach, it is particularly important to randomize the order of the trials so that any trends in the noise are unlikely to be correlated with the systematic changes in the control factors. (See step 4.)

- Run replicates of each row with *compounded noise.* In this method, selected noise factors are combined to create several representative noise conditions or extreme noise conditions. This approach also yields measurable variance for each row, which can be attributed to the effect of noise.

The Ford team chose to utilize the compounded noise approach in the seat belt experiment. The team tested each row using the two combinations of the three noise factors representing the best- and worst-case conditions. This resulted in 16 experimental runs for the L8 DOE plan, as shown in Exhibit 15-5.

	A	B	C	D	E	F	G	N–	N+	Avg	Range
1	1	1	1	1	1	1	1	0.3403	0.2915	0.3159	0.0488
2	1	1	1	2	2	2	2	0.4608	0.3984	0.4296	0.0624
3	1	2	2	1	1	2	2	0.3682	0.3627	0.3655	0.0055
4	1	2	2	2	2	1	1	0.2961	0.2647	0.2804	0.0314
5	2	1	2	1	2	1	2	0.4450	0.4398	0.4424	0.0052
6	2	1	2	2	1	2	1	0.3517	0.3538	0.3528	0.0021
7	2	2	1	1	2	2	1	0.3758	0.3580	0.3669	0.0178
8	2	2	1	2	1	1	2	0.4504	0.4076	0.4290	0.0428

EXHIBIT 15-6   Data obtained from the seat belt experiment.

Step 4: Run the Experiment

To execute the experiment, the product is tested under the various treatment conditions described by each row in the experimental plan. Randomizing the sequence of the experimental runs ensures that any systematic trend over the duration of the experiment is not correlated with the systematic changes to the levels of the factors. For example, if the experiments of the L8 plan are not randomized, and the test conditions drift over time, this effect may be incorrectly attributed to factor A because this column changes halfway through the experiment. For some experiments, changing certain factors may be so difficult that all trials at each level of that factor are run together and only partial randomization may be achieved. In practice, randomize the trials whenever practical, and when not possible, validate the results with a confirmation run. (See step 6.)

In the seat belt experiment, each of the eight factor combinations in the L8 design was tested under the two compounded noise conditions. The 16 data points containing the back angle data are shown in Exhibit 15-6 in the columns titled N– and N+.

Step 5: Conduct the Analysis

There are many ways to analyze the experimental data. For all but the most basic analysis, the team benefits from consulting with a DOE expert or from referring to a good book on statistical analysis and experimental design. The basic analytical method is summarized here.

Computing the Objective Function

The team will have already devised the objective functions for the experiment and will generally have an objective related to the mean performance and the variance in performance. Sometimes the mean and variance will be combined and expressed as a single objective in the form of a signal-to-noise ratio. The values of the objective function can be computed for each row of the experiment. For the seat belt experiment, the columns on the right side of the table in Exhibit 15-6 show the computed objective function values (average back angle and range of back angle) for each row. Recall that these are both objectives to be minimized.

324   *Chapter* 15

Computing Factor Effects by Analysis of Means

The most straightforward analysis to conduct will simply yield the main effect of each factor assigned to a column in the experiment. These main effects are called the *factor effects*. The *analysis of means* involves simply averaging all the computed objective functions for each factor level. In the L8 DOE example, the effect of factor level A1 (factor A at level 1) is the average of trials 1, 2, 3, and 4. Similarly, the effect of factor level E2 is the average of trials 2, 4, 5, and 7. The results of an analysis of means are conventionally shown on factor effects charts.

Exhibit 15-7 presents the factor effects charts for the seat belt example. These effects are plotted for each of the objective functions. Exhibit 15-7(a) plots the *average performance* at each factor level (the first objective function). This chart shows which factor levels can be used to raise or lower the mean performance. Recall that back angle at peak is to be minimized, and note that the chart suggests that factor levels [A1 B2 C2 E1 F1 G1] will

EXHIBIT 15-7
Factor effects charts for the seat belt experiment.

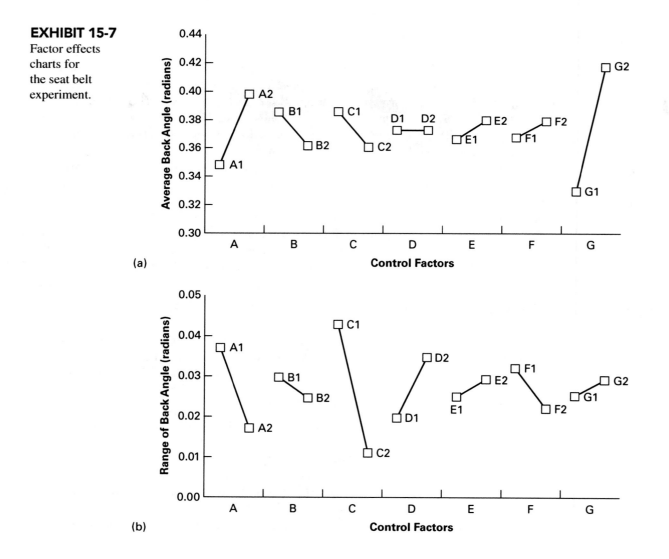

(a)

(b)

minimize the average back angle metric. (Factor D appears to have no effect upon mean performance.) However, these levels will not necessarily achieve robust performance. Exhibit 15-7(b) is based on the *range of performance* at each factor level (the second objective function). This chart suggests that levels [A2 B2 C2 D1 E1 F2 G1] will minimize the range of back angle at peak.

Taguchi recommends that the signal-to-noise ratio for each factor level be plotted in order to identify robust setpoints. Because the signal-to-noise ratio includes the mean performance in the numerator and the variance in the denominator, it represents a combination of these two objectives or a trade-off between them. Rather than specifically plotting the signal-to-noise ratio, many engineers and statisticians prefer to simply interpret the two objectives together, giving more control over the trade-off. To do so, the factor effects charts shown in Exhibit 15-7 can be compared in order to choose a robust setpoint in the next step.

Step 6: Select and Confirm Factor Setpoints

Analysis of means and the factor effects charts help the team determine which factors have a strong effect on mean performance and variance, and therefore how to achieve robust performance. These charts help to identify which factors are best able to reduce the product's variance (robustness factors) and which factors can be used to improve the performance (scaling factors). By choosing setpoints based on these insights, the team should be able to improve the overall robustness of the product.

For example, consider the effects of factor A on both average and range of back angle in the experiment. The charts in Exhibit 15-7 show that level A1 would minimize back angle, but level A2 would minimize the range of back angle, representing a trade-off between performance and robustness. A similar trade-off is evident in factor F; however, for factors B, C, D, E, and G, there is no such trade-off, and levels B2, C2, D1, E1, and G1 minimize both objectives.

Using factors B, C, D, E, and G to achieve the desired robustness and factors A and F to increase performance, Ford engineers selected the setpoint [A1 B2 C2 D1 E1 F1 G1]. As is usually the case, the chosen setpoint is not one of the eight orthogonal array rows tested in the experiment. Given that this setpoint has never been tested, a confirmation run should be used to ensure that the expected robust performance has been achieved.

Step 7: Reflect and Repeat

One round of experiments may be sufficient to identify appropriately robust setpoints. Sometimes, however, further optimization of the product's performance is worthwhile, and this may require several additional rounds of experimentation.

In subsequent experimentation and testing, the team may choose to:

- Reconsider the setpoints chosen for factors displaying a trade-off of performance versus robustness.
- Explore interactions among some of the factors in order to further improve the performance.
- Fine-tune the parameter setpoints using values between the levels tested or outside this range.

- Investigate other noise and/or control factors that were not included in the initial experiment.

As with all product development activities, the team should take some time to reflect on the DOE process and the robust design result. Did we run the right experiments? Did we achieve an acceptable result? Could it be better? Should we repeat the process and seek further performance/robustness improvement?

Caveats

Design of experiments is a well-established field of expertise. This chapter summarizes only one very basic approach in order to encourage the use of experimentation in product design to achieve more robust product performance. Most product development teams should include team members with DOE training or have access to engineers and/or statisticians with specialized expertise in design and analysis of experiments.

Obviously many assumptions underlie the type of analysis used in DOE. One basic assumption made in interpreting analysis of means is that the factor effects are independent, without interactions across the factors. In fact, most actual systems exhibit many interactions, but these interactions are often smaller than the main effects. Verification of this assumption is another motive for running confirming experiments at the chosen setpoints.

If necessary, experiments can be designed to specifically test interaction effects. This type of experiment is outside the scope of this chapter. DOE texts generally provide a number of ways to explore interactions across the factors, including the following:

- Assign specific interactions to be explored in certain columns of the orthogonal array (instead of using the column for a control factor).
- Execute a larger fractional factorial design.
- Use an adaptive one-at-a-time experimental plan (Frey et al., 2003).

Many advanced graphical and analytical techniques are available to assist in interpretation of the experimental data. Analysis of variance (ANOVA) provides a way to assess the significance of the factor effects results in light of the experimental error observed in the data. ANOVA takes into account the number of observations made of each degree of freedom in the experiment and the scale of the results to determine whether each effect is statistically significant. This helps determine to what extent detailed design decisions should be based on the experimental results. However, ANOVA makes many more assumptions and can be difficult to set up properly, so it is also beyond the scope of this chapter. Refer to a DOE text (Ross, 1996; Montgomery, 2012) or consult with a DOE expert to assist with ANOVA.

Summary

Robust design is a set of engineering design methods used to create robust products and processes.

- A robust product (or process) is one that performs properly even in the presence of noise effects. Noises are due to many kinds of uncontrolled variation that may affect performance, such as manufacturing variations, operating conditions, and product deterioration.

- We suggest an approach to the development of robust products based on design of experiments (DOE). This seven-step process for robust design is:

    1. Identify control factors, noise factors, and performance metrics.
    2. Formulate an objective function.
    3. Develop the experimental plan.
    4. Run the experiment.
    5. Conduct the analysis.
    6. Select and confirm factor setpoints.
    7. Reflect and repeat.

- Orthogonal array experimental plans provide a very efficient method for exploring the main effects of each factor chosen for the experiment.
- To achieve robust performance, use of objective functions helps in capturing both mean performance due to each control factor and variance of performance due to noise factors.
- Analysis of means and factor effects charts facilitate the choice of robust parameter setpoints.
- Because many nuances are involved in successful DOE, most teams applying these methods will benefit from assistance by a DOE expert.

References and Bibliography

Many current resources are available on the Internet via
www.ulrich-eppinger.net

Phadke provides numerous examples and practical advice on application of DOE. Ross emphasizes insights gained through ANOVA analysis. Taguchi's methods for experimental design and details about orthogonal array experimentation plans are explained in several texts, including Taguchi's classic two-volume text translated into English.

Phadke, Madhav S., *Quality Engineering Using Robust Design,* Prentice Hall, Englewood Cliffs, NJ, 1989.

Ross, Phillip J., *Taguchi Techniques for Quality Engineering,* McGraw-Hill, New York, 1996.

Taguchi, Genichi, *Introduction to Quality Engineering: Designing Quality into Products and Processes,* Asian Productivity Organization (trans. and pub.), Tokyo, 1986.

Taguchi, Genichi, *System of Experimental Design: Engineering Methods to Optimize Quality and Minimize Costs,* two volumes, Louise Watanabe Tung (trans.), White Plains, NY, 1987.

Grove and Davis present a thorough explanation of experimental design techniques in engineering, including planning, running, and analyzing the experiments. A different analysis of Ford's seat belt experiment is included in this text, as well as many more automotive applications of robust design.

Grove, Daniel M., and Timothy P. Davis, *Engineering, Quality and Experimental Design,* Addison-Wesley Longman, Edinburgh Gate, UK, 1992.

Several excellent texts provide detailed explanations of the use of statistical methods, fractional factorial experimental plans, analytical and graphical interpretations, and response surface methods.

Box, George E. P., J. Stuart Hunter, and William G. Hunter, *Statistics for Experimenters: Design, Innovation, and Discovery,* second edition, John Wiley and Sons, New York, 2005.

Box, George E. P., and Norman R. Draper, *Empirical Model Building and Response Surfaces,* John Wiley and Sons, New York, 1987.

Montgomery, Douglas C., *Design and Analysis of Experiments,* eighth edition, John Wiley and Sons, New York, 2012.

Recent research has renewed interest in one-at-a-time DOE plans. An adaptive one-factor-at-a-time approach has been shown to yield better performance optimization than the corresponding orthogonal array design for systems where the interaction effects are more significant than the noise and error effects.

Frey, Daniel D., Fredrik Engelhardt, and Edward M. Greitzer, "A Role for One-Factor-at-a-Time Experimentation in Parameter Design," *Research in Engineering Design,* 2003, Vol. 14, No. 2, pp. 65–74.

DOE can be used in many aspects of product development. Almquist and Wyner explain how carefully planned experiments are effective in evaluating and tuning parameters of sales campaigns.

Almquist, Eric, and Gordon Wyner, "Boost Your Marketing ROI with Experimental Design," *Harvard Business Review,* Vol. 79, No. 9, October 2001, pp. 135–141.

Exercises

1. Design an experiment to determine a robust process for making coffee.
2. Explain why the 1/4-fractional-factorial and orthogonal array plans shown in Exhibit 15-4 are balanced.
3. Formulate an appropriate signal-to-noise ratio for the seat belt experiment. Analyze the experimental data using this metric. Is signal-to-noise ratio a useful objective function in this case? Why or why not?

Thought Questions

1. If you are able to afford a larger experiment (with more runs), how might you best utilize the additional runs?
2. When would you choose not to randomize the order of the experiments? How would you guard against bias?
3. Explain the importance of balance in an experimental plan.

Appendix

Orthogonal Arrays

DOE texts provide several orthogonal array plans for experiments. The simplest arrays are for two-level and three-level factor experiments. Using advanced techniques, DOE plans can also be created for mixed two-, three-, and/or four-level factor experiments and many other special situations. This appendix shows some of the basic orthogonal arrays from Taguchi's text *Introduction to Quality Engineering* (1986). These plans are shown in row/column format, with the factor level assignments in the columns and the experimental runs in the rows. The numbers 1, 2, and 3 in each cell indicate the factor levels. (Alternatively, factor levels can be labeled as − and + for two-level factors or −, 0, and + for three levels.) Recall that the orthogonal arrays are named according to the number of rows in the design. Included here are the two-level arrays L4, L8, and L16 and the three-level arrays L9 and L27. Also shown is a DOE plan using the L8 inner array for seven control factors and the L4 outer array for three noise factors. This plan allows analysis of the effects of the three noise factors.

Two-Level Orthogonal Arrays

L4: 3 Factors at 2 Levels Each

	A	B	C
1	1	1	1
2	1	2	2
3	2	1	2
4	2	2	1

L8: 7 Factors at 2 Levels Each

	A	B	C	D	E	F	G
1	1	1	1	1	1	1	1
2	1	1	1	2	2	2	2
3	1	2	2	1	1	2	2
4	1	2	2	2	2	1	1
5	2	1	2	1	2	1	2
6	2	1	2	2	1	2	1
7	2	2	1	1	2	2	1
8	2	2	1	2	1	1	2

L16: 15 Factors at 2 Levels Each

	A	B	C	D	E	F	G	H	I	J	K	L	M	N	O
1	1	1	1	1	1	1	1	1	1	1	1	1	1	1	1
2	1	1	1	1	1	1	1	2	2	2	2	2	2	2	2
3	1	1	1	2	2	2	2	1	1	1	1	2	2	2	2
4	1	1	1	2	2	2	2	2	2	2	2	1	1	1	1
5	1	2	2	1	1	2	2	1	1	2	2	1	1	2	2
6	1	2	2	1	1	2	2	2	2	1	1	2	2	1	1
7	1	2	2	2	2	1	1	1	1	2	2	2	2	1	1
8	1	2	2	2	2	1	1	2	2	1	1	1	1	2	2
9	2	1	2	1	2	1	2	1	2	1	2	1	2	1	2
10	2	1	2	1	2	1	2	2	1	2	1	2	1	2	1
11	2	1	2	2	1	2	1	1	2	1	2	2	1	2	1
12	2	1	2	2	1	2	1	2	1	2	1	1	2	1	2
13	2	2	1	1	2	2	1	1	2	2	1	1	2	2	1
14	2	2	1	1	2	2	1	2	1	1	2	2	1	1	2
15	2	2	1	2	1	1	2	1	2	2	1	2	1	1	2
16	2	2	1	2	1	1	2	2	1	1	2	1	2	2	1

Three-Level Orthogonal Arrays

L9: 4 Factors at 3 Levels Each

	A	B	C	D
1	1	1	1	1
2	1	2	2	2
3	1	3	3	3
4	2	1	2	3
5	2	2	3	1
6	2	3	1	2
7	3	1	3	2
8	3	2	1	3
9	3	3	2	1

L27: 13 Factors at 3 Levels Each

	A	B	C	D	E	F	G	H	I	J	K	L	M
1	1	1	1	1	1	1	1	1	1	1	1	1	1
2	1	1	1	1	2	2	2	2	2	2	2	2	2
3	1	1	1	1	3	3	3	3	3	3	3	3	3
4	1	2	2	2	1	1	1	2	2	2	3	3	3
5	1	2	2	2	2	2	2	3	3	3	1	1	1
6	1	2	2	2	3	3	3	1	1	1	2	2	2
7	1	3	3	3	1	1	1	3	3	3	2	2	2
8	1	3	3	3	2	2	2	1	1	1	3	3	3
9	1	3	3	3	3	3	3	2	2	2	1	1	1
10	2	1	2	3	1	2	3	1	2	3	1	2	3
11	2	1	2	3	2	3	1	2	3	1	2	3	1
12	2	1	2	3	3	1	2	3	1	2	3	1	2
13	2	2	3	1	1	2	3	2	3	1	3	1	2
14	2	2	3	1	2	3	1	3	1	2	1	2	3
15	2	2	3	1	3	1	2	1	2	3	2	3	1
16	2	3	1	2	1	2	3	3	1	2	2	3	1
17	2	3	1	2	2	3	1	1	2	3	3	1	2
18	2	3	1	2	3	1	2	2	3	1	1	2	3
19	3	1	3	2	1	3	2	1	3	2	1	3	2
20	3	1	3	2	2	1	3	2	1	3	2	1	3
21	3	1	3	2	3	2	1	3	2	1	3	2	1
22	3	2	1	3	1	3	2	2	1	3	3	2	1
23	3	2	1	3	2	1	3	3	2	1	1	3	2
24	3	2	1	3	3	2	1	1	3	2	2	1	3
25	3	3	2	1	1	3	2	3	2	1	2	1	3
26	3	3	2	1	2	1	3	1	3	2	3	2	1
27	3	3	2	1	3	2	1	2	1	3	1	3	2

Combined Inner and Outer Arrays

L8 × L4: 7 Control Factors and 3 Noise Factors at 2 Levels Each

	A	B	C	D	E	F	G	1	1	2	2	Na
								1	2	1	2	Nb
								1	2	2	1	Nc
1	1	1	1	1	1	1	1					
2	1	1	1	2	2	2	2					
3	1	2	2	1	1	2	2					
4	1	2	2	2	2	1	1					
5	2	1	2	1	2	1	2					
6	2	1	2	2	1	2	1					
7	2	2	1	1	2	2	1					
8	2	2	1	2	1	1	2					

CHAPTER SIXTEEN

Patents and Intellectual Property

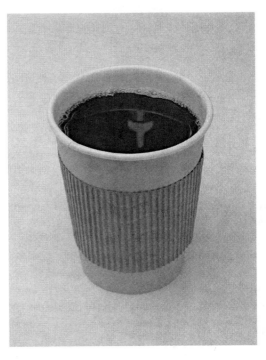

EXHIBIT 16-1
Hot beverage insulating sleeve by David W. Coffin Sr. (U.S. Patent 5,205,473).

David Coffin, an individual inventor, developed a product concept and prototype for an insulating sleeve that would make a hot beverage cup more comfortable to hold (Exhibit 16-1). The product opportunity arose in the 1980s after many food vendors had abandoned polystyrene foam hot beverage cups in favor of paper cups. The inventor was interested in commercialization and/or licensing his invention and sought protection of the intellectual property that he had created. This chapter provides an overview of intellectual property in the context of product development and provides specific guidance for preparing an invention disclosure or provisional patent application.

Within the context of product development, the term *intellectual property* refers to the legally protectable ideas, concepts, names, designs, and processes associated with a new product. Intellectual property can be one of the most valuable assets of firms. Unlike physical property, intellectual property cannot be secured with lock and key to prevent its unwanted transfer; therefore, legal mechanisms have been developed to protect the rights of intellectual property owners. These mechanisms are intended to provide an incentive and reward to those who create new useful inventions, while at the same time encouraging the dissemination of information for the long-run benefit of society.

What Is Intellectual Property?

Four types of intellectual property are relevant to product design and development. Exhibit 16-2 presents a taxonomy of types of intellectual property. Although some areas overlap, and all four types of intellectual property may be present in a single product, a particular invention usually falls into one of these categories.

- *Patent:* A patent is a temporary monopoly granted by a government to an inventor to exclude others from using an invention. In most countries, a patent expires 20 years from the filing date. Most of the balance of this chapter focuses on patents.
- *Trademark:* A trademark is an exclusive right granted by a government to a trademark owner to use a specific name or symbol in association with a class of products or services. In the context of product development, trademarks are typically brands or product names. For example, *JavaJacket* is a trademark for an insulated cup holder, and companies other than Java Jacket, Inc., may not make unauthorized use of the word JavaJacket to refer to their own cup-holder products. In the United States, registration of a trademark is possible, but not strictly necessary to preserve the trademark rights. In most other countries, the rights of a trademark are gained through registration.
- *Trade secret:* A trade secret is information used in a trade or business that offers its owner a competitive advantage and that can be kept secret. A trade secret is not a right conferred by a government but is the result of vigilance on the part of an organization in preventing the dissemination of its proprietary information. Perhaps the most famous trade secret is the formula for the beverage Coca-Cola.
- *Copyright:* A copyright is an exclusive right granted by a government to copy and distribute an original work of expression, whether literature, graphics, music, art, entertainment, or software. Registration of a copyright is possible but not necessary. A copyright comes into being upon the first tangible expression of the work and lasts for up to 95 years.

EXHIBIT 16-2   Taxonomy of types of intellectual property relevant to product design and development.

This chapter focuses on patents. Appendix A to this chapter briefly discusses trademarks. We do not devote substantial attention here to copyrights and trade secrets, but several references to other resources appear at the end of the chapter.

Overview of Patents

For most engineered goods, two basic types of patents are relevant: *design patents* and *utility patents*. (A third type of patent covers plants.) Design patents provide the legal right to exclude someone from producing and selling a product with the identical ornamental design described by the design patent. A design patent can be thought of as a "copyright" for the ornamental design of a product. Because design patents must be limited to ornamental design, for most engineered goods, design patents are of very limited value. For this reason, the chapter focuses further on utility patents.

Patent law in most of the world evolved from English law and so patent laws in different countries are somewhat similar. This chapter uses U.S. law as a reference point, and so readers with intentions to obtain patents in other countries should carefully investigate the laws in those countries.

Utility Patents

United States law allows for patenting of an invention that relates to a new process, machine, article of manufacture, composition of matter, or a new and useful improvement of one of these things. Fortunately, these categories include almost all inventions embodied by new products. Note that inventions embodied in software are sometimes patented, but usually the invention is described as a process or machine. Exhibit 16-3 shows the first page of a patent for the insulating sleeve invented by Coffin.

In addition, the law requires that patented inventions be the following:

- *Useful:* The patented invention must be useful to someone in some context.
- *Novel:* Novel inventions are those that are not known publicly and therefore are not evident in existing products, publications, or prior patents. The definition of novelty relates to disclosures of the actual invention to be patented as well. In the United States, an invention to be patented must not have been revealed to the public more than a year before the patent is filed.
- *Nonobvious:* Patent law defines obvious inventions as those that would be clearly evident to those with "ordinary skill in the art" who faced the same problem as the inventor.

Usefulness is rarely a hurdle to obtaining a patent; however, the requirements that an invention be novel and nonobvious are the most common barriers to obtaining a patent.

About two-thirds of applications filed for patents result in issued patents; however, an issued patent is not necessarily *valid*. A patent may be challenged in a government court by a competitor at some point in the future. The validity of a patent is determined by, among other factors, the adequacy of the description in the patent and the novelty of the invention relative to the prior art. A tiny fraction of patents—a few hundred per year in the United States—are ever challenged in court. Of those challenged in recent years, just over half have been found to be valid.

An inventor associated with a patent is a person who actually created the invention individually or in collaboration with other inventors. In some cases the inventor is also the owner of the intellectual property; however, in most cases, the patent is *assigned* to some other entity, usually the inventor's employer. The actual intellectual property rights associated with a patent belong to the owner of the patent and not necessarily to the inventor. (Appendix B to this chapter provides some advice to individual inventors interested in commercializing their inventions.)

A patent owner has the right to exclude others from using, making, selling, or importing an infringing product. This is an *offensive right,* which requires that the patent owner sue the infringer. There are also *defensive rights* associated with patents. Any invention described in a patent, whether part of the claimed invention or not, is considered by the legal system to be known publicly and forms part of the *prior art.* This disclosure is a defensive act blocking a competitor from patenting the disclosed invention.

Preparing a Disclosure

This chapter is focused on a process for preparing an *invention disclosure*—in essence a detailed description of an invention. This disclosure will be in the form of a patent application, which can serve as a provisional patent application and with relatively little additional work could be a regular patent application. It is possible, even typical, for a patent attorney to do much of the work described in the chapter; however, our belief is

US005205473A

United States Patent [19]

Coffin, Sr.

[54] **RECYCLABLE CORRUGATED BEVERAGE CONTAINER AND HOLDER**

[75] Inventor: David W. Coffin, Sr., Fayetteville, N.Y.

[73] Assignee: Design By Us Company, Philadelphia, Pa.

[21] Appl. No.: 854,425

[22] Filed: Mar. 19, 1992

[51] Int. Cl. B65D 3/28

[52] U.S. Cl. .... 229/1.5 B; 206/813; 220/441; 220/DIG. 30; 229/1.5 H; 229/DIG. 2; 493/296;493/907

[38] Field of Search .....229/1.5 B, 1.3 H, 4.5, 229/DIG. 2; 220/441, 671, 737–739, DIG. 30; 493/287, 296, 907, 908; 209/8, 47, 215; 206/813

[56]   **References Cited**

U.S. PATENT DOCUMENTS

1,732,322	10/1929	Wilson et al.	220/DIG. 30
1,771,765	7/1930	Benson	229/4.5
2,266,828	12/1941	Sykes	229/1.5 B
2,300,473	11/1942	Winkle	229/4.5
2,503,815	3/1950	Harman	
2,617,549	11/1952	Egger	
2,641,402	6/1953	Bruun	229/4.5
2,661,889	12/1953	Phinney	229/4.5

[11] Patent Number: 5,205,473

[45] Date of Patent: Apr. 27, 1993

2,969,901	1/1961	Behrens	229/1.3 B
3,237,834	3/1966	Davis et al.	229/1.3 B
3,779,157	12/1973	Ross, Jr. et al.	53/527
3,785,254	1/1974	Mann	
3,890,762	6/1975	Ernst et al.	
3,908,523	9/1975	Shikays	229/1.5 B
4,080,880	3/1978	Shikay	493/296
4,146,660	3/1979	Hall et al.	
4,176,034	11/1979	Kelley	209/8
5,009,326	4/1991	Reaves et al.	
5,092,485	3/1992	Lee	229/1.3 B

OTHER PUBLICATIONS

"The Wiley Encyclopedia of Packaging Technology", John Wiley & Sons, pp. 66-69, 1986.

Primary Examiner—Gary E. Elkins
Attorney, Agent, or Firm—Synnestvedt & Lochner

[57]   **ABSTRACT**

Corrugated beverage containers and holders are which employ recyclable materials, but provide fluting structures for containing insulating air. These products are easy to hold and have a lesser impact on the environment than polystyrene containers.

18 Claims, 8 Drawing Sheets

EXHIBIT

16-3 The first page of U.S. Patent 5,205,473.

Coffin, David W., Recyclable Corrugated Beverage Container and Holder, United States Patent 5,205,473, April 27, 1993

that having the inventor draft a detailed disclosure is the best way to communicate the inventor's knowledge, even though in most cases a patent attorney will revise the disclosure to prepare the formal patent application. Although many readers will be able to complete a provisional patent application from the guidance provided here, this chapter is not a substitute for competent legal advice. Inventors pursuing serious commercial opportunities should consult with a patent attorney after preparing their disclosure.

The steps in the process are:

1. Formulate a strategy and plan.
2. Study prior inventions.
3. Outline claims.
4. Write the description of the invention.
5. Refine claims.
6. Pursue application.
7. Reflect on the results and the process.

Step 1: Formulate a Strategy and Plan

In formulating a patent strategy and plan, a product development team must decide on the timing of the filing of a patent application, the type of application to be filed, and the scope of the application.

Timing of Patent Applications

Legally, a U.S. patent application must be filed within one year of the first public disclosure of an invention. In much of the rest of the world, a patent must be filed before any public disclosure or within one year of filing a U.S. application, so long as the U.S. application is filed before public disclosure. In most cases, public disclosure is a description of the invention to an individual or group of people who are not obligated to keep the invention confidential. Examples of such disclosure include: publication of invention details in a magazine or journal, presentation of a product at a trade show, display of the invention on a publicly accessible Web site, or test marketing of a product. (Most experts agree that a student's class presentation of an invention is not public disclosure, as long as the class members have agreed to preserve the confidentiality of the invention and as long as members of the general public are not present.) We strongly recommend that inventors file patent applications before any public disclosure. This action ensures that the option to file an international patent is preserved for one year. Fortunately, a provisional patent application may be filed at relatively little expense to preserve these rights.

Although we recommend that filing precede public disclosure, the inventor may benefit by delaying the application until just before such disclosure. The principal advantage to waiting as long as possible is that the inventor has as much knowledge as possible about the invention and its commercialization. Very often what the inventor believes are the key features of an invention early in the innovation process turn out to be less important than refinements developed later in the innovation process. By waiting, the inventor can ensure that the most important elements of the invention are captured in the patent application; however, a risk in waiting is that someone else may file a patent for the same invention.

In most countries, including the United States, priority among competing patent applications is based on the filing date not the date of invention. If two inventors are working simultaneously on competing inventions, the first to file is given priority. Historically, U.S. law granted priority based on the date of invention. The current law harmonizes U.S. law with that of most of the rest of the world. A nuance in the law is that if one inventor discloses an invention publicly, then that invention is no longer novel from the perspective of competing inventors and so they may not patent the disclosed invention. This prevents rival inventors from rushing to file patents on newly disclosed inventions. The disclosing inventor preserves the right to file a patent for one year after public disclosure.

Type of Application

A team faces two basic choices about the type of patent application to be pursued. First, the team must decide whether to file a *regular patent application* or a *provisional patent application.* Second, the team must decide whether to pursue domestic and/or foreign patents.

A regular patent application was the only option available to an inventor in the United States until substantial changes were made to patent law in 1995. Under current U.S. patent law, an inventor may file a provisional patent application. A provisional patent application needs only to fully describe the invention. It does not need to contain claims or comply with the formal structure and language of a regular patent application. The principal advantage of a provisional patent application is that it requires less cost and effort to prepare and file than a regular patent application, but it preserves all options to pursue further patent filings for a period of one year. Once a provisional patent application has been filed, a company may label its products "patent pending," and it retains the right to file a foreign patent application and/or a regular patent application. The only fundamental disadvantage of a provisional patent application is that it delays the eventual issuance of a patent by up to one year, as the process of examining a patent application does not begin until a regular patent application is filed. Another possible disadvantage is that the preliminary nature of a provisional patent application may lead to the use of less care in preparing the description of the invention than might be the case with a regular application. The description of the invention must be complete in a provisional patent application, and the regular patent application that follows cannot contain features that were not described in the provisional application.

Filing patents internationally is expensive and somewhat complex. The team should therefore consult with a patent professional about international patent strategy, as patent law varies somewhat from country to country. To obtain foreign patent rights, an application must eventually be filed in each country in which a patent is sought. (The European Community, however, acts as a single entity with respect to patent filing.) Foreign applications can be expensive, costing up to $15,000 per country for filing fees, translation fees, and patent agent fees.

The expense of filing for foreign patents can be delayed, generally by 30 months, by filing a *Patent Cooperation Treaty* (PCT) application. A PCT application is filed in one country (e.g., the United States) but is designated as a PCT application, which is the beginning of a process by which foreign patents can be pursued. A PCT application costs only slightly more than a regular patent application in filing fees, but it allows for a substantial delay before application fees must be paid in the countries in which foreign patents are sought.

The provisional patent application and the PCT application together provide a vehicle for a small company or individual inventor to preserve most patent rights with relatively little cost. A typical strategy is to file a provisional patent application before any public disclosure of the invention; then, within one year, to file a PCT application with the U.S. patent office; then, when forced to act or abandon the application at some point in the future (usually a year or more away), to pursue actual foreign applications. This strategy allows a delay of two or more years before substantial legal and application fees must be paid. During this period, the team can assess the true commercial potential of the products embodying the invention and can estimate the value of more extensive patent protection.

Scope of Application

The team should evaluate the overall product design and decide which elements embody inventions that are likely to be patentable. Typically, the process of reviewing the product design will result in a list of elements that the team considers to be novel and nonobvious. The team should focus on those elements that present substantial barriers to competition, which are typically the elements that in the opinion of the team represent a substantial improvement over the publicly known methods of addressing similar problems.

Complex products often embody several inventions. For example, a printer may embody novel signal processing methods and novel paper handling techniques. Sometimes these inventions fall into very different *classes* within the patent system. As a result, a product development team may need to file multiple applications corresponding to the distinct classes of invention. For simple products or for products that embody a single type of invention, a single patent application usually suffices. The decision about whether to divide an application into multiple parts is complex and is best made in consultation with a patent attorney; however, all intellectual property rights are preserved even if a patent application is filed that contains multiple classes of inventions. In such cases, the patent office will inform the inventor that the application must be divided.

While defining the scope of the patent, the team should also consider who the inventors are. An inventor is a person who contributed substantially to the creation of the invention. The definition of an inventor for the purposes of patent law is subjective. For example, a technician who only ran experiments would not typically be an inventor, but a technician who ran experiments and then devised a solution to an observed problem with the device could be considered an inventor. There is no limit to the number of inventors named in a patent application. We believe that product development and invention are most often team efforts and that many members of the team who participated in concept generation and the subsequent design activities could be considered inventors. Failing to name a person who is an inventor can result in a patent being declared not valid.

Step 2: Study Prior Inventions

There are three key reasons for studying prior inventions, the so-called *prior art.* First, by studying the prior patent literature, design teams can learn whether an invention may infringe on existing unexpired patents. Although there is no legal barrier to patenting an invention that infringes on an existing patent, if anyone manufactures, sells, or uses a product that infringes upon an existing patent without a license, the patent owner may sue for damages. Second, by studying the prior art, the inventors get a sense of how similar their invention is to prior inventions and therefore how likely they are to be granted a broad patent. Third, the team will develop background knowledge enabling the members to craft novel claims.

In the course of product development efforts, most teams accumulate a variety of references to prior inventions. Some of the sources of information on prior inventions include:

- Existing and historical product literature.
- Patent searches.
- Technical and trade publications.

Several good online reference sources can be used for searching patents. Simple keyword searches are often sufficient to find most relevant patents. It is important for the team to keep a file containing the prior art they are aware of. This information must be provided to the patent office shortly after filing the patent application.

In the Coffin patent for the cup holder shown in Exhibit 16-1, references to 19 other U.S. patents are cited along with a reference to a book. (The references cited by the inventor and by the patent examiner are listed on the first page of a patent. The first page of the Coffin patent is reproduced as Exhibit 16-3.) Among the prior art for the Coffin patent, for example, is a 1930 patent by Benson (1,771,765; "Waterproof Paper Receptacle") in which a corrugated holder insulates a paper liner cup. The Benson patent describes a cup holder that fits underneath and into the bottom of the liner cup. This is one reason that the invention in the Coffin patent is described as a tube with an opening at the top and bottom.

Step 3: Outline Claims

Issuance of a patent gives the owner a legal right to exclude others from infringing on the invention specifically described in the patent's claims. Claims describe certain characteristics of the invention; they are written in formal legal language and must adhere to some rules of composition. In step 5 we describe how the formal legal language works; however, at this point in the process of preparing the disclosure, the team benefits from thinking carefully about what it believes is unique about the invention. We therefore recommend that the team outline the claims. Don't worry about legal precision at this point. Instead, make a list of the features and characteristics of the invention that the team believes are unique and valuable. For example, an outline of the claims for the Coffin invention might be:

- Use of corrugations as insulation, in many possible forms
  - Corrugations on the inside surface of the tube
  - Corrugations on the outside surface of the tube
  - Corrugations sandwiched between two flat layers of sheet material
  - Vertical orientation of flutes
    - Flutes open at top and bottom of holder
  - Corrugations with "triangle wave" cross section
  - Corrugations with "sine wave" cross section
- Tubular form with openings at both ends
  - In shape of truncated cone
- Recyclable materials
  - Recyclable adhesive
  - Recyclable sheeting
    - Cellulose material

- Biodegradable adhesive
- Surface to print on
- Holder folds flat along two fold lines

The outline of the claims provides guidance about what must be described in detail in the description.

Step 4: Write the Description of the Invention

The bulk of a patent application is formally known as the *specification.* To avoid confusion with our use of the word *specifications* in this book, we call the body of the patent application the *description* because this is the part of the application that actually describes the invention. The description must present the invention in enough detail that someone with "ordinary skill in the art" (i.e., someone with the skills and capabilities of a typical practitioner working in the same basic field as the invention) could implement the invention. The description should also be a marketing document promoting the value of the invention and the weaknesses in existing solutions. The patent application will be read by a patent examiner, who will search and study prior patents. The description must convince the examiner that the inventors developed something useful that is different from existing inventions and that is nonobvious. In these respects one can think of the description as essentially a technical report on the invention. There are some formatting conventions for patent applications, although these are not strictly necessary for an invention disclosure or a provisional patent application.

Patent law requires that the application "teach" with sufficient detail that someone "skilled in the art" could practice the invention. For example, in the Coffin patent, the inventor discloses that the adhesive to bond the flutes is "a recyclable, and preferably a biodegradable adhesive, for example, R130 adhesive by Fasson Inc., Grand Rapids, MI."[1] The requirement to completely teach the invention may be somewhat counterintuitive for someone accustomed to treating inventions confidentially. Patent law requires that inventors disclose what they know about the invention, but in exchange they are granted the right to exclude others from practicing the invention for a limited time period. This requirement reflects the basic tension in the patent system between granting a temporary monopoly to inventors in exchange for publication of information that will eventually be available for use by anyone.

A typical description includes the following elements:

- *Title:* Provide a short descriptive label for the invention, for example, "Recyclable Corrugated Beverage Container and Holder."
- *List of inventors:* All inventors must be listed. A person should be listed as an inventor if he or she originated any of the inventions claimed in the application. There are no legal limits to the number of inventors and no requirements about the order in which inventors are listed. A failure to list an inventor could result in a patent eventually being declared not valid.
- *Field of the invention:* Explain what type of device, product, machine, or method this invention relates to. For example, the Coffin patent reads, "This invention relates to insulating containers, and especially to those which are recyclable and made of cellulosic materials."[2]

---

[1]Coffin, David W., Recyclable Corrugated Beverage Container and Holder, United States Patent 5,205,473, April 27, 1993.
[2]Ibid.

- *Background of the invention:* State the problem that the invention solves. Explain the context for the problem, what is wrong with existing solutions, why a new solution is needed, and what advantages are offered by the invention.
- *Summary of the invention:* This section should present the substance of the invention in summarized form. The summary may point out the advantages of the invention and how it solves the problems described in the background.
- *Brief description of the drawings:* List the figures in the description along with a brief description of each drawing. For example, "Figure 10 is a perspective view of a preferred embodiment illustrating internal flute portions in breakaway views."
- *Detailed description of the invention:* This section of the description is usually the most comprehensive and contains detailed descriptions of embodiments of the invention along with an explanation of how these embodiments work. Further discussion of the detailed description is provided later.

Figures

Formal figures for patents must comply with a variety of rules about labeling, line weight, and types of graphical elements; however, for an invention disclosure or provisional patent application, informal figures are sufficient and hand sketches or CAD drawings are perfectly appropriate. At some point after filing a regular patent application, the patent office will request formal figures, at which time a professional drafter may be hired to prepare formal versions of the necessary figures. Prepare enough figures to clearly show the key elements of the invention in the preferred embodiments that have been considered. A simple invention like the cup holder would probably require 5 to 15 figures.

The features shown in the figures may be labeled with words (e.g., "outer layer"), although to facilitate preparation of a regular patent application, the team may wish to use "reference numerals" on the figures right from the beginning. No rule stipulates that reference numerals must be uninterrupted and consecutive, so a convenient numbering scheme uses reference numerals 10, 11, 12, and so on, for features that first appear in Figure 1; reference numerals 20, 21, 22, and so on, for features that first appear in Figure 2; and so on. This way adding numerals to one figure does not influence the use of numerals in another figure. The same feature shown in more than one figure must be labeled with the same reference numeral, so some numerals will be carried over from one figure to another.

Writing the Detailed Description

The detailed description describes *embodiments* of the invention. An embodiment is a physical realization of the claimed invention. Patent law requires that the application describe the *preferred embodiment*—that is, the best way of practicing the invention. Typically, a detailed description is organized as a collection of paragraphs, each describing an embodiment of the invention in terms of its physical structure along with an explanation of how that embodiment works.

A good strategy for writing the detailed description is to first create the figures that show embodiments of the invention. Next describe the embodiment by labeling each feature of the embodiment in the figure and explaining the arrangement of these features. Finally, explain how the embodiment works and why the features are important to this function. This process is repeated for each of the embodiments described in the detailed description.

344   *Chapter* 16

EXHIBIT 16-4
Figure 10
from the Coffin
patent.

Coffin, David W.,
Recyclable Corrugated
Beverage Container
and Holder, United
States Patent 5,205,473,
April 27, 1993

FIG. 10

Consider Figure 10 from the Coffin patent, shown here as Exhibit 16-4. A detailed description might include language like the following:

> A preferred embodiment of the invention is shown in Figure 10. A liner surface 22 and an outer surface 24 sandwich a corrugation 21. The assembly 200 forms a tubular shape whose diameter changes linearly with length so as to form a section of a truncated cone. The smooth outer surface 24 provides a smooth surface onto which graphics may be printed. Corrugation 21 is bonded to outer surface 24 and liner surface 22 with a recyclable adhesive.

The detailed description should show alternative embodiments of the invention. For example, in the Coffin patent, the invention features "flutes" that create an insulating air gap. In a preferred embodiment these flutes are formed by smooth wavy corrugations, with the smooth surface on the outside to allow for graphics to be easily printed on the sleeve. Alternative embodiments include triangle waves and/or sheet materials on either or both sides of the tube. These alternative embodiments are explained in the detailed description and shown in the figures. (See Exhibit 16-5.)

Defensive Disclosure

The primary benefit of a patent is that it grants the owner *offensive rights*; that is, the owner has the right to prevent others from practicing the invention. However, patents also offer a subtle mechanism for taking *defensive* actions. A patent is considered prior art and so an invention that appears in a patent may not be patented in the future. For this reason, inventors

EXHIBIT 16-5
Figures 6a, 6b,
7a, and 7b
from the Coffin
patent showing
alternative
embodiments of
the invention.

Coffin, David W.,
Recyclable Corrugated
Beverage Container
and Holder, United
States Patent 5,205,473,
April 27, 1993

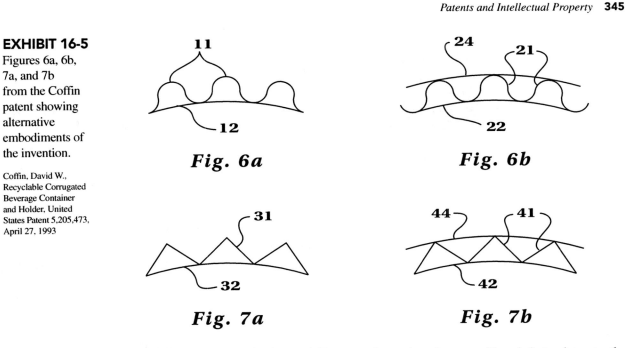

Fig. 6a

Fig. 6b

Fig. 7a

Fig. 7b

may benefit from disclosing essentially every invention they considered that relates to the claimed invention no matter how wide ranging. This may be done in the detailed description. Even though these inventions may not actually be reflected in the claims of the patent, their disclosure becomes part of the prior art and therefore prevents others from patenting them. This defensive strategy may offer competitive advantages in fields of emerging technologies.

Step 5: Refine Claims

The claims are a set of numbered phrases that precisely define the essential elements of the invention. The claims are the basis for all offensive patent rights. A patent owner can prevent others from practicing the invention described by the claims only. The rest of the patent application is essentially background and context for the claims.

Writing the Claims

Although claims must be expressed verbally, they adhere to a strict mathematical logic. Almost all claims are formulated as a recursive expression of the form

$$X = A + B + C \ldots , \qquad \text{where } A = u + v + w \ldots , \quad B = \ldots$$

This is expressed verbally as:

> An *X* comprising an *A*, a *B*, and a *C*, wherein said *A* is comprised of a *u*, a *v*, and a *w* and wherein said *B* is . . .

Note that claims comply with some verbal conventions. The word *comprising* means "including but not limited to" and is almost always used as the equal sign in the expression. The first time an element, say a *liner sheet*, is named in a claim the inventor uses the indefinite article *a* as in "comprises *a* liner sheet." Once this element has been named it is never referred to as *the* liner sheet, but always as *said* liner sheet. This is true for every subsequent instance in which *liner sheet* is used in the claims. Although these conventions are not difficult to remember once learned, inventors preparing a disclosure for subsequent editing by a patent attorney should not worry too much about formal correctness of the language. The language is easily corrected when the formal patent application is prepared.

Multiple claims are arranged hierarchically into *independent* claims and *dependent* claims. Independent claims stand alone and form the root nodes of a hierarchy of claims. Dependent claims always add further restrictions to an independent claim. Dependent claims are typically written in this form:

The invention of Claim N, further comprising *Q, R,* and *S* . . .

or

The invention of Claim N, wherein said *A* . . .

Dependent claims essentially inherit all of the properties of the independent claim on which they depend. In fact, a dependent claim can be read as if all of the language of the independent claim on which it depends were inserted as a replacement for the introductory phrase "The invention of Claim N."

The dependent claims are important in that the patent office may reject the independent claim as obvious or not novel while allowing one or more dependent claims. In such cases, patentable material remains; the original independent claim can be deleted and the original dependent claim can be rewritten as an independent claim.

The elements of a claim form a *logical and* relationship. To infringe on a claim, a device must include each and every element named in the claim. If, for example, a competitive product were to use only three of four elements named in a claim, it would not infringe on the claim.

Consider this example from the Coffin patent (edited slightly for clarity).[3]

Claim 1

A beverage container holder, comprising a corrugated tubular member comprising cellulosic material and at least a first opening therein for receiving and retaining a beverage container, said corrugated tubular member comprising fluting means for containing insulating air; said fluting means comprising fluting adhesively attached to a liner with a recyclable adhesive.

Claim 1 is an independent claim. Consider Claim 2, which is dependent on Claim 1.

Claim 2

The holder of claim 1, wherein said tubular member further comprises a second opening wherein said first opening and said second opening are of unequal cross-sectional dimensions.

This claim adheres to the logical structure shown in Exhibit 16-6.

Let us reinforce the idea that a claim is formed of a logical "and" relation among its elements. Claim 1 is for a holder that includes all of these elements:

- Corrugated tube
  - Made of cellulosic material
  - With a first opening
  - With fluting means
    - Made of flutes adhesively attached to a liner
      - Using recyclable adhesive

---

[3]Coffin, David W., Recyclable Corrugated Beverage Container and Holder, United States Patent 5,205,473, April 27, 1993

EXHIBIT 16-6
The logical structure of Claims 1 and 2 from the Coffin patent. Note that Claim 2 is dependent on Claim 1 and simply adds further restrictions, a second opening and a relationship between the first and second openings.

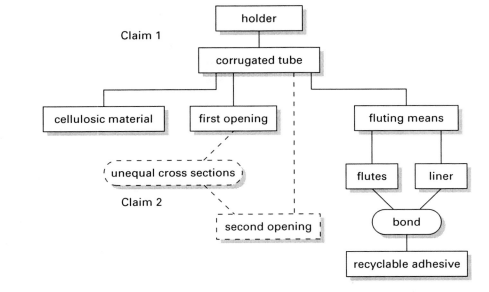

If a competing cup holder does not have every one of these elements, it does not infringe upon this claim. So, for example, if it were made of polystyrene, it would not infringe on this claim (no cellulosic material). Consider a patent by Jay Sorensen filed shortly after the Coffin patent. Sorensen's patent is for a cup holder with a dimpled surface. (See Exhibit 16-7.) Because this invention does not have "fluting means" it does not infringe upon the Coffin patent. Sorensen's claims include the following (edited slightly for clarity):

Claim 4

A cup holder comprising a band of material formed with an open top and an open bottom through which a cup can extend and an inner surface immediately adjacent to said cup, said band comprising a plurality of discrete, spaced-apart, approximately semi-spherically shaped depressions distributed on substantially the entire inner surface of said band so that each depression defines a non-contacting region of said band creating an air gap between said band and said cup, thereby reducing the rate of heat transfer through said holder.[4]

At least two lessons can be derived from comparing the Coffin and Sorensen inventions. First, patents often provide relatively limited commercial advantages. In this case, by creating a cup holder with dimples instead of flutes, Sorensen was able to avoid infringing on the Coffin patent. In fact, both inventions are embodied by successful commercial products, but neither patent provides ironclad protection from competition. The second lesson is that the inventor should invest in considering as many ways as possible to achieve the desired function of the invention, in this case an insulating layer. Had Coffin thought of a dimpled surface, then this feature could have been described in his patent application. In the best case, the dimpled invention may have formed the basis for additional claims in the patent. In the worst case, the description of the dimpled embodiment in the patent application would have been prior art and therefore prevented Sorensen from obtaining his patent. (It would not prevent Sorensen and others from practicing the dimpled invention unless it were claimed.)

[4]Sorensen, Jay, Cup Holder, United States Patent 5,425,497, June 20, 1995.

348   *Chapter* 16

Sorensen, Jay, Cup Holder, United States Patent 5,425,497, June 20, 1995

EXHIBIT 16-7   Figure from the Sorensen patent (U.S. Patent 5,425,497, "dimpled cup holder").

Guidelines for Crafting Claims

Several guidelines are helpful in crafting claims. Writing great claims is tricky, so we advise inventors to seek the help of an experienced patent attorney in refining a patent application.

- Always try to make a claim as general as possible. When a specific descriptor is used, try making it general. For example, Coffin's patent speaks of a "tubular member" and not a "tube."
- Avoid absolute definitions by using modifiers like "substantially," "essentially," and "approximately."
- Attempt to create an invention that does not infringe on the draft claim, and then try to rewrite the claim or add an additional claim such that the hypothetical invention would infringe.

Step 6: Pursue Application

In most cases, the inventor will deliver the draft application to a patent attorney or other intellectual property professional for refinement and formal application. It is possible to file a patent application as an individual if severely budget constrained. Pressman provides detailed guidelines for doing this (Pressman, 2014). Note that the statutory requirements are administratively complex, and so we highly recommend that commercial product development teams retain a competent specialist to pursue any application to the patent office.

Once an invention disclosure is prepared, the team can proceed in four different ways, with the specific course of action dictated by the business context.

- ***The team can file a provisional patent application.*** An individual or small company can file a provisional patent application for less than $100 in filing fees. The application need contain only a description of the invention and need not comply with the formalities of a regular patent application. Once a provisional application is filed, a product may be labeled "patent pending." If the team wishes to pursue a regular patent application, this application must be filed within one year of the filing of the provisional patent application. A provisional patent therefore acts as an option to pursue a regular patent application and allows the team time to pursue licensing or further investigation before incurring the expense of a regular patent application.

- ***The team may file a regular patent application in the United States.*** This process costs about $500 in filing fees for a small company or individual, in addition to the legal fees for a patent attorney.

- ***The team may file a patent cooperation treaty or PCT application.*** A PCT application allows a single patent application in a single country, say the United States, to initiate the process of pursuing international patent protection. Eventually, the inventor must pursue patent protection in individual countries or collections of countries (e.g., European Union); however, the PCT process allows the first steps of the process to be carried out relatively efficiently and with a single point of contact. The entire process of pursuing foreign patent rights is beyond the scope of this chapter. Consult a patent attorney for details.

- ***The team can defer application indefinitely.*** The team may delay in hope that future information will make a course of action obvious. In some cases, the team may decide not to pursue the invention and therefore may decide to abandon the patent application process. The consequences of delay may be substantial. If the invention is disclosed publicly, then all international patent rights are forgone. If a year passes after public disclosure without filing a regular patent application, then U.S. patent rights are also forgone. Nevertheless, the team may be able to defer any action for several months before these eventualities are realized.

At some point after the team files a regular patent application or a PTO application, the patent office will issue an *office action* responding to the application. In almost all cases, a patent examiner will reject many or all of the claims as either obvious or not novel. This is the norm and it is part of a back-and-forth exchange between the patent office and inventor that should eventually result in claims that are patentable. Next, the inventor and patent attorney sharpen arguments, edit claims to reflect comments from the examiner, and respond to the office action with an amended application. Most applications eventually result in an issued patent, although the claims rarely remain exactly as originally written.

The patent office does not review or act on provisional patent applications. It merely records their filing and stores the application for review when and if a regular application is filed.

Step 7: Reflect on the Results and the Process

In reflecting on the patent application or invention disclosure, the team should consider at least the following questions:

- What are the essential and distinctive features of the product concept, and therefore the invention? Are these features reflected in the description of the invention and in the claims? Does the description communicate the best way of practicing the invention?

- What is the timing of future required actions? The team's patent attorney will typically maintain a *docket*—essentially a calendar indicating when further actions must be taken to preserve patent rights; however, the inventor or someone within the team's company should also be responsible for thinking about the actions that must be taken in the coming months.

- Which aspects of the process of preparing the patent application or invention disclosure went smoothly and which aspects require further efforts in the future?

- What did the team learn about the prior art that may inform future product development efforts? For example, are there valuable technologies that might be licensed from existing patent holders? Are competitors' patents expiring, possibly allowing the team to use a convenient solution to a long-standing problem?

- How strong an intellectual property position does the team have? Are the features of the invention in the patent application so novel and valuable that they really prevent competitors from direct competition, or is the patent likely to be merely a deterrent to the most direct copies of the products that embody the invention?

- Did the team begin the process too early or too late? Was the effort rushed? What is the ideal timing for the next effort to prepare a patent application?

Summary

- A patent is a temporary monopoly granted by a government to exclude others from using, making, or selling an invention. Patent law is intended to balance an incentive for invention with the free dissemination of information.

- Utility patents are the central element of the intellectual property for most technology-based product development efforts.

- An invention can be patented if it is useful, novel, and nonobvious.

- The final invention that is patented is defined by the patent claims. The rest of the patent application essentially serves as background and explanation in support of the claims.

- We recommend a seven-step process for pursuing a patent:
  1. Formulate a strategy and plan.
  2. Study prior inventions.
  3. Outline claims.
  4. Write the description of the invention.
  5. Refine claims.

6. Pursue application.

7. Reflect on the results and the process.

- Provisional patent applications and patent cooperation treaty (PCT) applications can be used to minimize the costs of pursuing patent protection while preserving all future options.

References and Bibliography

Many current resources are available on the Internet via
www.ulrich-eppinger.net

The examples in the chapter are derived from the Coffin and Sorensen patents.

Coffin, David W., *Recyclable Corrugated Beverage Container and Holder,* United States Patent 5,205,473, April 27, 1993.

Sorensen, Jay, *Cup Holder,* United States Patent 5,425,497, June 20, 1995.

Pressman's book is a comprehensive guide to the details of patent law and provides a step-by-step process for writing a patent application and pursuing the application with the patent office. The book also contains valuable related information on licensing inventions.

Pressman, David, and Thomas J. Tuytschaevers, *Patent It Yourself,* seventeenth edition, Nolo Press, Berkeley, CA, 2014.

Stim provides an in-depth discussion of most aspects of intellectual property, including trademarks and copyrights.

Stim, Richard, *Patent, Copyright & Trademark: An Intellectual Property Desk Reference,* thirteenth edition, Nolo Press, Berkeley, CA, 2014.

Exercises

1. Find a patent number on a product that interests you. Look up the patent using an online reference tool.

2. Draft a claim for the self-stick notepad invention marketed by 3M Corporation as the Post-it note.

3. Draw a logic diagram of two claims for the patent in Exercise 1.

4. Generate one or more product concepts that are very different from the Coffin and Sorensen inventions to address the problem of handling a hot coffee cup and that don't infringe the Coffin and Sorensen patents.

Thought Questions

1. Controversy erupted in 1999 when the J.M. Smucker Company sued a Michigan bakery, Albie's, for infringing on its patent by marketing a crustless peanut butter and jelly sandwich crimped on the edges. (See U.S. patent 6,004,596.) Albie's argued that the patent was issued in error because the invention was obvious. Look up the Smucker patent. Do you believe that the Smucker's invention is nonobvious? Why or why not?

2. Why might an inventor describe but not claim an invention in a patent?

Appendix A

Trademarks

A trademark is a word or symbol associated with the products of a particular manufacturer. Trademarks can form an important element of the portfolio of intellectual property owned by a company. Trademarks can be words, "word marks" (stylized graphics spelling out words), and/or symbols. Trademarks usually correspond to brands, product names, and sometimes to company names.

Trademark law is intended to prevent unfair competition, which could result if one manufacturer named its products like those of another in an attempt to confuse the public. In fact, to avoid confusion, when a manufacturer uses a competitor's trademark in advertising, say for the purposes of comparison, it must by law indicate that the name is a trademark of the competitor.

Trademarks must not be purely descriptive. For example, although a company could not obtain a trademark on "Insulating Sleeve," it could for names that are suggestive but not purely descriptive such as "Insleev," "ThermaJo," or "CupPup."

In the United States, a federal trademark may be established merely by using the mark in interstate commerce. This is done by attaching "TM" to the word or symbol when used in advertising or labeling the product (e.g., JavaJacket™). Trademarks may also be registered at modest cost through the United States Patent and Trademark Office using a simple process. When registered, a trademark is denoted with the symbol ® (e.g., Coke®).

Given the importance of the Internet for communicating with customers, when creating new product names, the team should strive to create trademarks that correspond exactly to domain names on the Internet.

Appendix B

Advice to Individual Inventors

Most students of product development and product development professionals have at some point had an idea for a novel product. Often further thought results in a product concept, which sometimes embodies a patentable invention. A common misconception among inventors is that a raw idea or even a product concept is highly valuable. Here is some advice based on observations of many inventors and product commercialization efforts.

- A patent can be a useful element of a plan for developing and commercializing a product; however, it is not really a central element of that activity. Patenting an invention can usually wait until many of the technical and market risks have been addressed.

- A patent by itself rarely has any commercial value. (An idea by itself has even less value.) To extract value from a product opportunity, an inventor must typically complete a product design, resolving the difficult trade-offs associated with addressing customer needs while minimizing production costs. Once this hard work is completed, a product design may have substantial value. In most cases, pursuing a patent is not worth the effort except as part of a larger effort to take a product concept through to a substantial development milestone such as a working prototype. If the design is proven through prototyping and testing, a patent can be an important mechanism for increasing the value of this intellectual property.

- Licensing a patent to a manufacturer as an individual inventor is very difficult. If you are serious about your product opportunity, be prepared to pursue commercialization of your product on your own or in partnership with a smaller company. Once you have demonstrated a market for the product, licensing to a larger entity becomes much more likely.

- File a provisional patent application. For very little money, an individual using the guidelines in this chapter can file a provisional application. This action provides patent protection for a year, while you evaluate whether your idea is worth pursuing.

CHAPTER EIGHTEEN

Product Development Economics

© Niels Poulsen std/Alamy

EXHIBIT 18-1
A home coffee maker using single-serving capsules.

A product development team working for a manufacturer of kitchen appliances was in the midst of developing a new coffee maker, referred to by the project name AB-100. The new coffee maker would provide high-quality coffee using an existing capsule system and would compete in the market against products by Nespresso, Illy, Keurig, and others. Exhibit 18-1 shows a coffee maker and coffee capsule by Nespresso.

During the AB-100 development, the product development team was faced with several decisions that it knew could have a significant impact on the product's profitability. For example:

- Should the team increase development spending and production cost to add an additional feature that could lead to greater sales volume?

- Would the project be profitable if the retail price is reduced by 10% due to competitive pricing pressure?

The team used the financial analysis tools presented in this chapter to help answer these and other questions relating to the project's ability to generate profit for the manufacturer. The emphasis in this chapter is on fairly quick, approximate methods for supporting decision making within the project team. This analysis is generally referred to as product development economics, financial modeling, or break-even analysis. It is essentially a prediction of the expected payback and profitability deriving from a specific project, in this case the development and production of a new product.

Elements of Economic Analysis

This chapter describes a method consisting of two types of analysis, *quantitative* and *qualitative*. We will see in this chapter that this analysis supports a wide variety of project decisions in the product development context.

Quantitative Analysis

There are several basic cash inflows (revenues) and cash outflows (costs) over the life cycle of a successful new product. Cash inflows come from sales of the product and related goods and services. Cash outflows include spending on product and process development; costs of production ramp-up such as equipment purchases and tooling; costs of marketing and supporting the product; and ongoing production costs such as raw materials, components, and labor. The cumulative cash inflows and outflows over the life cycle of a typical successful product are presented schematically in Exhibit 18-2.

Economically successful products are profitable; that is, they generate more cumulative inflows than cumulative outflows. A measure of the degree to which inflows are greater than outflows is the *net present value* (NPV) of the project, or the value in today's dollars of all of the expected future cash flows. The quantitative part of the economic analysis method described in this chapter estimates the NPV of a project's expected cash flows. The method uses NPV techniques because they are easily understood and used widely in business. (Appendix A at the end of this chapter provides a brief tutorial on NPV.) The purpose of quantitative analysis is not only to provide objective evaluations of projects and alternatives but also to bring a measure of structure and discipline to the assessment of product development projects.

EXHIBIT 18-2

Typical cash flows for a new product.

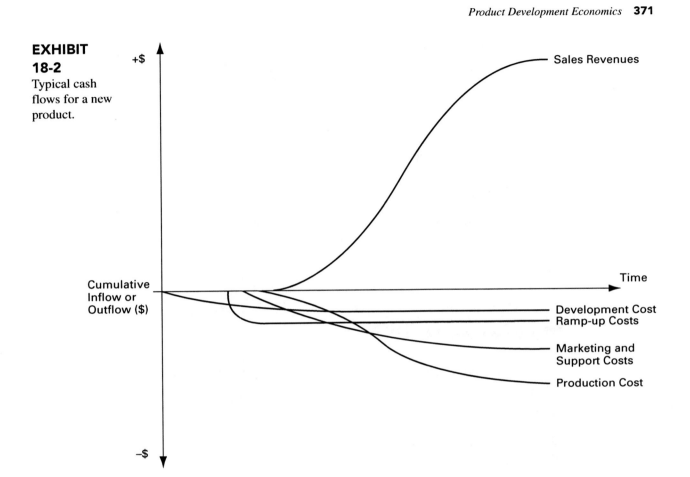

Qualitative Analysis

Quantitative analysis can capture only those factors that are measurable, yet projects often have both positive and negative implications that are difficult to quantify. Also, quantitative analysis rarely captures the characteristics of a dynamic and competitive environment. In fact, a product development project with negative NPV may be a worthwhile investment in certain circumstances; for example, where the expenditure (loss) on one project enables valuable learning that can lead to profitable future products. The method in this chapter uses qualitative analysis to capture some of these issues. Our approach to qualitative analysis is to consider specifically the interactions between the project and (1) the firm, (2) the market, and (3) the macroeconomic environment.

When Should Economic Analysis Be Performed?

Economic analysis, including both quantitative and qualitative approaches, is useful in at least two different circumstances:

* *Go/no-go milestones:* Go/no-go decisions are typically made at the end of each phase of development. These decisions may involve questions such as: Should we try to develop a product to address this market opportunity? Should we proceed with the implementation of the selected concept? Should we launch the product we have developed?

- *Operational design and development decisions:* Operational decisions involve questions such as: Should we spend $100,000 to hire an outside firm to develop this component to save two months of development time? Should we launch the product in one year at a unit price of $260 or wait another quarter when we can reduce the price to $240?

The financial modeling done at the beginning of a project can usually be updated with current information so that it does not have to be re-created in its entirety each time. Used in this way, the analysis becomes one of the information systems the team uses to manage the development project. Economic analysis can be carried out by any member of the development team. In small companies, the project leader or one of the members of the core project team will implement the details of the analysis. In larger companies, a representative from a finance or planning group may be appointed to assist the development team in performing the analysis. We emphasize that even when someone with formal training in financial modeling takes responsibility for this analysis, the core team should fully understand the analysis and be involved in its formulation and use.

Economic Analysis Process

We recommend the following four-step method for the economic analysis of a product development project. The balance of this chapter is organized around these four steps.

1. Build a base-case financial model to compute expected profit.
2. Perform sensitivity analysis to understand the key assumptions of the model.
3. Use sensitivity analysis to understand project trade-offs.
4. Consider the influence of qualitative factors on project success.

Step 1: Build a Base-Case Financial Model

Constructing the base-case model consists of estimating the future cash flows and then computing the NPV of those cash flows.

Estimate the Timing and Magnitude of Future Cash Inflows and Outflows

The timing and magnitude of the cash flows is estimated by merging the project schedule with the project budget and estimates of ongoing revenues and expenses. The level of detail of cash flows should be coarse enough to be convenient to work with, yet it should contain enough resolution to facilitate effective decision making. The most basic categories of cash flow for a typical new product development project are:

- Sales revenues
- Development and testing cost
- Equipment and tooling cost
- Production and distribution ramp-up cost
- Market launch, ongoing marketing, and product support costs
- Production direct and indirect costs

Depending on the types of decisions the model will support, greater levels of detail for one or more areas may be required. More detailed modeling may consider these same types of cash flows in greater detail, or it may consider other flows. Typical refinements include:

- Breakdown of seasonal sales by quarter
- Inclusion of growth or decline of sales volume and/or pricing
- Breakdown of development cost into design, testing, and refinement costs
- Breakdown of production costs into direct costs and indirect costs (overhead)
- Breakdown of marketing and support costs into launch costs, promotion costs, direct sales costs, and service costs
- Inclusion of tax effects, including depreciation and investment tax credits
- Inclusion of cannibalization (the impact of the new product on existing product sales), salvage costs, and opportunity costs
- Inclusion of working capital cash flows and interest on accounts

The financial model we use in this chapter is simplified to include only the major cash flows that are typically considered in practice, but conceptually it is identical to more complex models. The numerical values of the cash flows generally come from budgets and other estimates made by the development team, the manufacturing organization, and the marketing organization. Note that all revenues and expenses to date are *sunk costs* and are irrelevant to NPV calculations. (The concept of sunk costs is reviewed in Appendix A.) Exhibit 18-3 shows the relevant financial estimates for the new coffee maker AB-100.

To complete the model, the financial estimates must be merged with timing information. This can be done by considering the project schedule and sales plan. (For most projects, quarter-year time increments are used.) Exhibit 18-4 shows the AB-100 project timing information in Gantt chart form. The remaining time to market is estimated to be four quarters, and product sales are anticipated to last 12 quarters.

EXHIBIT 18-3

AB-100 project expenses, sales forecasts, marketing and production costs used to create the base-case model.

Model Parameter	Base-Case Value
Product development	$5M over 1 year
Equipment and tooling	$4M over 1/2 year
Production ramp-up	$2M over 1/2 year
Market launch	$10M over 1/2 year
Marketing and support	$5M/year after launch
Production direct cost	$55/unit
Production overhead	$1M/year
Initial sales and production volume	200,000 units/year
Quarterly sales profile	Q1 20%, Q2 25%, Q3 25%, Q4 30%
Sales volume growth	15%/year after first year
Initial retail sale price	$260/unit
Retail price growth	−10%/year after first year
Distributor and retail margin	40% combined
Discount rate	7%/year

374   *Chapter* 18

	Year 1				Year 2				Year 3				Year 4				Year 5			
	Q1	Q2	Q3	Q4	Q1	Q2	Q3	Q4	Q1	Q2	Q3	Q4	Q1	Q2	Q3	Q4	Q1	Q2	Q3	Q4
Sales					▓	▓	▓	▓	▓	▓	▓	▓	▓	▓	▓	▓	▓	▓	▓	▓
Product development	▓	▓	▓																	
Equipment and tooling			▓	▓																
Production ramp up				▓																
Marketing and support				▓	▓	▓	▓	▓	▓	▓	▓	▓	▓	▓	▓	▓	▓	▓	▓	▓
Production					▓	▓	▓	▓	▓	▓	▓	▓	▓	▓	▓	▓	▓	▓	▓	▓

EXHIBIT 18-4   AB-100 project schedule from inception through production and sales.

A common method of representing project cash flow is a table in a spreadsheet. The rows of the table are the different cash flow categories, while the columns represent successive time periods. For this model, the product development team made several assumptions based on experience with their earlier projects and their products already in the market. Based on recent industry trends, the team assumed an annual sales growth of 15%, but that the unit retail price would decline by 10% annually after the first year of sales. We multiply the unit sales quantity by the net wholesale price to find the total product revenues in each period. We also multiply the unit production quantity (assumed same as sales volume) by the unit direct production cost and add the overhead cost to find the total production cost in each period. Exhibit 18-5 illustrates the resulting table.

Compute the Net Present Value of the Cash Flows

Computing the NPV involves simply summing the cash flow for each period and then converting (discounting) this cash flow to its *present value* (its value in today's dollars) using the appropriate *discount rate*. The discount rate is an interest rate reflecting the cost of the capital invested in the project. (The concepts of present value, net present value,

Values in $M *(except where noted)*	Year 1				Year 2				Year 3				Year 4			
	Q1	Q2	Q3	Q4	Q1	Q2	Q3	Q4	Q1	Q2	Q3	Q4	Q1	Q2	Q3	Q4
Sales, machines					6.24	7.80	7.80	9.36	6.46	8.07	8.07	9.69	6.68	8.36	8.36	10.03
Sales Volume, machines (units/qtr)					40,000	50,000	50,000	60,000	46,000	57,500	57,500	69,000	52,900	66,125	66,125	79,350
Unit Wholesale Revenue, machines ($/unit)					156	156	156	156	140	140	140	140	126	126	126	126
Total Revenue					6.24	7.80	7.80	9.36	6.46	8.07	8.07	9.69	6.68	8.36	8.36	10.03
Product Development	1.25	1.25	1.25	1.25												
Equipment and Tooling			2.00	2.00												
Production Ramp-up				1.00	1.00											
Marketing and Support				6.25	6.25	1.25	1.25	1.25	1.25	1.25	1.25	1.25	1.25	1.25	1.25	1.25
Production, machines					2.45	3.00	3.00	3.55	2.78	3.41	3.41	4.05	3.16	3.89	3.89	4.61
Total Costs	1.25	1.25	3.25	10.50	9.70	4.25	4.25	4.80	4.03	4.66	4.66	5.30	4.41	5.14	5.14	5.86

EXHIBIT 18-5   Merging the project financials and schedule into a cash flow table (values in millions of dollars, except for unit revenue and volume, as noted).

and discount rate are reviewed in Appendix A.) Consider, for example, the calculations for year 2, second quarter:

Sales revenue	$7.80M
Marketing and support	− $1.25M
Production	−$3.00M
Period cash flow	$3.55M
Period present value	$3.20M

The period cash flow is the sum of revenues minus costs, $3.55M. The present value of this period cash flow discounted at 7% per year (1.75% per quarter) back to before the first quarter of year 1 (a total of six quarters) is $3.55M ÷ $(1 + 1.75\%)^6 =$ $3.20M.

Project NPV is the sum of the discounted cash flows for all of the periods, $13.1M, as shown in Exhibit 18-6. The positive NPV suggests that development, production, and sales of the AB-100 coffee maker is a profitable project. It pays back the investment at 7% interest and more. Next we consider also sales of the coffee capsules associated with sales of the machines.

Other Cash Flows

Many products generate revenues from associated sales and/or services. For example, the sale of a computer system may also result in revenues from software, accessories, and repair services. They may also have other expenses such as warranty costs related to the computer sales. Furthermore these sales may cannibalize sales of other product lines. If any such cash flows are significant and can be directly associated with sales of the new product being analyzed, we would consider them also in the cash flow projection and the NPV calculation.

The AB-100 uses the manufacturer's existing coffee capsule system in which brewing each cup of coffee requires one capsule. Our analysis assumes that the capsule system requires no additional development or production investment and that each machine results in the (incremental) sale of 400 capsules per year. (Customers typically consume

Values in $M *(except where noted)*	Year 1				Year 2				Year 3				Year 4			
	Q1	Q2	Q3	Q4	Q1	Q2	Q3	Q4	Q1	Q2	Q3	Q4	Q1	Q2	Q3	Q4
Sales, machines					6.24	7.80	7.80	9.36	6.46	8.07	8.07	9.69	6.68	8.36	8.36	10.03
Sales Volume, machines *(units/qtr)*					40,000	50,000	50,000	60,000	46,000	57,500	57,500	69,000	52,900	66,125	66,125	79,350
Unit Wholesale Revenue, machines *($/unit)*					156	156	156	156	140	140	140	140	126	126	126	126
Total Revenue					6.24	7.80	7.80	9.36	6.46	8.07	8.07	9.69	6.68	8.36	8.36	10.03
Product Development	1.25	1.25	1.25	1.25												
Equipment and Tooling			2.00	2.00												
Production Ramp-up				1.00	1.00											
Marketing and Support				6.25	6.25	1.25	1.25	1.25	1.25	1.25	1.25	1.25	1.25	1.25	1.25	1.25
Production, machines					2.45	3.00	3.00	3.55	2.78	3.41	3.41	4.05	3.16	3.89	3.89	4.61
Total Costs	1.25	1.25	3.25	10.50	9.70	4.25	4.25	4.80	4.03	4.66	4.66	5.30	4.41	5.14	5.14	5.86
Period Cash Flow	-1.25	-1.25	-3.25	-10.50	-3.46	3.55	3.55	4.56	2.43	3.41	3.41	4.39	2.27	3.22	3.22	4.16
Period Present Value	-1.23	-1.21	-3.09	-9.80	-3.17	3.20	3.14	3.97	2.08	2.87	2.82	3.57	1.82	2.52	2.48	3.15
Net Present Value	$13.1 million															

EXHIBIT 18-6   Cash flows and net present value.

EXHIBIT 18-7

AB-100 capsule production and sales parameters for the base-case model.

Model Parameter	Base-Case Value
Production cost, capsules	$0.05/unit
Sales volume, capsules per machine	400/year
Initial retail price, capsules	$0.60/unit
Retail price growth, capsules	5%/year

Values in $M *(except where noted)*	Year 1				Year 2				Year 3				Year 4			
	Q1	Q2	Q3	Q4	Q1	Q2	Q3	Q4	Q1	Q2	Q3	Q4	Q1	Q2	Q3	Q4
Sales, machines					6.24	7.80	7.80	9.36	6.46	8.07	8.07	9.69	6.68	8.36	8.36	10.03
Sales Volume, machines (units/qtr)					40,000	50,000	50,000	60,000	46,000	57,500	57,500	69,000	52,900	66,125	66,125	79,350
Unit Wholesale Revenue, machines ($/unit)					156	156	156	156	140	140	140	140	126	126	126	126
Sales, capsules					1.44	3.24	5.04	7.20	9.30	11.47	13.65	16.25	19.17	21.79	24.42	27.56
Sales Volume, capsules (units/qtr)					4,000,000	9,000,000	14,000,000	20,000,000	24,600,000	30,350,000	36,100,000	43,000,000	48,290,000	54,902,500	61,515,000	69,450,000
Unit Wholesale Revenue, capsules ($/unit)					0.36	0.36	0.36	0.36	0.38	0.38	0.38	0.38	0.40	0.40	0.40	0.40
Total Revenue					7.68	11.04	12.84	16.56	15.76	19.55	21.72	25.94	25.85	30.15	32.77	37.59
Product Development	1.25	1.25	1.25	1.25												
Equipment and Tooling		2.00	2.00													
Production Ramp-up			1.00	1.00												
Marketing and Support				6.25	6.25	1.25	1.25	1.25	1.25	1.25	1.25	1.25	1.25	1.25	1.25	1.25
Production, machines					2.45	3.00	3.00	3.55	2.78	3.41	3.41	4.05	3.16	3.89	3.89	4.61
Production, capsules					0.20	0.45	0.70	1.00	1.23	1.52	1.81	2.15	2.41	2.75	3.08	3.47
Total Costs	1.25	1.25	3.25	10.50	9.90	4.70	4.95	5.80	5.26	6.18	6.47	7.45	6.82	7.88	8.21	9.34
Period Cash Flow	-1.25	-1.25	-3.25	-10.50	-2.22	6.34	7.89	10.76	10.50	13.37	15.25	18.50	19.03	22.26	24.56	28.25
Period Present Value	-1.23	-1.21	-3.09	-9.80	-2.04	5.71	6.99	9.37	8.98	11.24	12.60	15.02	15.19	17.46	18.93	21.41
Net Present Value	**$125.5 million**															

EXHIBIT 18-8 Cash flows and net present value for coffee makers and capsules.

more than 400 capsules per machine per year; however, it is assumed that some machine sales are to existing consumers of the capsules, and thus not all the capsule sales are incremental.) Accordingly we will augment the financial model to include ongoing capsule sales for each coffee maker sold. Capsules cost $0.05/unit to produce and have a retail price of $0.60/unit, a price that is increasing at 5%/year, and the same margins at the retail and distributor levels. These additional base-case model parameters are listed in Exhibit 18-7.

Exhibit 18-8 displays the cash flows and NPV analysis for coffee makers and capsules. The resulting NPV of $125.5M shows that considering the capsule sales has a tremendous impact on the business projection of the AB-100, with a profit almost ten times that of selling machines alone. In fact, the coffee makers could be sold at a financial loss if customers would still purchase the coffee capsules.

Supporting Go/No-Go and Major Investment Decisions

The NPV of this project, according to the base-case model, is positive, so the model supports and is consistent with the decision to proceed with development. This decision would typically be considered at each major project milestone, and in particular at the reviews concluding each project phase.

It is helpful to put the NPV into context of the overall investment budget. In the AB-100 case, to achieve the expected return of $125.5M in NPV, an investment of $17.4M is necessary. This is seen in Exhibit 18-8 as the sum of the negative present values of cash flows for the first five quarters (until the project begins to yield positive cash flow).

This type of financial modeling can also be used to support major investment decisions. Say, for example, that the company was deciding between two different production facilities with different production, equipment, and ramp-up costs. The team could develop a model for each of the two scenarios and then compare the NPVs. The scenario with the higher NPV would be the one with greater profitability. We now consider sensitivity analysis as a technique for readily understanding multiple scenarios for various product development decisions.

Step 2: Perform Sensitivity Analysis

Sensitivity analysis modifies the base-case financial model to answer "what-if" questions by calculating the change in NPV corresponding to a change in specific factors included in the model. Both internal and external factors influence project value. *Internal factors* are those over which the development team has a high degree of influence, including development program expense, development speed, production cost, and product performance. *External factors* are those that the team cannot arbitrarily change, including the competitive environment (e.g., market response, actions of competitors), sales volume, product price, and cost of capital. (There may be disagreement over whether price is an internal or external factor. Nevertheless, there is little disagreement that price is strongly influenced by the prices of competitive products and that it is coupled to sales volume.) While external factors are not directly controlled by the product development team, it is still useful to understand the project's sensitivity to such influences. The external and internal factors are shown in Exhibit 18-9.

Development Cost Example

As a first example, let us consider the sensitivity of NPV to changes in product development cost. By making incremental changes to development cost while holding other factors constant, we can see the incremental impact on project NPV. For example, what will be the change in NPV if development cost is decreased by 20%? This would lower the total development spending from $5M to $4M. If development time remains one year, then the spending per quarter would decrease from $1.25M to $1M.

EXHIBIT 18-9
Key factors influencing product development profitability.

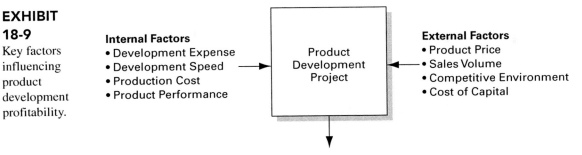

Values in $M *(except where noted)*	Year 1				Year 2				Year 3				Year 4			
	Q1	Q2	Q3	Q4	Q1	Q2	Q3	Q4	Q1	Q2	Q3	Q4	Q1	Q2	Q3	Q4
Sales, machines					6.24	7.80	7.80	9.36	6.46	8.07	8.07	9.69	6.68	8.36	8.36	10.03
Sales Volume, machines (units/qtr)					40,000	50,000	50,000	60,000	46,000	57,500	57,500	69,000	52,900	66,125	66,125	79,350
Unit Wholesale Revenue, machines ($/unit)					156	156	156	156	140	140	140	140	126	126	126	126
Sales, capsules					1.44	3.24	5.04	7.20	9.30	11.47	13.65	16.25	19.17	21.79	24.42	27.56
Sales Volume, capsules (units/qtr)					4,000,000	9,000,000	14,000,000	20,000,000	24,600,000	30,350,000	36,100,000	43,000,000	48,290,000	54,902,500	61,515,000	69,450,000
Unit Wholesale Revenue, capsules ($/unit)					0.36	0.36	0.36	0.36	0.38	0.38	0.38	0.38	0.40	0.40	0.40	0.40
Total Revenue					7.68	11.04	12.84	16.56	15.76	19.55	21.72	25.94	25.85	30.15	32.77	37.59
Product Development	1.00	1.00	1.00	1.00												
Equipment and Tooling		2.00	2.00													
Production Ramp-up				1.00	1.00											
Marketing and Support				6.25	6.25	1.25	1.25	1.25	1.25	1.25	1.25	1.25	1.25	1.25	1.25	1.25
Production, machines					2.45	3.00	3.00	3.55	2.78	3.41	3.41	4.05	3.16	3.89	3.89	4.61
Production, capsules					0.20	0.45	0.70	1.00	1.23	1.52	1.81	2.15	2.41	2.75	3.08	3.47
Total Costs	1.00	1.00	3.00	10.25	9.90	4.70	4.95	5.80	5.26	6.18	6.47	7.45	6.82	7.88	8.21	9.34
Period Cash Flow	-1.00	-1.00	-3.00	-10.25	-2.22	6.34	7.89	10.76	10.50	13.37	15.25	18.50	19.03	22.26	24.56	28.25
Period Present Value	-0.98	-0.97	-2.85	-9.56	-2.04	5.71	6.99	9.37	8.98	11.24	12.60	15.02	15.19	17.46	18.93	21.41
Net Present Value	$126.5 million															

EXHIBIT 18-10   AB-100 financial model with 20% decrease in development spending.

This change is simply entered into the model and the resulting NPV is calculated. This change to the AB-100 base-case model is shown in Exhibit 18-10. In doing so we find that a 20% decrease in product development cost will change NPV to $126.5M. This represents an increase of slightly less than $1M, which is 0.76% of the base NPV. This is an extremely simple case; we assume we can achieve the same project goals by spending $1M less on development, and we therefore have increased the project value by the present value of the $1M in savings accrued over a time period of one year.

The AB-100 product development cost sensitivity analysis for a range of changes is shown in Exhibit 18-11. The values in the table are computed by entering the changes corresponding to each scenario into the base-case model and noting the results. It is often useful to know the absolute dollar changes in NPV as well as the relative percentage changes, so we show both in the sensitivity table.

Change in Product Development Cost, %	Product Development Cost, $M	Change in Product Development Cost, $M	Change in NPV, %	NPV, $M	Change in NPV, $M
50	7.5	2.5	−1.91	123.14	−2.39
20	6.0	1.0	−0.76	124.58	−0.96
10	5.5	0.5	−0.38	125.06	−0.48
base	5.0	base	0	125.54	0
−10	4.5	−0.5	0.38	126.02	0.48
−20	4.0	−1.0	0.76	126.50	0.96
−50	2.5	−2.5	1.91	127.93	2.39

EXHIBIT 18-11   AB-100 product development cost sensitivities.

Development Time Example

As a second example, we calculate the development time sensitivities for the AB-100 model. Consider the impact on project NPV of a 25% increase in development time from four quarters to five quarters. This increase in development time would also delay the start of production ramp-up, marketing efforts, and product sales. To perform the sensitivity analysis, we must make several assumptions about the changes. In this case, we assume the same total amount of development cost, even though we will increase the time period over which the spending occurs, thus lowering the rate of spending from $1.25M to $1.0M per quarter. We also assume that there is a fixed window for sales, which starts as soon as the product enters the market and ends at a fixed date in the future (the fourth quarter of year 4). Note that these assumptions are unique to this development project; other projects would require different assumptions. For example, we might have instead assumed that the sales window simply shifts in time by one quarter. The change to the AB-100 financial model is shown in Exhibit 18-12. We find that a 25% increase in development time will decrease NPV to $110.4M. This represents a decrease of $15.1M, or 12.1% of base NPV.

Exhibit 18-13 presents the development time sensitivities for a range of changes one to two quarters faster or slower than the base case. This analysis also makes certain assumptions regarding the sales window, timing of price increases, and seasonal sales distribution in the partial years. Note the relationship between changes in development time and changes in NPV, and in particular the huge benefit of getting to market early in this case.

Sensitivities can be computed for each of the external and internal factors included in the base-case model. Note that the competitive environment is not explicitly contained in the model, so we would explore sensitivity to competition by considering the effects of pricing and sales volume changes in the model. These sensitivity analyses inform the team about which factors in the model have a substantial influence on NPV. This information is useful in helping the team understand which factors should be studied in more detail to refine and improve the base-case model. The information is also useful in making trade-off decisions, as discussed later.

Values in $M *(except where noted)*	Year 1				Year 2				Year 3				Year 4			
	Q1	Q2	Q3	Q4	Q1	Q2	Q3	Q4	Q1	Q2	Q3	Q4	Q1	Q2	Q3	Q4
Sales, machines						7.80	7.80	9.36	6.46	8.07	8.07	9.69	6.68	8.36	8.36	10.03
Sales Volume, machines (units/qtr)						50,000	50,000	60,000	46,000	57,500	57,500	69,000	52,900	66,125	66,125	79,350
Unit Wholesale Revenue, machines ($/unit)						156	156	156	140	140	140	140	126	126	126	126
Sales, capsules						1.80	3.60	5.76	7.79	9.96	12.13	14.74	17.58	20.20	22.83	25.98
Sales Volume, capsules (units/qtr)						5,000,000	10,000,000	16,000,000	20,600,000	26,350,000	32,100,000	39,000,000	44,290,000	50,902,500	57,515,000	65,450,000
Unit Wholesale Revenue, capsules ($/unit)						0.36	0.36	0.36	0.38	0.38	0.38	0.38	0.40	0.40	0.40	0.40
Total Revenue						9.60	11.40	15.12	14.25	18.03	20.21	24.43	24.26	28.56	31.18	36.00
Product Development	1.00	1.00	1.00	1.00	1.00											
Equipment and Tooling				2.00	2.00											
Production Ramp-up				1.00	1.00											
Marketing and Support				6.25	6.25	1.25	1.25	1.25	1.25	1.25	1.25	1.25	1.25	1.25	1.25	1.25
Production, machines					3.00	3.00	3.55	2.78	3.41	3.41	4.05	3.16	3.89	3.89	4.61	
Production, capsules					0.25	0.50	0.80	1.03	1.32	1.61	1.95	2.21	2.55	2.88	3.27	
Total Costs	1.00	1.00	1.00	3.00	10.25	10.50	4.75	5.60	5.06	5.98	6.27	7.25	6.62	7.68	8.01	9.14
Period Cash Flow	-1.00	-1.00	-1.00	-3.00	-10.25	-0.90	6.65	9.52	9.19	12.05	13.94	17.18	17.64	20.88	23.17	26.87
Period Present Value	-0.98	-0.97	-0.95	-2.80	-9.40	-0.81	5.89	8.29	7.86	10.13	11.52	13.95	14.08	16.37	17.86	20.35
Net Present Value	$110.4 million															

EXHIBIT 18-12   AB-100 financial model with 25% increase in development time.

Change in Product Development Time, %	Product Development Time, Quarters	Change in Product Development Time, Quarters	Change in NPV, %	NPV, $M	Change in NPV, $M
50	6	2	−30.31	87.49	−38.05
25	5	1	−12.06	110.40	−15.14
base	4	base	0	125.54	0
−25	3	−1	13.01	141.87	16.33
−50	2	−2	25.84	157.98	32.44

EXHIBIT 18-13   AB-100 product development time sensitivities.

Understanding Uncertainties

Sensitivity analysis generally reveals that NPV is highly dependent on uncertainties in some base-case input values and less dependent on others. In addition, some of the input values used to compute the base case are more uncertain than others. For example, forecasted sales volume may be more uncertain than estimated unit production cost. By assuming a range of high and low values for any uncertain inputs in the financial analysis, the team can compute a range of predicted values for NPV. The high and low values can be thought of as defining the range within which the team is highly confident the actual outcomes will fall. This analysis can be summarized graphically in a *tornado chart*, showing the effect of each uncertainty on NPV. Parameters are shown in order of decreasing impact, giving the graph its tornado (funnel) shape.

Indeed, some of the input values in the AB-100 base-case analysis are fairly precisely known (e.g., estimated production costs), while other model values are less certain (e.g., sales volume). Uncertainty ranges of key parameter values are given in Exhibit 18-14. Changing these inputs in the model one at a time, holding everything else constant, yields the listed changes in NPV. Exhibit 18-15 shows these results as a tornado chart. As expected, variances of sales volumes and capsule price show the greatest impact on NPV; however, note that while capsule sales provide the vast majority of revenues and profits, several of the largest effects are due to ranges of the coffee machine sales values (because coffee machine sales lead to coffee capsule sales).

Step 3: Use Sensitivity Analysis to Understand Trade-Offs

Why would a product development team want to change the factors under its control? For instance, why should development time be increased if the change lowers the NPV of the project? Typically, the development team will make such a change only if some other offsetting gain is expected, such as a better-quality product with higher sales volumes. We therefore need to understand the relative magnitude of these financial interactions.

Model Parameter	Base-Case Value	Worst-Case Analysis			Best-Case Analysis		
		Value	NPV	% Δ NPV	Value	NPV	% Δ NPV
Product development	$5M	$7M	123.6	−1.5%	$4M	126.5	0.8%
Equipment and tooling	$4M	$5M	124.6	−0.7%	$3M	126.5	0.7%
Production ramp-up	$2M	$2.5M	125.1	−0.4%	$1.5M	126.0	0.4%
Market launch	$10M	$15M	120.9	−3.7%	$8M	127.4	1.5%
Marketing and support	$5M/year	$6M	122.8	−2.2%	$4M	128.3	2.2%
Production direct cost, machines	$55/unit	$60	122.7	−2.3%	$50	128.4	2.3%
Production overhead	$1M/year	$1.2M	125.0	−0.4%	$0.8M	126.0	0.4%
Initial sales volume, machines	200K units/year	100K	44.8	−64.3%	250K	165.9	32.1%
Sales volume growth, machines	15%/year	−5%	105.9	−15.6%	25%	136.1	8.4%
Initial retail sale price, machines	$260/unit	$225	114.7	−8.6%	$295	136.4	8.6%
Retail price growth, machines	−10%/year	−15%	121.2	−3.4%	5%	139.4	11.0%
Production cost, capsules	$0.05/unit	$0.055	123.9	−1.3%	$0.045	127.2	1.3%
Sales volume, capsules per machine	400/year	250	83.4	−33.6%	600	181.7	44.8%
Initial retail price, capsules	$0.60/unit	$0.55	114.8	−8.6%	$0.70	147.1	17.1%
Retail price growth, capsules	5%/year	0%	116.8	−6.9%	5%	125.5	0.0%
Distributor and retail margin	40% combined	50%	90.6	−27.8%	35%	143.0	13.9%

EXHIBIT 18-14 Base-case, worst-case, and best-case values for the model parameters and their effects on the base-case NPV of $125.5M. Note that each case considers changing only one parameter at a time, keeping all others at base-case values.

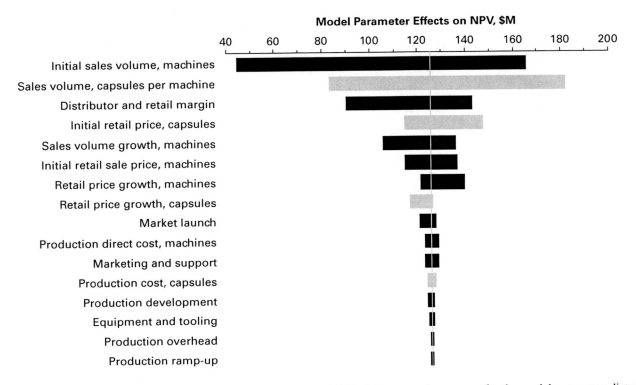

EXHIBIT 18-15 Tornado chart illustrating the effects on NPV of the uncertainty ranges for the model parameters listed in Exhibit 18-14. Dark bars represent machine values. Light bars represent capsule values.

Potential Interactions

Development teams attempt to manage numerous potential interactions between the internally driven factors or with external ones. These interactions are shown schematically in Exhibit 18-16. Coupling between any two factors depends on the characteristics of the specific product and its context. In many cases the interactions are trade-offs. For example, decreasing development time may lead to lower product performance. Increased product performance may require additional product cost; however, some of these interactions are more complex than a simple trade-off. For example, decreasing product development time may require an increase in development spending but may allow the product to reach the market sooner and thus increase sales volume. On the other hand, increasing development cost or time may enhance product performance and therefore increase sales volume and/or allow higher prices.

While accurate modeling of externally driven factors (e.g., price, sales volume) is often very difficult, the quantitative model can nevertheless support critical decisions. Recall from our initial examples that the AB-100 development team was considering increasing development spending to develop a higher-quality product, which they hoped would lead to greater sales volume. The quantitative model can support this decision by answering the question of how much the sales volume would have to increase to justify the additional spending on development. We have calculated the sensitivity of NPV to changes in development cost (Exhibit 18-11). We can also calculate the sensitivity of NPV to changes in sales volume, as shown in Exhibit 18-17.

Say that the AB-100 development team is considering actions that will incur a 20% increase in development cost. From Exhibit 18-11 we found that this increase in spending will decrease NPV by $0.96M. Now, what increase in initial sales volume of coffee makers would be necessary to compensate for the decrease in NPV? From Exhibit 18-17 we know that a 10% increase in sales volume would increase NPV by $16.1M. It follows, under assumptions of linearity, that a 0.60% increase (10% × $0.96M/$16.1M) in initial sales volume to 201,200 units/yr would increase NPV by $0.96M. To summarize, a 20% *increase* in development cost would *decrease* NPV by $0.96M. Merely a 0.60% *increase* in sales volume is needed to offset the drop.

EXHIBIT 18-16

Potential interactions between project factors.

Adapted from Smith, Preston G., and Donald G. Reinertsen, Developing Products in Half the Time: New Rules, New Tools, second edition, Wiley, New York, 1997

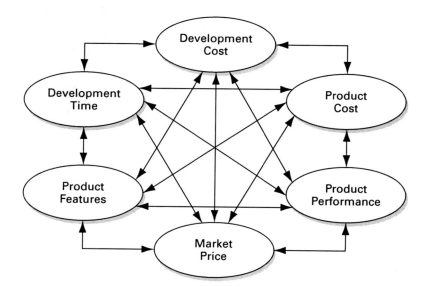

Change in Initial Sales Volume, %	Initial Sales Volume, thousands/year	Change in Initial Sales Volume, thousands/year	Change in NPV, %	NPV, $M	Change in NPV, $M
30	260	60	38.6	174.0	48.4
20	240	40	25.7	157.8	32.3
10	220	20	12.9	141.7	16.1
base	200	base	0	125.5	0
−10	180	−20	−12.9	109.4	−16.1
−20	160	−40	−25.7	93.3	−32.3
−30	140	−60	−38.6	77.1	−48.4

EXHIBIT 18-17   AB-100 sales volume sensitivities.

While the precise impact of the increased development spending on sales volume is not known, the model does provide a helpful guide for what magnitude of sales volume increase is needed to offset particular increases in development cost. Note that these sensitivities are highly project specific. Surely a different product without associated sales of highly profitable consumables would exhibit very different sensitivities and trade-offs.

Trade-Off Rules

The near linearity of many sensitivity analyses allows the team to compute some *trade-off rules* to inform day-to-day decision making. These rules take the form of change in NPV per unit change of the internal and external factors. For example, what is the reduction in NPV due to a one-quarter delay in development time? What is the impact of a 10% development budget overrun? What is the effect of a $1 per unit increase in manufacturing cost? The trade-off rules are easily computed from the financial model and can be used to inform the team of the relative magnitude of the sensitivities of the project profitability on factors (at least partially) under its control. Exhibit 18-18 shows several rules for the AB-100.

The trade-off rules can help answer questions such as the two asked in the chapter introduction.

- *Should the team increase development spending and production cost to add an additional feature, which could lead to greater sales volume?* The feature in question would add 10% to the product development budget and increase production costs by approximately $3/unit. These changes would reduce the expected NPV by $2.2M. To offset this would require only a 1.4% increase in sales of the coffee machines; however, a marketing study concluded that the feature would not likely have a positive effect on overall sales because the feature was already included on other models in the product line.

- *Would the project be profitable if the retail price is reduced by 10% due to competitive pricing pressure?* Dropping the price by 10% would reduce NPV by $8M. While this is significant, the resulting NPV of $117.5M is still highly attractive.

Factor	Trade-Off Rule	Comments
Product development cost	$480,000 per 10% change	Additional funds spent or saved on development is worth the present value of those funds.
Product development time	$16.3M for 1 quarter less −$15.1M for 1 quarter more	This nonlinear trade-off makes specific assumptions about timing of sales and pricing.
Equipment and tooling cost	$376,000 per 10% change	Incremental capital expenditures such as tooling are worth the present value of those expenses.
Production cost, machines	$575,000 per $1 change	A $1 decrease in unit cost raises unit profits margins by the same amount.
Retail price, machines	$310,000 per $1 change	A $1 increase in retail price raises profits by the manufacturer's share, which is 60% of retail.
Sales volume, machines	$1.6M per 1% change	Increasing sales is a powerful way to increase profits. Coffee maker sales also drives sales of coffee capsules.
Capsule consumption per machine	$1.1M per 1% change	Capsule sales make up the largest portion of revenues.

EXHIBIT 18-18   Trade-off rules for the AB-100 project highlight the effects on NPV of various operation factors in the financial model.

Limitations of Quantitative Analysis

Base-case financial modeling and sensitivity analysis are powerful tools for supporting product development decisions, but these techniques have important limitations. One school of thought believes that rigorous financial analyses are required to bring discipline and control to the product development process; however, detractors argue that quantitative analysis suffers from some of the following problems:

- *Analysis focuses only on measurable quantities.* Quantitative techniques like NPV emphasize and rely on that which is measurable; however, many critical factors impacting product development projects are difficult to measure accurately. In effect, quantitative techniques encourage investment in measurable assets and discourage investment in intangible assets.

- *Analysis depends on validity of assumptions and data.* Product development teams may be given a false sense of security by the seemingly precise result of an NPV calculation; however, *such precision in no way implies accuracy.* We can develop a highly sophisticated financial model of a product development project that computes project NPV to the fifth decimal place, yet if the assumptions and data of our model are not correct, the value calculated will not be correct. Consider the AB-100 development time sensitivity example's assumption of a fixed product sales window. This assumption was useful, but its integrity can easily be questioned. Indeed, a different assumption could give dramatically different results.

- *Teams can easily game the analysis.* It has been said that one can achieve any NVP they like by tweaking the model values. This is certainly true. In the AB-100 example, changing all of the model parameters to the best-case or worst-case values would either triple the NPV or make it negative, respectively. This illustrates the necessity for both the team and its managers to understand the model in sufficient depth to challenge the underlying assumptions.

These concerns are generally quite valid; however, in our opinion, they are largely associated with naive application of the methods of the quantitative analysis or arise from the use of financial analysis within a poorly managed product development process. We reject the notion that quantitative analysis should not be done just because problems can arise from the blind application of the results. Rather, development teams should understand the strengths and limitations of the techniques and should be fully aware of how the models work and on what assumptions they are based. Furthermore, qualitative analysis, as discussed in the next section, can remedy some of the inherent weaknesses in the quantitative techniques.

Step 4: Consider the Influence of Qualitative Factors

Many factors influencing development projects are difficult to quantify because they are complex or uncertain. We refer to such factors as *qualitative* factors. After providing a conceptual framework for qualitative analysis, we use examples from the AB-100 to illustrate how the analysis is carried out.

Consider the following questions about the AB-100 project: Will knowledge gained from the AB-100 development spill over and be of benefit to other development projects? How will competitors react to the introduction of the AB-100? Will competitors modify their own product lines in response? Will there be significant fluctuations in the dollar/euro exchange rate that would change the cost of component parts?

Our quantitative model implicitly accounts for these and many other issues with several broad assumptions. The model assumes that decisions made by the project team do not affect actions of groups external to the project, or alternatively that the external forces do not change the team's actions. This important assumption of our model is common to many financial models and is called the *ceteris paribus* (other things being equal) assumption.

Projects Interact with the Firm, the Market, and the Macro Environment

Decisions made within a project in general do have important consequences for the firm as a whole, for competitors and customers in the market, and even for the macroeconomic (macro) environment in which the market operates (Exhibit 18-19). Similarly, events and actions outside of a development project often significantly impact its value. Qualitative analysis focuses largely on these interactions. The most basic approach to qualitative analysis is to consider (1) the interactions between the project and the firm as a whole, (2) the interactions between the project and the market in which the product is sold, and (3) the interactions between the project and the macro environment.

EXHIBIT 18-19
The broader context of a development project.

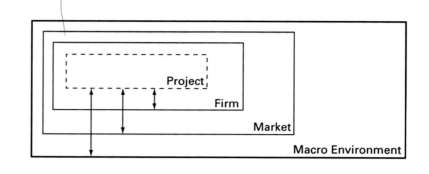

Interactions between the Project and the Firm as a Whole

One assumption embedded in the quantitative model is that firm profit will be maximized if project profit is maximized; however, development decisions must be made in the context of the firm as a whole. The two key interactions between the project and the firm are *externalities* and *strategic fit*.

Externalities   An externality is an "unpriced" cost or benefit imposed on one part of the firm by the actions of another; costs are known as negative externalities and benefits as positive externalities. An example of a positive externality would be development learning on one project that benefits other current or future projects but is paid for by the first project. An example of a negative externality could be cannibalization of sales of existing products due to the launch of the new product. How should projects account for such benefits gained at no additional cost? How should a project account for resources spent that benefit not only itself, but also other current or future projects?

Strategic fit   Decisions of the development team must not only benefit the project, but also be consistent with the firm's overall product plan and technology strategy. For example, how well does a proposed new product, technology, or feature fit with the firm's resources and objectives? Is it compatible with the firm's need to maintain its technical excellence? Is it compatible with the firm's branding emphasis on uniqueness? Even if the project NPV is favorable, does the firm have other projects that (perhaps as a portfolio) offer superior NPV?

Because of their complexity and uncertainty, externalities and strategic fit are very difficult to quantify. Sometimes cross-project externalities are modeled quantitatively using a multi-project NPV analysis, possibly including multiple scenarios; however, generally they are considered qualitatively. See Chapter 4, Product Planning, for discussion of some strategic planning issues that cut across multiple projects. See also Appendix B at the end of this chapter for an overview of scenario analysis using decision trees.

Interactions between the Project and the Market

We have modeled explicitly only price and volume as the key externally driven factors. In effect, we have held the actions and reactions of the market constant. To model project value accurately, we must relax the *ceteris paribus* assumption to recognize that a development team's decisions impact the market and that market events impact the development project. The market environment is impacted by the actions of not only the development team but also three other groups:

- *Competitors:* Competitors may provide products in direct competition or products that compete indirectly as substitutes.
- *Customers:* Customers' expectations, incomes, or tastes may change. Changes may be independent or may be driven by new conditions in markets for complementary or substitute products.
- *Suppliers:* Suppliers of components and resources to the new product are subject to their own markets' competitive pressures. These pressures may, indirectly through the value chain, impact the new product.

Actions and reactions of these groups most often impact expected price and volume, but they can have second-order effects as well. For example, consider a new competitor that has rapid product development cycles and that seems to value market share rather than short-term profitability. Clearly, the entrance of such a new competitor would change our expected price and volume. Further, we may attempt to accelerate our own development efforts in response. Thus, the competitor's actions may impact not only our sales volume forecasts but also our planned development schedule. Often these cases can be considered analytically by simulating a range of market scenarios and their impact on the project.

Interactions between the Project and the Macro Environment
We must relax the *ceteris paribus* assumption to take into account key macro factors:

- *Major economic shifts:* Examples of economic shifts that impact the value of development projects include changes in foreign exchange rates, materials prices, labor costs, consumer disposable incomes, business investment levels, and cost of investment capital.
- *Government regulations:* New regulations can destroy a product development opportunity. On the other hand, a shift in the regulatory structure of an industry can also spawn entire new industries.
- *Social trends:* As with government regulations, new social concerns such as increased environmental awareness can also destroy existing industries and/or create new ones.

Macro factors can have important impacts on development project value; however, these effects are difficult to model quantitatively because of inherent complexity and uncertainty. The product development team for the AB-100 faced many qualitative issues during development of the product. We present two of the key qualitative issues that the team encountered and describe the impacts of these issues on the project. The examples illustrate not only the limitations of quantitative analysis but also the importance of qualitative analysis.

Carrying Out Qualitative Analysis

For most project teams, the most appropriate qualitative analysis method is simply to consider and discuss the interactions between the project and the firm, the project and the market, and the project and the macro environment. Then the team considers these interactions in concert with the results of the quantitative analysis to determine the most appropriate relative emphasis on development speed, development expense, manufacturing cost, and product performance. We provide two examples that follow of the qualitative analysis for the AB-100.

While we believe this informal approach is most appropriate for decisions made at the level of the project team, more structured techniques are available, including strategic analysis, game theory, Monte Carlo simulation, and scenario analysis techniques. References for each of these techniques are included in the bibliography.

Decrease in Price of a Substitute Product

Several competing coffee makers can be considered substitute products for the AB-100. Even though the AB-100 team initially priced the product competitively, after the market introduction a competitor lowered the price of their most similar product. The AB-100 project was faced with a change in the competitive environment caused by market conditions responding to the AB-100.

Here it is clear that the AB-100 project cannot be considered in isolation. The original sales volume assumptions were no longer valid. While this change could not be anticipated with certainty, the quantitative analysis was able to show the sensitivity of NPV to changes in sales volume, and the team was able to quickly grasp the magnitude of the change in project value. The combination of quantitative and qualitative analysis convinced the team to move quickly and to respond by reducing the retail price of the AB-100.

Option Value of a Platform Product

The AB-100 was not the first coffee maker in its product line using the capsule system as a platform. The initial development of the coffee capsules and the key components of the coffee machine was a very large investment. Many of the development decisions made at that time determined the ease with which future generation products could be built around the same basic technological platform. Development of a platform gives the firm the option to produce future models based on market response to the initial products and other future considerations. In some cases it makes sense to invest in a platform even if doing so would not make economic sense in the context of a single product. Success of a platform-based product strategy therefore relies upon not only a suitable product architecture but also consideration of the long-term payback from the resulting product family.

Summary

Economic analysis is a useful tool for supporting decisions made during a product development project and to compute the expected payback time and financial returns.

- The method consists of four steps:

    1. Build a base-case financial model to compute expected profit.
    2. Perform sensitivity analysis to understand the key assumptions of the model.
    3. Use sensitivity analysis to understand project trade-offs.
    4. Consider the influence of qualitative factors on project success.

- Quantitative financial analysis based on NPV is practiced widely in business. The technique forces product development teams to look objectively at their projects and their decisions. At the very least, they must go through the process of creating realistic project schedules and budgets. Financial modeling provides a method for quantitatively understanding the key profit drivers and uncertainties of the project.

- Quantitative techniques such as financial modeling and analysis rest upon assumptions about the external environment. This environment is constantly changing and may be influenced by a development team's decisions or by other uncontrollable factors. Further, quantitative analysis, by its very nature, considers only that which is measurable, yet many key factors influencing the project are highly complex or uncertain and are thus difficult to quantify.

- Qualitative analysis emphasizes the importance of such difficult-to-quantify issues by asking specifically what the interactions are between the project and the rest of the firm, the market, and the macro environment.

- Together, quantitative and qualitative techniques can help ensure that the team makes economically sound development decisions.

References and Bibliography

Many current resources are available on the Internet via
www.ulrich-eppinger.net

For a thorough review of discounted cash flow techniques as well as option theory from a general financial perspective, see the classic text on corporate finance.

Brealey, Richard A., Stewart C. Myers, and Franklin Allen, *Principles of Corporate Finance*, eleventh edition, McGraw-Hill, New York, 2013.

Bayus provides an interesting analysis of trade-offs involving development time and product performance factors.

Bayus, Barry L., "Speed-to-Market and New Product Performance Trade-offs," *Journal of Product Innovation Management*, Vol. 14, 1997, pp. 485–497.

Smith and Reinertsen include a thorough discussion of how to model the economics of development time.

Smith, Preston G., and Donald G. Reinertsen, *Developing Products in Half the Time: New Rules, New Tools*, second edition, Wiley, New York, 1997.

Michael Porter's strategic analysis techniques have become standard fare for business school students. His 1980 text on strategic analysis has been very influential. In his 1985 book, Porter presents a general structured approach to scenario analysis, a technique originally developed by Royal Dutch Shell for planning under uncertainty.

Porter, Michael E., *Competitive Strategy: Techniques for Analyzing Industries and Competitors*, The Free Press, New York, 1980.

Porter, Michael E., *Competitive Advantage: Creating and Sustaining Superior Performance*, The Free Press, New York, 1985.

Game theory can be used to analyze competitive interactions. Oster provides a view of strategic analysis and game theory from a microeconomic perspective.

Oster, Sharon M., *Modern Competitive Analysis*, third edition, Oxford University Press, New York, 1999.

Copeland and Antikarov provide a detailed treatment of real options and analysis of projects with uncertainty and decision points.

    Copeland, Tom, and Vladimir Antikarov, *Real Options: A Practitioner's Guide*, Texere, New York, 2003.

Exercises

1. List five reasons firms may choose to pursue a product even if the quantitative analysis reveals a negative NPV.

2. Build a quantitative model to analyze the development and sale of a bicycle light. Assume that you could sell 20,000 units per year for five years at a sales price (wholesale) of $20 per unit and a manufacturing cost of $10 per unit. Assume that production ramp-up expenses would be $20,000, ongoing marketing and support costs would be $2,000 per month, and development would take another 12 months. How much development spending could such a project justify?

3. Compute the trade-off rules for the case described in Exercise 2.

4. Revise the tornado chart in Exhibit 18-15 to show the effect of an increase in development time. Assume that the minimum change in development time is zero, and the maximum change in development time is an increase of one quarter.

5. Consider the economic impact to the AB-100 project if the coffee capsules are recyclable. Assume that 50% of the capsules are returned, with a scrap material value of $0.001/unit, variable cost to recycle capsules of $0.01/unit, and $500,000 per year fixed costs to operate the recycling program. What increased sales volume would compensate for the cost of this recycling program?

Thought Questions

1. Can you think of successful products that never would have been developed if their creators had relied exclusively on a quantitative financial model to justify their efforts? Do these products share any characteristics?

2. One model of the impact of a delay in product introduction is that sales are simply shifted later in time. Another model is that some of the sales are pushed beyond the "window of opportunity" and are lost forever. Can you suggest other models for the implications of an extension of product development time? Is such an extension ever beneficial?

3. How would you use the quantitative analysis method to capture the economic performance of an entire line of products to be developed and introduced over several years?

4. What are various ways that you could consider in a quantitative analysis the effect of cannibalization of an existing product offered by the same firm?

Appendix A

Time Value of Money and the Net Present Value Technique

This appendix provides a very basic tutorial on net present value for those who are unfamiliar with this concept.

Net present value (NPV) is an intuitive and powerful concept. In essence, NPV is simply a recognition of the fact that a dollar today is worth more than a dollar tomorrow. NPV calculations evaluate the value today *(present value)* of some future income or expense. Say that a bank will give an *interest rate* of 8 percent per time period (the time period could be a month, a quarter, or a year long). If we invest $100 today for one time period at an interest rate of 8 percent, how much will the bank pay out after one time period? If we let r be the interest rate and C be the amount invested, then the amount received after one time period is

$$(1 + r) \times C = (1 + 0.80) \times 100 = (1.08) \times 100 = \$108$$

Thus, if we invest $100 for one time period at an interest rate of 8 percent, we will receive $108 at the end of the time period. In other words, $100 today is worth $108 received in the next time period.

Now, let's say that we have invested some amount, C', for one time period at an interest rate r. Let's also say that after the one time period, the amount received back is $100, and the interest rate is 8 percent. How much, then, was invested originally? We can find C', the original investment, by doing the reverse of what we did in the previous example:

$$(1 + r) \times C' = \$100$$

$$C = \frac{\$100}{1 + r} = \frac{\$100}{1 + 0.08} = \frac{\$100}{1.08} = \$92.59$$

Thus, if we invest $92.59 for one time period at an interest rate of 8 percent, we will receive $100 at the end of the time period. In other words, $92.59 today is worth $100 received in the next time period.

We have just shown how a dollar today is worth more than a dollar tomorrow. Of course, $100 today is worth $100. But what is $100 received *next* time period worth in *today's* dollars? The answer is $92.59 as we showed in the last example. Stated another way, the *present value* of $100 received in the next time period is $92.59 at a *discount rate* of 8 percent. So, present value is the value in today's dollars of some income received or expense paid out in a future period.

Now let's look at the result of investing $100 at 8 percent for longer periods:

One time period: $(1 + r) \times C = (1 + 0.08) \times \$100 = \$108$

Two time periods: $(1 + r) \times (1 + r) \times \$100 = (1 + 0.08)^2 \times \$100 = \$116.64$

Three time periods: $(1 + r) \times (1 + r) \times (1 + r) \times \$100 = (1 + 0.08)^3 \times \$100 = \$125.97$

As we did earlier, let's find the present value of three separate investments of $100 received after one, two, and three time periods:

One time period: $(1 + r) \times C' = \$100$

$$C' = \frac{\$100}{1 + 0.08} = \$92.59$$

The present value of $100 received next time period is $92.59.

Two time periods: $(1 + r) \times (1 + r) \times C' = \$100$

$$C' = \frac{\$100}{(1 + 0.08)^2} = \$85.7$$

The present value of $100 received after two time periods is $85.73.

Three time periods: $(1 + r) \times (1 + r) \times (1 + r) \times C' = \$100$

$$C' = \frac{\$100}{(1 + 0.08)^3} = \$79.38$$

The present value of $100 received after three time periods is $79.38.

We found the present value of these three separate investments. Let's say instead that we had one investment that paid out $100 in each of time periods one, two, and three. What would that investment be worth today? The answer is simply the sum of the individual present values, or $257.70. The sum of the present values is called the *net present value,* or NPV. NPV is the present value of all cash inflows and all cash outflows. The present value of a cash *outflow* is just the negative of a cash *inflow* of the same amount.

We can summarize the present value calculation into a convenient formula. The present value (PV) of an amount C received (or paid out) *t* time periods from now is

$$PV = \frac{C}{(1 + r)^t}$$

Some calculators have a special present value function on them that can do the calculations quickly. Most computer spreadsheet programs have special financial functions that automatically do the present value calculations. The information required for these special functions is the future amount paid out, the interest rate, and the number of time periods of the investment.

What Discount Rate Should We Use?

The discount rate (also called the discount factor or hurdle rate) to use is the interest rate of our own or our company's "opportunity cost of capital." It is called the opportunity cost of capital because it is the return forgone by investing in the project rather than in other in-vestments. Stated another way, the discount factor is the reward that investors demand for accepting delayed payment. A project that has a positive NPV must be earning more than the opportunity cost of capital and is thus a good investment. Note that many firms apply a constant hurdle rate to all their investment decisions. In recent years most firms have been using discount factors of 5 to 15 percent. Large companies generally have an established guideline to determine the discount factor to use in NPV-based analyses. Smaller companies can use their estimated weighted average cost of capital or the rate of return the firm's investors expect. See Brealey and Myers (2013).

Sunk Costs Are Irrelevant for Net Present Value Calculations

In the context of product development decision making, costs that have already been incurred are termed sunk costs. Because sunk costs are past and irreversible outflows, they cannot be affected by present or future decisions, so they should be ignored for NPV calculations. To clarify this point, let's consider an example of the familiar "cut our losses" argument: "We've already spent over $600 million and nine years with no product to show for it, and you want me to approve another $90 million? That's crazy!" While this type of argument might sound logical, in fact the amount of money already spent is not important for the decision of whether or not to spend $90 million more. What is important is how much extra profit will be gained from investing the additional $90 million. Say that the expected profit from product sales is $350 million. Let's look at the NPV of the two options (assume all numbers given are present values):

"Cut Our Losses"		"Invest $90 Million More"	
Additional amount invested:	$0	Additional amount invested:	–$90
Profits from product sales:	0	Profits from product sales:	350
NPV of "cut losses" decision:	$0	NPV of "invest" decision:	$260
Total invested:	–$600	Total invested:	–$690
Total project return:	–$600	Total project return:	–$340

Because the "invest" decision has a positive NPV, the firm should proceed. While it is clear that the firm will lose money on the project in either case, the $600 million already spent is a sunk cost and should not impact the invest-or-cut-losses decision. Of course, the sunk cost argument is a cold analytical perspective; there is a saying that "sunk costs are only relevant to the manager who sunk them." Project managers with a long record of negative total project returns may find that sunk costs are extremely relevant to their ability to get support for future projects.

Appendix B

Modeling Uncertain Cash Flows Using Net Present Value Analysis

Product development projects face many perils. For example, the team may think that the manufacturing cost for a particular new product will be $40 per unit; however, the cost could be much higher or it might even be lower. The team does not

394 *Chapter* 18

know for sure until the product is actually built. The team may forecast sales for the new product, but the forecasts depend on (among other things) when competitors get their versions to the market, and this information will not be available until their products are actually introduced. These uncertainties that are particular to a project are called *project-specific risks*. How should project-specific risks be accounted for? Some development teams increase the discount rate to offset uncertainty about the outcomes; however, such an arbitrary increment in the discount rate would be applied uniformly to both certain and uncertain cash flows. Fortunately, better approaches are available if the team is able to estimate the probabilities of uncertain cash flows.

Instead of using arbitrary adjustments to the discount rate, development teams should strive for realistic forecasting of cash flows. These forecasts can be supplemented with sensitivity analysis to understand the impact of the full range of possible outcomes for the uncertain factors. Project-specific risks should be considered only in the expected cash flows and not in the discount rate.

Sensitivity analysis can be performed by systematically varying the model parameters, such as product price or manufacturing cost, to understand how critically the net present value depends on specific values for these parameters. A basic analysis can be performed one variable at a time, as explained in the body of this chapter, or combinations of variables can be adjusted to form realistic scenarios. A more sophisticated analysis can be performed using Monte Carlo simulation based on assumed probability distributions for the parameters in the model.

Note that there is a second type of risk, *general market risk*, which is not specific to the project. General market risk stems from the fact that there are economywide perils, which threaten all businesses and projects. Although entire books on calculating market risk have been written, for our purposes it suffices to say that market risk is typically accounted for by inflating the discount rate.

Analyzing Scenarios

Sometimes project teams face discrete scenarios that are clearly foreseeable and that will have a direct and significant influence on the project outcome. For example, a team may have filed a patent application on a novel and distinctive product concept. If the patent is allowed, then the team expects to face much less of a competitive threat than if the patent is not allowed. These two scenarios can be modeled as a *decision tree*, as shown in Exhibit 18-20. (In this case, there is not an explicit decision,

EXHIBIT 18-20
A situation in which two discrete scenarios can be envisioned.

$P_a = 60\%$ Patent Allowed $PV_a = \$6,500,000$

Launch Product

$P_b = 40\%$ Patent not Allowed $PV_b = \$1,500,000$

but rather an outcome of an uncertain process. These diagrams are nevertheless called decision trees by convention.) The two branches of this tree represent the two scenarios the team envisions. The present value of the project can be analyzed for each scenario taken independently. The team can also assign a probability to each scenario. Given these inputs, the team can now calculate the expected net present value for the project accounting for the two possible scenarios:

$$NPV = P_a \times PV_a + P_b \times PV_b \quad \text{where } P_a + P_b = 1$$

For the situation depicted by the decision tree shown in Exhibit 18-20,

$$NPV = 0.60 \times \$6,500,000 + 0.40 \times \$1,500,000 = \$4,500,000$$

This kind of analysis is appropriate when discrete and distinct scenarios can be envisioned and when these scenarios have substantially different cash flows.

Analyzing Scenarios with Decision Points

When analyzing product development projects, the team should recognize that most development projects can be discontinued or redirected based on the latest information available. Such decision points may occur at the time of major milestones or reviews. This flexibility to expand or contract a project is financially valuable. The notion of decision points with the ability to change an investment is the subject of an entire field of analysis called *real options*. Copeland and Antikarov (2003) provide a detailed treatment of this subject. Here we provide a way to think about scenarios containing decision points.

Consider the scenario depicted in Exhibit 18-21. A team is contemplating the launch of a product in an entirely new category, which is an inherently risky type of project. The team could just launch the project and hope for success, or it could spend time and money

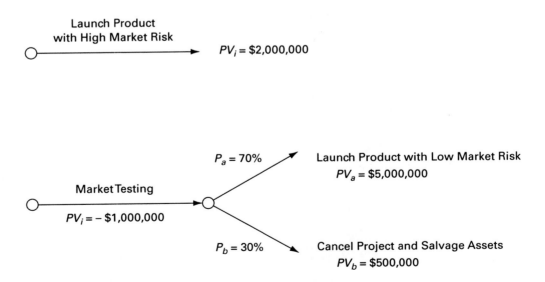

EXHIBIT 18-21   In this situation, the team can either launch the product immediately and face a great deal of market risk or it can test the market and then decide whether to launch the product.

testing the product in the marketplace. If it invests in market testing, the team may discover that the product is not viable, in which case it has the option to cancel the project. Alternatively, it may discover that the market is highly responsive to the new product, in which case it can launch with confidence and a much higher associated expected value of the future cash flows.

As a base case, the team analyzes the value of just launching the product without investigation. Given the team's assessment of the likelihood of success, the present value is $2 million for this plan. The value of market testing followed by a decision to proceed or not can be analyzed as follows. In this case, the team spends an additional $1 million for investigation. After investigation there is a 70 percent chance that the team will launch the product and reap positive cash flow of $5 million. There is a 30 percent chance that the team will decide to cancel the project, reaping only $0.5 million in salvage value. Thus, the net present value of the project is

$$NPV = PV_i + P_a \times PV_a + P_b \times PV_b$$
$$= -\$1,000,000 + 0.70 \times \$5,000,000 + 0.30 \times \$500,000$$
$$= \$2,650,000$$

Based on these estimates, because the net present value exceeds that of just launching the product without testing, the team would be better off spending the $1 million to test the market. There are, of course, many factors that influence a decision about whether to launch a product with high uncertainty or to perform further investigation. Economic modeling can be used as one perspective for informing this kind of decision.

CHAPTER NINETEEN

Managing Projects

Courtesy of Eastman Kodak Company

EXHIBIT 19-1
The Cheetah microfilm cartridge.

A manufacturer of microfilm imaging equipment approached the Eastman Kodak Company to design and supply the microfilm cartridges for use with a new machine under development (Exhibit 19-1). The target specifications were similar to previous products developed by the cartridge group at Kodak; however, in contrast to the usual 24-month development time, the customer needed prototype cartridges for demonstration at a trade show in just 8 months, and production was to begin 4 months later. Kodak accepted this challenge of cutting its normal development time in half and called its efforts the Cheetah project. Effective project management was crucial to the successful completion of the project.

For all but the simplest products, product development involves many people completing many different tasks. Successful product development projects result in high-quality, low-cost products while making efficient use of time, money, and other resources. *Project management* is the activity of planning and coordinating resources and tasks to achieve these goals.

Project management activities occur during *project planning* and *project execution.* Project planning involves scheduling the project tasks and determining resource requirements. The project plan is first laid out during the concept development phase, although it is a dynamic entity and continues to evolve throughout the development process.

Project execution, sometimes called *project control,* involves coordinating and facilitating the myriad tasks required to complete the project in the face of inevitable unanticipated events and the arrival of new information. Execution is just as important as planning; many teams fail because they do not remain focused on their goals for the duration of the project.

This chapter contains five remaining sections. We first present the fundamentals of task dependencies and timing, along with three tools for representing relationships among project tasks. In the second section we show how these principles are used to develop an effective product development plan. In the third section we provide a set of guidelines for completing projects more quickly. After that, we discuss project execution, and finally we present a process for project evaluation and continuous improvement.

Understanding and Representing Tasks

Product development projects involve the completion of hundreds or even thousands of tasks. This section discusses some of the fundamental characteristics of interacting tasks—the "basic physics" of projects. We also present three ways to represent the tasks in a project.

Sequential, Parallel, and Coupled Tasks

Exhibit 19-2 displays the tasks for three portions of the Cheetah project. The tasks are represented by boxes, and the information (data) dependencies among the tasks are represented by arrows. We refer to this representation as an *information-processing view* or a *data-driven perspective* of product development because most of the dependencies involve transfer of information (data) between the tasks. We say that task B is *dependent* on task A if an output of task A is required to complete task B. This dependency is denoted by an arrow from task A to task B.

EXHIBIT 19-2
The three basic
types of task
dependencies:
(a) sequential,
(b) parallel, and
(c) coupled.

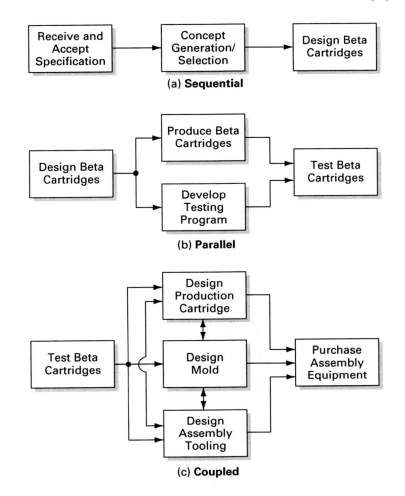

Exhibit 19-2(a) shows three tasks, two of which are dependent on the output of another task. These tasks are *sequential* because the dependencies impose a sequential order in which the tasks must be completed. (Note that when we refer to tasks being "completed" sequentially, we do not necessarily mean that the later task cannot be started before the earlier one has been completed. Generally the later task can begin with partial information but cannot finish until the earlier task has been completed.) Exhibit 19-2(b) shows four development tasks. The middle two tasks depend only on the task on the left, but not on each other. The task on the right depends on the middle two tasks. We call the middle two tasks *parallel* because they are both dependent on the same task but are independent of each other. Exhibit 19-2(c) shows five development tasks, three of which are *coupled*. Coupled tasks are mutually dependent; each task requires the result of the other tasks to be completed. Coupled tasks either must be executed simultaneously with continual exchanges of information or must be carried out in an iterative fashion. When coupled tasks are completed iteratively, the tasks are performed either sequentially or simultaneously with the understanding that the results are tentative and that each task will most likely be repeated one or more times until the team converges on a solution.

400   *Chapter* 19

The Design Structure Matrix

A useful tool for representing and analyzing task dependencies is the *design structure matrix* (DSM). This representation was originally developed by Steward (1981) for the analysis of design descriptions and has more recently been used to analyze development projects modeled at the task level (Eppinger and Browning, 2012). Exhibit 19-3 shows a DSM for the 14 major tasks of the Cheetah project. (Kodak's actual plan included more than 100 tasks.)

In a DSM model, a project task is assigned to a row and a corresponding column. The rows and columns are named and ordered identically, although generally only the rows list the complete names of the tasks. Each task is defined by a row of the matrix. We represent a task's dependencies by placing marks in the columns to indicate the other tasks (columns) on which it depends. Reading across a row reveals all of the tasks whose output is required to perform the task corresponding to the row. Reading down a column reveals which tasks receive information from the task corresponding to the column. The diagonal cells are usually filled in with dots or the task labels, simply to separate the upper and lower triangles of the matrix and to facilitate tracing dependencies.

The DSM is most useful when the tasks are listed in the order in which they are to be executed. In most cases, this order will correspond to the order imposed by sequential dependencies. Note that if only sequentially dependent tasks were contained in the DSM, then the tasks could be sequenced such that the matrix would be lower triangular; that is, no marks would appear above the diagonal. A mark appearing above the diagonal has special significance; it indicates that an earlier task is dependent on a later task. An above-diagonal mark could mean that two sequentially dependent tasks are ordered backward, in which case the order of the tasks can be changed to eliminate the above-diagonal mark; however, when there is no ordering of the tasks that will eliminate an above-diagonal mark, the mark reveals that two or more tasks are coupled.

Changing the order of tasks is called *sequencing* or *partitioning* the DSM. Simple algorithms are available for partitioning DSMs such that the tasks are ordered as much as possible according to the sequential dependencies of the tasks. Inspection of a partitioned DSM reveals which tasks are sequential, which are parallel, and which are coupled and will require simultaneous solution or iteration. In a partitioned DSM, a task is part of a sequential group if its row contains a mark just below the diagonal. Two or more tasks are parallel if there are no marks linking them. As noted, coupled tasks are

EXHIBIT 19-3

Simplified design structure matrix for the Kodak Cheetah project.

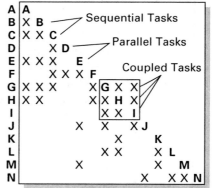

identified by above-diagonal marks. Exhibit 19-3 shows how the DSM reveals all three types of relationships.

More sophisticated use of the DSM method has been a subject of research at MIT since the 1990s. Much of this work has applied the method to larger projects and to the development of complex systems such as automobiles and airplanes. Analytical methods have been developed to help understand the effects of complex task coupling, to predict the distribution of possible project completion times and costs, and to help plan organization designs based on product architectures (Eppinger and Browning, 2012).

DSM practitioners have found that creative uses of the DSM's graphical display of project task relationships can be highly insightful for project managers in both the planning and execution phases. The chapter appendix presents a larger DSM model in which several overlapping phases of coupled development activities are represented.

Gantt Charts

The traditional tool for representing the timing of tasks is the Gantt chart. Exhibit 19-4 shows a Gantt chart for the Cheetah project. The chart contains a horizontal time line created by drawing a horizontal bar representing the start and end of each task. The filled-in portion of each bar represents the fraction of the task that is complete. The vertical line in Exhibit 19-4 shows the current date, so we can observe directly that task D is behind schedule, while task E is ahead of schedule.

A Gantt chart does not explicitly display the dependencies among tasks. Task dependencies constrain, but do not fully determine, the timing of the tasks. The dependencies dictate which tasks must be completed before others can begin (or finish, depending on the nature of the dependency) and which tasks can be completed in parallel. When two

EXHIBIT 19-4 Gantt chart for the Cheetah project.

tasks overlap in time on a Gantt chart, they may be parallel, sequential, or iteratively coupled. Parallel tasks can be overlapped in time for convenience in project scheduling because they do not depend on one another. Sequential tasks might be overlapped in time, depending on the exact nature of the information dependency, as described later in the section on accelerating projects. Coupled tasks must be overlapped in time because they need to be addressed simultaneously or in an iterative fashion.

PERT Charts

PERT (program evaluation and review technique) charts explicitly represent both dependencies and timing, in effect combining some of the information contained in the DSM and Gantt chart. While there are many forms of PERT charts, we prefer the "activities on nodes" form of the chart, which corresponds to the process diagrams that most people are familiar with. The PERT chart for the Cheetah project is shown in Exhibit 19-5. The blocks in the PERT chart are labeled with both the task and its expected duration. Note that the PERT representation does not allow for loops or feedback and so cannot explicitly show iterative coupling. As a result, the coupled tasks G, H, and I are grouped together into one task. The graphical convention of PERT charts is that all links between tasks must proceed from left to right, indicating the temporal sequence in which tasks can be completed. When the blocks are sized to represent the duration of tasks, as in a Gantt chart, then a PERT diagram can also be used to represent a project schedule.

The Critical Path

The dependencies among the tasks in a PERT chart, some of which may be arranged sequentially and some of which may be arranged in parallel, lead to the concept of a *critical path*. The critical path is the longest chain of dependent events. This is the single sequence of tasks whose combined required times define the minimum possible completion

EXHIBIT 19-5
PERT chart for the Cheetah project. The critical path is designated by the thicker lines connecting tasks. Note that tasks G, H, and I are grouped together because the PERT representation does not depict coupled tasks explicitly.

A	Receive & accept specification	H	Design mold
B	Concept generation/selection	I	Design assembly tooling
C	Design beta cartridges	J	Purchase assembly equipment
D	Produce beta cartridges	K	Fabricate molds
E	Develop testing program	L	Debug molds
F	Test beta cartridges	M	Certify cartridge
G	Design production cartridge	N	Initial production run

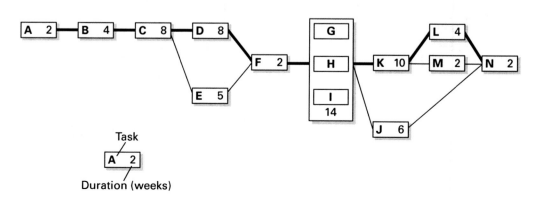

time for the entire set of tasks. Consider for example the Cheetah project represented in Exhibit 19-5. Either the sequence C-D-F or the sequence C-E-F defines how much time is required to complete the four tasks C, D, E, and F. In this case, the path C-D-F requires 18 weeks and the path C-E-F requires 15 weeks, so the critical path for the whole project includes C-D-F. The critical path for the project is denoted by the thick lines in Exhibit 19-5. Identifying the critical path is important because a delay in any of these *critical tasks* would result in an increase in project duration. All other paths contain some *slack,* meaning that a delay in one of the noncritical tasks does not necessarily create a delay for the entire project. Exhibit 19-4 shows that task D is behind schedule. Because task D is on the critical path, this delay, if not corrected, will result in a delay of the completion of the entire project.

Several software packages are available for producing Gantt charts and PERT charts; these programs can also compute the critical path.

Baseline Project Planning

The project plan is the roadmap for the remaining development effort. The plan is important in coordinating the remaining tasks and in estimating the required development resources and development time. Some measure of project planning occurs at the earliest stages of product development, but the importance of the plan is highest at the end of the concept development phase, just before significant development resources are committed. This section presents a method for creating a *baseline project plan.* After establishing this baseline, the team considers whether it should modify the plan to change the planned development time, budget, or project scope. The results of the concept development phase plus the project plan make up the *contract book.*

The Contract Book

We recommend that a contract book be used to document the project plan and the results of the concept development phase of the development process. The concept of a contract book is detailed by Wheelwright and Clark (1992). The word *contract* is used to emphasize that the document represents an agreement between the development team and the senior management of the company about project goals, direction, and resource requirements. The book is sometimes actually signed by the key team members and the senior managers of the company. A table of contents for a contract book is shown in Exhibit 19-6, along with references to the chapters in this book where some of these contents are discussed.

Later we discuss elements of the project plan: the project task list, team staffing and organization, the project schedule, the project budget, and the project risk areas.

Project Task List

We have already introduced the idea that a project consists of a collection of tasks. The first step in planning a project is to list the tasks that make up the project. For most product development projects the team will not be able to list every task in great detail; too much uncertainty remains in the subsequent development activities; however, the team will be able to list its best estimate of the remaining tasks at a general level of detail. To be most useful during project planning, the task list should contain from 50 to 200 items.

404 *Chapter* 19

EXHIBIT 19-6
Table of contents of a contract book for a project of moderate complexity.

Item	Approximate Pages	See Chapter(s)
Mission Statement	1	4
Customer Needs List	1–2	5
Competitive Analysis	1–2	3, 4, 5, 8, 9
Product Specifications	1–3	6
Sketches of Product Concept	1–2	7, 11
Concept Test Report	1–2	9
Sales Forecast	1–3	9, 18
Economic Analysis/Business Case	1–3	18
Environmental Impact Assessment	1–2	12
Manufacturing Plan	1–5	13
Project Plan		
Task List	1–5	2, 19
Design Structure Matrix	2–3	19
Team Staffing and Organization	1	2, 19
Schedule (Gantt and/or PERT)	1–2	19
Budget	1	19
Risk Plan	1	19
Project Performance Measurement Plan	1	19
Incentives	1	19
	Total 19–40 Pages	

For small projects, such as the development of a hand tool, each task may correspond, on average, to a day or two of work for a single individual. For medium-sized projects, such as the development of a computer printer, each task may correspond to a week of work for a small group of people. For a large project, such as the development of an automobile, each task may correspond to one or more months of efforts for an entire division or subteam. For large projects, each of the tasks identified at this level may be treated as its own development project with its own project plan.

An effective way to tackle the generation of the task list is to consider the tasks in each of the remaining phases of development. For our generic development process, the phases remaining after concept development are system-level design, detail design, testing and refinement, and production ramp-up. (See Chapter 2, Development Processes and Organizations.) In some cases, the current effort will be very similar to a previous project. In these cases, the list of tasks from the previous project is a good starting point for the new task list. The Cheetah project was very similar to dozens of previous efforts. For this reason, the team had no trouble identifying the project tasks. (Its challenge was to complete them quickly.)

After listing all of the tasks, the team estimates the effort required to complete each task. Effort is usually expressed in units of person-hours, person-days, or person-weeks, depending on the size of the project. Note that these estimates reflect the "actual working time" that members of the development team would have to apply to the task and not the "elapsed calendar time" the team expects the task to require. Because the speed with which a task is completed has some influence on the total amount of effort that must be applied to the task, the estimates embody preliminary assumptions about the overall project schedule and how quickly the team will attempt to complete tasks. These estimates are typically derived from past experience or the judgment of experienced members of the development team. A task list for the Cheetah project is shown in Exhibit 19-7.

EXHIBIT 19-7
Task list for the
Cheetah project.
(This task list is
abbreviated for
clarity; the
actual list
contained over
100 tasks.)

Task	Estimated Person-Weeks
Concept Development	
Receive and accept specification	8
Concept generation/selection	16
Detail Design	
Design beta cartridges	62
Produce beta cartridges	24
Develop testing program	24
Testing and Refinement	
Test beta cartridges	20
Design production cartridge	56
Design mold	36
Design assembly tooling	24
Purchase assembly equipment	16
Fabricate molds	16
Debug molds	24
Certify cartridge	12
Production Ramp-up	
Initial production run	16
Total	**354**

Team Staffing and Organization

The project team is the collection of individuals who complete project tasks. Whether or not this team is effective depends on a wide variety of individual and organizational factors. Smith and Reinertsen (1997) propose seven criteria as determinants of the speed with which a team will complete product development; in our experience these criteria predict many of the other dimensions of team performance as well:

1. There are 10 or fewer members of the team.
2. Members volunteer to serve on the team.
3. Members serve on the team from the time of concept development until product launch.
4. Members are assigned to the team full-time.
5. Members report directly to the team leader.
6. The key functions, including at least marketing, design, and manufacturing, are on the team.
7. Members are located within conversational distance of each other.

While few teams are staffed and organized ideally, these criteria raise several key issues: How big should the team be? How should the team be organized relative to the larger enterprise? Which functions should be represented on the team? How can the development team of a very large project exhibit some of the agility of a small team? Here we address the issues related to team size. Chapter 1, Introduction, and Chapter 2, Development Processes and Organizations, address some of the other team and organizational issues.

The minimum number of people required on the project team can be estimated by dividing the total estimated time to complete the project tasks by the planned project duration. For example, the estimated task time for the Cheetah project was 354 person-weeks. The team hoped to complete the project in 12 months (or about 50 weeks), so the minimum possible team size would be seven people. All other things being equal, small teams seem to be more efficient than large teams, so the ideal situation would be to have a team made up of the minimum number of people, each dedicated 100 percent to the project.

Three factors make realizing this ideal difficult. First, specialized skills are often required to complete the project. For example, one of the Cheetah tasks was to design molds. Mold designers are highly specialized, and the team could not use a mold designer for a full year. Second, one or more key team members may have other unavoidable responsibilities. For example, one of the engineers on the Cheetah project was responsible for assisting in the production ramp-up of a previous project. As a result, she was only able to commit half of her time to the Cheetah project initially. Third, the work required to complete tasks on the project is not constant over time. In general, the work requirement increases steadily until the beginning of production ramp-up and then begins to taper off. As a result, the team will generally have to grow in size as the project progresses to complete the project as quickly as possible.

After considering the need for specialized skills, the reality of other commitments of the team members, and the need to accommodate an increase and subsequent decrease in workload, the project leader, in consultation with his or her management, identifies the full project staff and approximately when each person will join the team. When possible, team members are identified by name, although in some cases they will be identified only by area of expertise (e.g., mold designer, industrial designer). The project staffing for the Cheetah project is shown in Exhibit 19-8.

Project Schedule

The project schedule is the merger of the project tasks and the project time line. The schedule identifies when major project milestones are expected to occur and when each project task is expected to begin and end. The team uses this schedule to track progress

Person	Month:	1	2	3	4	5	6	7	8	9	10	11	12
Team Leader		100	100	100	100	100	100	100	100	100	100	100	100
Schedule Coordinator		25	25	25	25	25	25	25	25	25	25	25	25
Customer Liaison		50	50	50	50	25	25	25	25	25	25	25	25
Mechanical Designer 1		100	100	100	100	100	100	100	100	50	50	50	50
Mechanical Designer 2			50	100	100	100	100	100	100	50			
CAD Technician 1			50	100	100	100	100	100	100	100	50	50	50
CAD Technician 2					50	100	100	100	100	100	50		
Mold Designer 1		25	25	25	25	100	100	100	100	25	25	25	
Mold Designer 2						100	100	100	100				
Assembly Tool Designer		25	25	25	25	100	100	100	100	100	100	50	50
Manufacturing Engineer		50	50	100	100	100	100	100	100	100	100	100	100
Purchasing Engineer			50	50	100	100	100	100	100	100	100	100	100

EXHIBIT 19-8   Project staffing for the Cheetah project. Numbers shown are approximate percentages of full time.

and to orchestrate the exchange of materials and information between individuals. It is therefore important that the schedule is viewed as credible by the entire project team.

We recommend the following steps to create a baseline project schedule:

1. Use the DSM or PERT chart to identify the dependencies among tasks.
2. Position the key project milestones along a time line in a Gantt chart.
3. Schedule the tasks, considering the project staffing and other critical resources.
4. Adjust the timing of the milestones to be consistent with the time required for the tasks.

Project milestones are useful as anchor points for the scheduling activity. Common milestones include design reviews (also called phase reviews or design gates), comprehensive prototypes (e.g., alpha prototype, beta prototype), and trade shows. Because these events typically require input from almost everyone on the development team, they serve as powerful forces for integration and act as anchor points on the schedule. Once the milestones are laid out on the schedule, the tasks can be arranged between these milestones.

The Cheetah schedule was developed by expanding the typical project phases into a set of approximately 100 tasks. The major milestones were the concept approval, the testing of beta prototype cartridges, the trade show demonstration, and production ramp-up. Relationships among these activities and the critical path were documented using a combined PERT/Gantt chart.

Project Budget

Budgets are customarily represented with a simple spreadsheet, although many companies have standard budgeting forms for requests and approvals. The major budget items are staff, materials and services, project-specific facilities, and spending on outside development resources.

For most projects the largest budget item is the cost of staff. For the Cheetah project, personnel charges made up 80 percent of the total budget. The personnel costs can be derived directly from the staffing plan by applying the *loaded* salary rates to the estimated time commitments of the staff on the project. Loaded salaries include employee benefits and overhead and are typically between two and three times the actual salary of the team member. Many companies use only one or two different rates to represent the cost of the people on a project. Average staff costs for product development projects range from $2,000 to $5,000 per person-week. For the Cheetah project, assuming an average cost of $3,000 per person-week, the total cost for the 354 person-weeks of effort would be $1,062,000.

Early in the development project, uncertainty of both timing and costs are high, and the forecasts may only be accurate within 30 to 50 percent. In the later stages of the project the program uncertainty is reduced to perhaps 5 percent to 10 percent. For this reason some margin should be added to the budget as a contingency. A summary of the Cheetah project budget is shown in Exhibit 19-9.

Project Risk Plan

Projects rarely proceed exactly according to plan. Some of the deviations from the plan are minor and can be accommodated with little or no impact on project performance. Other deviations can cause major delays, budget overruns, poor product performance, or high manufacturing costs. Often the team can assemble, in advance, a list of what might go wrong, that is,

Item		Amount
Staff salaries		
354 person-weeks @ $3,000/week		$1,062,000
Materials and Services		125,000
Prototype Molds		75,000
Outside Resources, Consultants		25,000
Travel		50,000
	Subtotal	$1,337,000
	Contingency (20%)	$267,400
	Total	$1,604,400

EXHIBIT 19-9   Summary budget for the Cheetah project. The production tooling and equipment are accounted for as manufacturing costs rather than as part of the development project budget. (Kodak figures are disguised and listed here only for illustration.)

EXHIBIT 19-10

Risk plan for the Cheetah project.

Risk	Risk Level	Actions to Minimize Risk
Change in customer specifications	Moderate	• Involve the customer in process of refining specifications. • Work with the customer to estimate time and cost penalties of changes.
Poor feeding characteristics of cartridge design	Low	• Build early functional prototype from machined parts. • Test prototype in microfilm machine.
Delays in mold-making shop	Moderate	• Reserve 25% of shop capacity for May–July.
Molding problems require rework of mold	High	• Involve mold maker and mold designer in the part design. • Perform mold filling computer analysis. • Establish design rules for part design. • Choose materials at end of concept development phase.

the areas of risk for the project. To identify risks the team asks what uncertainties could affect the project's technical, financial, and schedule performance. Uncertainties may relate to task timing, technical developments, market acceptance, material costs, competition, and so on.

After identifying each risk, the team can prioritize the risks. To do so, some teams use a scale combining severity and likelihood of each risk. A complete risk plan also includes a list of actions the team will take to minimize the risk. It is good project management practice to address the biggest risks as early as possible in the project. This is done by scheduling early actions to reduce the uncertainty underlying the high risks that have been identified. In addition to pushing the team to work to minimize risk, the explicit focus on risk during the project planning activity helps to minimize the number of surprises the team will have to communicate to its senior management later in the project. The risk plan for the Cheetah project is shown in Exhibit 19-10.

Modifying the Baseline Plan

The baseline project plan embodies assumptions about how quickly the project should be completed, about the performance and cost goals for the product, and about the resources to be applied to the project. After completing a baseline plan, the team should consider whether some of these assumptions should be revisited. In particular, the team can usually choose to trade off development time, development cost, product manufacturing cost, product performance, and risk. For example, a project can sometimes be completed more quickly by spending more money. Some of these trade-offs can be explored quantitatively using the economic analysis techniques described in Chapter 18, Product Development Economics. The team may also develop contingency plans in case certain risks cannot be overcome. The most common desired modification to the baseline plan is to compress the schedule. For this reason, we devote the next section to ways the team can accelerate the project.

Accelerating Projects

Product development time is often the dominant concern in project planning and execution. This section provides a set of guidelines for accelerating product development projects. Most of these guidelines are applicable at the project planning stage, although a few can be applied throughout a development project. Accelerating a project before it has begun is much easier than trying to expedite a project that is already under way.

The first set of guidelines applies to the project as a whole.

- *Start the project early.* Saving a month at the beginning of a project is just as helpful as saving a month at the end of a project, yet teams often work with little urgency before development formally begins. For example, the meeting to approve a project plan and review a contract book is often delayed for weeks because of difficulty in scheduling a meeting with senior managers. This delay at the beginning of a project costs exactly as much time as the same delay during production ramp-up. The easiest way to complete a project sooner is to start it early.

- *Manage the project scope.* There is a natural tendency to add additional features and capabilities to the product as development progresses. Some companies call this phenomenon "feature creep" or "creeping elegance," and in time-sensitive contexts it may result in an elegant product without a market. Disciplined teams and organizations are able to "freeze the design" and leave incremental improvements for the next generation of the product.

- *Facilitate the exchange of essential information.* As shown in the DSM representation, a tremendous amount of information must be transferred within the product development team. Every task has one or more internal customers for the information it produces. For small teams, frequent exchange of information is quite natural and is facilitated by team meetings and colocation of team members. Larger teams may require more structure to promote rapid and frequent information exchange. Blocks of coupled tasks revealed by the DSM identify the specific needs for intensive information exchange. Computer networks and collaboration software tools can facilitate regular information transfer within large and dispersed product development teams.

The second set of guidelines is aimed at decreasing the time required to complete the tasks on the critical path. These guidelines arise from the fact that the only way to reduce the time required to complete a project is to shorten the critical path. Note that a decision to allocate additional resources to shortening the critical path should be based on the value of accelerating the entire project. For some projects, time reductions on the critical path can be worth hundreds of thousands, or even millions, of dollars per week.

- *Complete individual tasks on the critical path more quickly.* The benefit of recognizing the critical path is that the team can focus its efforts on this vital sequence of tasks. The critical path generally represents only a small fraction of the total project effort, and so additional spending on completing a critical task more quickly can usually quite easily be justified. Sometimes completing critical tasks more quickly can be achieved simply by identifying a task as critical so that it gets special attention, starts earlier, and is not interrupted. Note that the accelerated completion of a critical task may cause the critical path to shift to include previously noncritical tasks.

- *Aggregate safety times.* The estimated duration of each task in the project generally includes some amount of "safety time." This time accounts for the many normal but unpredictable delays that occur during the execution of each task. Common delays include: waiting for information and approvals, interruptions from other tasks or projects, and tasks being more difficult than anticipated. Goldratt (1997) estimates that built-in safety doubles the nominal duration of tasks. Although safety time is added to the expected task duration to account for random delays, these estimates become targets during execution of the tasks, which means that tasks are rarely completed early and many tasks overrun. Goldratt recommends removing the safety time from each task along the critical path and aggregating all of the safety time from the critical path into a single *project buffer* placed at the end of the project schedule. Because the need to extend task duration occurs somewhat randomly, only some of the tasks will actually need to utilize time from the project buffer. Therefore, a single project buffer can be smaller than the sum of the safety times that would be included in each estimate of task duration, and the critical path may be completed sooner. In practice, the project buffer may only need to start with time equal to half of the shortened critical path duration. Goldratt has developed these ideas into a project management method called *Critical Chain.* In addition to the project buffer, the method uses *feeder buffers* to protect the critical path from delays where noncritical tasks feed into the critical path. Each feeder buffer aggregates the safety times of the tasks on a noncritical path. Exhibit 19-11 illustrates the use of project and feeder buffers.

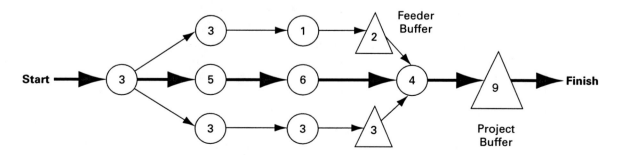

EXHIBIT 19-11   The Critical Chain method aggregates the safety time along the critical path into the project buffer. Feeder buffers protect the critical path from delays. In this illustration, nominal task durations (in days) are given for each task, and the critical path is shown with thicker arrows linking the critical tasks.

- *Eliminate some critical path tasks entirely.* Scrutinize each and every task on the critical path and ask whether it can be removed or accomplished in another way.
- *Eliminate waiting delays for critical path resources.* Tasks on the critical path are sometimes delayed by waiting for a busy resource. The waiting time is frequently longer than the actual time required to complete the task. Delays due to waiting are particularly prominent when procuring special components from suppliers. Sometimes such delays can be avoided by ordering an assortment of materials and components to be sure to have the right items on hand, or by purchasing a fraction of the capacity of a vendor's production system to expedite the fabrication of prototype parts. These expenses may make perfect economic sense in the context of the overall development project, even though the expenditure may seem extravagant when viewed in isolation. In other cases, administrative tasks such as purchase order approvals may become bottlenecks. Because in past cartridge development projects periodic budget approvals had caused delays, the Cheetah project leader began early to pursue aggressively the necessary signatures so as not to hold up the activities of the entire team.
- *Overlap selected critical tasks.* By scrutinizing the relationships between sequentially dependent tasks on the critical path, the tasks can sometimes be overlapped or executed in parallel. In some cases, this may require a significant redefinition of the tasks or even changes to the architecture of the product. (See Chapter 10, Product Architecture, for more details on dependencies arising from the architecture of the product.) In other cases, overlapping entails simply transferring partial information earlier and/or more frequently between nominally sequential tasks or freezing the critical upstream information earlier. Krishnan (1996) provides a framework for choosing various overlapping strategies.
- *Pipeline large tasks.* The strategy of *pipelining* is applied by breaking up a single large task into smaller tasks whose results can be passed along as soon as they are completed. For example, the process of finding and qualifying the many vendors that supply the components of a product can be time-consuming and can even delay the production ramp-up if not completed early enough. Instead of waiting until the entire bill of materials is complete before the purchasing department begins qualifying vendors, purchasing could qualify vendors as soon as each component is identified. Pipelining in effect allows nominally sequential tasks to be overlapped.
- *Outsource some tasks.* Project resource constraints are common. When a project is constrained by available resources, assigning tasks to an outside firm or to another group within the company may prove effective in accelerating the overall project.

The final set of guidelines is aimed at completing coupled tasks more quickly. Recall that coupled tasks are those that must be completed simultaneously or iteratively because they are mutually dependent.

- *Perform more iterations quickly.* Much of the delay in completing coupled tasks is in passing information from one person to another and in waiting for a response. If the iteration cycles can be completed at a higher frequency, then the coupled tasks can sometimes be completed more quickly. Faster iterations can be achieved through faster and more frequent information exchanges. In the Cheetah project, the mechanical engineer would work closely with the mold designer, who would in turn work closely with the mold maker. In many cases, these three would share a single computer display

412 *Chapter* 19

for the purpose of exchanging ideas about how the design was evolving from their three different perspectives.

- *Decouple tasks to avoid iterations.* Iterations can often be reduced or eliminated by taking actions to decouple tasks. For example, by clearly defining an interface between two interacting components early in the design process, the subsequent design of the two components can proceed independently and in parallel. The definition of the interface may take some time in advance, but the avoidance of time-consuming iterations may result in net time savings. (See Chapter 10, Product Architecture, for a discussion of establishing interfaces to allow the independent development of components.)

- *Consider sets of solutions.* Iterations involve the exchange of information about the evolving product design. Rather than exchanging point-value estimates of design parameters, in some cases the use of ranges or sets of values may facilitate faster convergence of coupled tasks. Researchers have recently described the application of such set-based approaches to concurrent engineering at Toyota (Sobek et al., 1999).

Project Execution

Smooth execution of even a well-planned project requires careful attention. Three problems of project execution are particularly important: (1) What mechanisms can be used to coordinate tasks? (2) How can project status be assessed? and (3) What actions can the team take to correct for undesirable deviations from the project plan? We devote this section to these issues.

Coordination Mechanisms

Coordination among the activities of the different members of the team is required throughout a product development project. The need for coordination is a natural outgrowth of dependencies among tasks. Coordination needs also arise from the inevitable changes in the project plan caused by unanticipated events and new information. Difficulties in coordination can arise from inadequate exchanges of information and from organizational barriers to cross-functional cooperation. Here are several mechanisms used by teams to address these difficulties and facilitate coordination.

- *Informal communication:* A team member engaged in a product development project may communicate with other team members dozens of times per day. Many of these communications are informal; they involve a spontaneous stop by someone's desk, a telephone call, or e-mail to request or provide a piece of information. Good informal communication is one of the mechanisms most useful in breaking down individual and organizational barriers to cross-functional cooperation. While professionals today are generally comfortable interacting with collaborators around the globe, informal communication is dramatically enhanced by locating the core members of the development team in the same work space. Allen (2007) has shown that communication frequency is inversely related to physical separation and falls off rapidly when people are located more than a few meters from one another (Exhibit 19-12). In our experience, e-mail and, to a lesser extent, voice mail also provide effective means of fostering informal communication among people who are already well acquainted with one another.

- *Meetings:* The primary formal communication mechanism for project teams is meetings. Most teams meet formally at least once each week. Many teams meet twice each week, and some teams meet every day. Teams located in the same work space need

**EXHIBIT
19-12**

Communication
frequency versus
separation
distance. This
relationship
shown is for
individuals with
an organizational
bond, such as
belonging to the
same product
development
team.

Source: Based on
Allen, Thomas J., and
Gunter W. Henn, The
Organization and
Architecture of
Innovation: Managing
the Flow of
Technology, Elsevier,
Burlington, MA, 2007

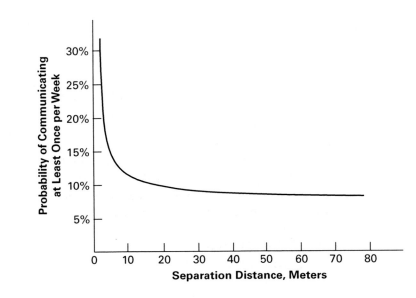

fewer formal meetings than those whose members are geographically separated. Time spent exchanging information in meetings is time not spent completing other project tasks. To minimize the amount of time wasted in meetings, some teams that hold frequent meetings meet standing up to emphasize that the meeting is intended to be quick. Other techniques for controlling the length of meetings include preparing a written agenda, appointing someone to run the meeting, and holding the meeting just before lunchtime or near the end of the day when people are anxious to leave. We recommend that team meetings be held at a regular time and place so that no extra effort is expended in scheduling the meeting and in informing the team of its time and location.

- *Schedule display:* The most important information system in project execution is the project schedule, usually in the form of a PERT or Gantt chart. Most successful projects have a single person who is responsible for monitoring the schedule. On small projects, this is usually the team leader. Larger projects generally have a designated person other than the project leader who watches and updates the schedule regularly. On the Cheetah project, Kodak provided a part-time project analyst who kept the schedule current on a weekly basis and reported to the project team leader. The team members understood the importance of accurate schedule projections and were very cooperative in this effort. Schedule updates are usually displayed in Gantt chart form (Exhibit 19-4).

- *Weekly updates:* The *weekly status memo* is written by the project leader and is distributed on paper, by e-mail, or even by voice mail to the entire extended project team, usually on Friday or over the weekend. The memo is usually one or two pages long and lists the key accomplishments, decisions, and events of the past week. It also lists the key events of the coming week. It is sometimes accompanied by an updated schedule.

- *Incentives:* Some of the most basic organizational forms, such as functional organizations that use functional performance reviews, may inhibit the productive collaboration of team members across functions. The implementation of project-based performance measures creates incentives for team members to contribute more fully to the project. Having both a project manager and a functional manager contribute to individual performance reviews leading to promotions, merit increases, and bonuses sends a strong message that project results are highly valued. (See Chapter 2, Development Processes and Organizations, for a discussion of various organizational forms, including project, functional, and matrix organizations.)

- *Process documents:* Each of the methods presented in this book also has an associated information system that assists the project team in making decisions and provides documentation. (By information systems we mean all of the structured means the team uses to exchange information, not only the computer systems used by the team.) For example, the concept selection method uses two concept selection matrices to both document and facilitate the selection process. Similarly, each of the other information systems serves both to facilitate the logical execution of the process step and to document its results. Exhibit 19-13 lists some of the important information systems used at the various stages of the development process.

Assessing Project Status

Project leaders and senior managers need to be able to assess project status to know whether corrective actions are warranted. In projects of modest size (say, fewer than 50 people) project leaders are fairly easily able to assess the status of the project. The project leader assesses project status during formal team meetings, by reviewing the project schedule, and by gathering information in informal ways. The leader constantly interacts with the project team, meets regularly with individuals to work through difficult problems, and is able to observe all of the information systems of the project. A team may also engage an expert from outside the core team to review the status of the project. The goal of these reviews is to highlight areas of risk and to generate ideas for addressing these risk areas.

Project reviews, conducted by senior managers, are another common method of assessing progress. These reviews tend to correspond to the end of each phase of development and are key project milestones. These events serve not only to inform senior managers of the status of a project but also to bring closure to a wide variety of development tasks. While these reviews can be useful milestones and can enhance project performance, they can also hinder performance. Detrimental results arise from devoting too much time to preparing formal presentations, from delays in scheduling reviews with busy managers, and from excessive meddling in the details of the project by those reviewing the project.

The Critical Chain method uses a novel approach to monitoring the project schedule. By simply monitoring the project buffer and the feeder buffers of the project (described briefly earlier), the project manager can quickly assess the criticality of each path and the estimated project completion time. If tasks consume the project buffer faster than the critical path is being completed, the project runs the risk of slipping the end date. A buffer report therefore provides a concise update on the project status in terms of progress of the critical path and its feeder paths.

Corrective Actions

After discovering an undesirable deviation from the project plan, the team attempts to take corrective action. Problems almost always manifest themselves as potential schedule slippage, and so most of these corrective actions relate to arresting potential delays. Some of the possible actions include:

- *Changing the timing or frequency of meetings:* Sometimes a simple change from weekly to daily meetings increases the "driving frequency" of the information flow

EXHIBIT 19-13
Information systems that facilitate product development decision making, team consensus, and the exchange of information.

Development Activity	Information Systems Used
Product planning	Product segment map Technology roadmap Product-process change matrix Aggregate resource plan Product plan Mission statement
Customer needs identification	Customer needs lists
Concept generation	Function diagrams Concept classification tree Concept combination table Concept descriptions and sketches
Concept selection	Concept screening matrix Concept scoring matrix
Product specifications	Needs-metrics matrix Competitive benchmarking charts Specifications lists
System-level design	Schematic diagram Geometric layout Differentiation plan Commonality plan
Detailed design	Bill of materials Prototyping plan Environmental impact assessment
Industrial design	Aesthetic/ergonomic importance survey
Testing	Performance test reports Durability test reports
Product development economics	NPV analysis spreadsheet
Project management	Contract book Task list Design structure matrix Gantt chart PERT chart Staffing matrix Risk analysis Weekly status memo Buffer report Postmortem project report

among team members and enables more rapid completion of tasks. This is particularly true of teams that are not already colocated (although if the team is highly dispersed geographically, meetings can consume a great deal of travel time). Sometimes simply moving a weekly meeting from a Tuesday morning to a Friday afternoon increases the urgency felt by the team to "get it done this week."

- *Changing the project staff:* The skills, capabilities, and commitment of the members of the project team in large measure determine project performance. When the project team is grossly understaffed, performance can sometimes be increased by adding the necessary staff. When the project team is overstaffed, performance can sometimes be increased by removing staff. Note that adding staff in a panic at the end of a project can lead to delays in project completion because the increased coordination requirements may outweigh the increase in human resources.

- *Locating the team together physically:* If the team is geographically dispersed, one way to increase project performance is to locate the team in the same work space. This action invariably increases communication among the team members. Some benefit of "virtual colocation" is possible with e-mail, video conferencing, and other network-based collaboration tools.

- *Soliciting more time and effort from the team:* If some team members are distributing their efforts among several projects, project performance may be increased by relieving them of other responsibilities. Needless to say, high-performance project teams include team members who regularly deliver more than a 40-hour work week to the project. If a few critical tasks demand extraordinary effort, most committed teams are willing to devote a few weeks of 14-hour days to get the job done; however, 60- or 70-hour weeks cannot reasonably be expected from most team members for more than a few weeks without causing fatigue and burnout.

- *Focusing more effort on the critical tasks:* By definition, only one sequence of tasks forms the critical path. When the path can be usefully attacked by additional people, the team may choose to temporarily drop some or all other noncritical tasks to ensure timely completion of the critical tasks.

- *Engaging outside resources:* The team may be able to retain an outside resource such as a consulting firm or a supplier to perform some of the development tasks. Outside firms are typically fast and relatively economical when a set of tasks can be clearly defined and when coordination requirements are not severe.

- *Changing the project scope or schedule:* If all other efforts fail to correct undesirable deviations from the project plan, then the team must narrow the scope of the project, identify an alternative project goal, or extend (slip) the project schedule. These changes are necessary to maintain a credible and useful project plan.

Postmortem Project Evaluation

An evaluation of the project's performance after it has been completed is useful for both personal and organizational improvement. This review is often called a *postmortem project evaluation* or *postproject review.* The postmortem evaluation is usually an open-ended discussion of the strengths and weaknesses of the project plan, development processes employed, commercial and technical results, and quality of execution. This discussion is sometimes facilitated by an outside consultant or by someone within the company who was not involved in the project. Several questions help to guide the discussion:

- Did the team achieve the mission articulated in the mission statement (including strategic, technical, and financial goals)?
- Which aspects of project performance (development time, development cost, product quality, manufacturing cost, environmental impacts) were most positive?
- Which aspects of project performance were most negative?
- Which tools, methods, and practices contributed to the positive aspects of performance?

- Which tools, methods, and practices detracted from project success?
- What problems did the team encounter?
- What specific actions can the organization take to improve project performance?
- What specific technical lessons were learned? How can they be shared with the rest of the organization?

A postmortem report is then prepared as part of the formal closing of the project. These reports are used in the project planning stage of future projects to help team members know what to expect and to help identify what pitfalls to avoid. The reports are also a valuable source of historical data for studies of the firm's product development practices. Together with the project documentation, and particularly the contract book, they provide "before and after" views of each project.

For the Cheetah project, the postmortem discussion involved six members of the core team and lasted two hours. The discussion was facilitated by a consultant. The project was completed on time, and despite the aggressive schedule, so much of the discussion focused on what the team had done to contribute to project success. The team agreed that the most important contributors to project success were:

- Empowerment of a team leader.
- Effective team problem solving.
- Emphasis on adherence to schedule.
- Effective communication links.
- Full participation from multiple functions.
- Building on prior experience in cartridge development.
- Use of computer-aided design (CAD) tools for communication and analysis.
- Early understanding of manufacturing capabilities.

The Cheetah team also identified a few opportunities for improvement:

- Use of 3D CAD tools and plastic molding analysis tools.
- Earlier participation by the customer in the design decisions.
- Improved integration of tooling design and production system design.

Summary

Successful product development requires effective project management. Some of the key ideas in this chapter are:

- Projects consist of tasks linked to each other by dependencies. Tasks can be sequential, parallel, or coupled.
- The longest chain of dependent tasks defines the critical path, which dictates the minimum possible completion time of the project.
- The design structure matrix (DSM) can be used to represent dependencies. Gantt charts are used to represent the timing of tasks. PERT charts represent both dependencies and timing and are frequently used to compute the critical path.

- Project planning results in a task list, a project schedule, staffing requirements, a project budget, and a risk plan. These items are key elements of the contract book.

- Most opportunities for accelerating projects arise during the project planning phase. There are many ways to complete development projects more quickly.

- Project execution involves coordination, assessment of progress, and taking action to address deviations from the plan.

- Evaluating the performance of a project encourages and facilitates personal and organizational improvement.

References and Bibliography

Many current resources are available on the Internet via
www.ulrich-eppinger.net

There are many basic texts on project management, although most do not focus on product development projects. PERT, critical path, and Gantt techniques are described in most project management books, including Kerzner's classic text. Kerzner also discusses project staffing, planning, budgeting, risk management, and control.

Kerzner, Harold, *Project Management: A Systems Approach to Planning, Scheduling, and Controlling,* eleventh edition, Wiley, New York, 2013.

The product management and the project management professions each have professional organizations that maintain a compendium of the tools and best practices of their profession. Known respectively as the ProdBOK and the PMBOK, these "bodies of knowledge" serve not only as professional handbooks, but also as the basis for training and certification programs.

Product Management Educational Institute, *The Guide to the Product Management and Marketing Body of Knowledge: ProdBOK,* 2013.

Project Management Institute, *A Guide to the Project Management Body of Knowledge: PMBOK Guide,* fifth edition, 2013.

Several authors have written specifically about the management of product development. Wheelwright and Clark discuss team leadership and other project management issues in depth.

Wheelwright, Stephen C., and Kim B. Clark, *Revolutionizing Product Development: Quantum Leaps in Speed, Efficiency, and Quality,* The Free Press, New York, 1992.

The design structure matrix (DSM) was originally developed by Steward in the 1970s. More recently, this method has been applied to industrial project planning and improvement by Eppinger and his research group at MIT.

Eppinger, Steven D., and Tyson R. Browning, *Design Structure Matrix Methods and Applications,* MIT Press, Cambridge, MA, 2012.

Steward, Donald V., *Systems Analysis and Management: Structure, Strategy, and Design,* Petrocelli Books, New York, 1981.

Krishnan provides a framework for overlapping nominally sequential tasks, explaining under what conditions it is better to transfer preliminary information from upstream to downstream and when it may be better to freeze the upstream task early.

Krishnan, Viswanathan, "Managing the Simultaneous Execution of Coupled Phases in Concurrent Product Development," *IEEE Transactions on Engineering Management,* Vol. 43, No. 2, May 1996, pp. 210–217.

Goldratt developed the Critical Chain method of project management. This approach aggregates safety times from each task into project and feeder buffers, allowing the project to be tracked by monitoring these buffers. Critical Chain has been developed into a management technique focusing on prioritization of work and project efficiency by Newbold and Lynch.

Goldratt, Eliyahu M., *Critical Chain,* North River Press, Great Barrington, MA, 1997.

Newbold, Rob, and Bill Lynch, *The Project Manifesto: Transforming Your Life and Work with Critical Chain Values,* ProChain Press, Lake Ridge, VA, 2014.

Smith and Reinertsen provide many ideas for accelerating product development projects, along with interesting insights on team staffing and organization.

Smith, Preston G., and Donald G. Reinertsen, *Developing Products in Half the Time: New Rules, New Tools,* second edition, Wiley, New York, 1997.

Sobek, Ward, and Liker present the principles of set-based concurrent engineering, in which product development teams reason about sets of possible design solutions rather than using only point-based values to describe the evolving design.

Sobek II, Durward K., Allen C. Ward, and Jeffrey K. Liker, "Toyota's Principles of Set-Based Concurrent Engineering," *Sloan Management Review,* Vol. 40, No. 2, Winter 1999, pp. 67–83.

Allen has extensively studied communication in R&D organizations. With Henn, he discusses the results of his seminal empirical studies of the influence of architecture and workspace design on communication and organizational effectiveness.

Allen, Thomas J., and Gunter W. Henn, *The Organization and Architecture of Innovation: Managing the Flow of Technology,* Elsevier, Burlington, MA, 2007.

Kostner offers guidance for leaders of geographically dispersed teams.

Kostner, Jaclyn, *Virtual Leadership: Secrets from the Round Table for the Multi-Site Manager,* Warner Books, New York, 1994.

Markus explains that electronic mail can facilitate rich interactions between project team members, in addition to traditional rich media such as face-to-face meetings.

Markus, M. Lynne, "Electronic Mail as the Medium of Managerial Choice," *Organization Science,* Vol. 5, No. 4, November 1994, pp. 502–527.

Hall presents a structured process for risk identification, analysis, and management, with application examples in software and systems engineering. (See also Kerzner, 2013.)

Hall, Elaine M., *Methods for Software Systems Development,* Addison-Wesley, Reading, MA, 1998.

Smith presents a 12-step process for project review and evaluation, leading to ongoing improvement of the product development process.

Smith, Preston G., "Your Product Development Process Demands Ongoing Improvement," *Research-Technology Management,* Vol. 39, No. 2, March–April 1996, pp. 37–44.

Exercises

1. The tasks for preparing a dinner (along with the normal completion times) might include:

    a. Wash and cut vegetables for the salad (15 minutes).
    b. Toss the salad (2 minutes).
    c. Set the table (8 minutes).
    d. Start the rice cooking (2 minutes).
    e. Cook rice (25 minutes).
    f. Place the rice in a serving dish (1 minute).
    g. Mix casserole ingredients (10 minutes).
    h. Bake the casserole (25 minutes).

    Prepare a DSM for these tasks.

2. Prepare a PERT chart for the tasks in Exercise 1. How fast can one person prepare this dinner? What if there were two people?

3. What strategies could you employ to prepare dinner more quickly? If you thought about dinner 24 hours in advance, are there any steps you could take to reduce the time between arriving home the next day and serving dinner?

4. Interview a project manager (not necessarily from product development). Ask him or her to describe the major obstacles to project success.

Thought Questions

1. When a task on the critical path (e.g., the fabrication of a mold) is delayed, the completion of the entire project is delayed, even though the total amount of work required to complete the project may remain the same. How would you expect such a delay to impact the total cost of the project?

2. This chapter has focused on the "hard" issues in project management related to tasks, dependencies, and schedules. What are some of the "soft," or behavioral, issues related to project management?

3. What would you expect to be some of the characteristics of individuals who successfully lead project teams?

4. Under what conditions might efforts to accelerate a product development project also lead to increased product quality and/or decreased product manufacturing costs? Under what conditions might these attributes of the product deteriorate when the project is accelerated?

Appendix

Design Structure Matrix Example

One of the most useful applications of the design structure matrix (DSM) method is to represent well-established, but complex, engineering design processes. This rich process modeling approach facilitates:

- Understanding of the existing development process.
- Communication of the process to the people involved.
- Process improvement.
- Visualization of progress during the project.

Exhibit 19-14 shows a DSM model of a critical portion of the development process at a major automobile manufacturer. The model includes 50 tasks involved in the digital mock-up (DMU) process for the layout of all of the many components in the engine compartment of the vehicle. The process takes place in six phases, depicted by the blocks of activities along the diagonal. The first two of these phases (project planning and CAD data collection) occur in parallel, followed by the development of the digital assembly model (DMU preparation). Each of the last three phases involves successively more accurate analytical verification that components represented by the digital assembly model actually fit properly within the engine compartment area of the vehicle.

In contrast to the simpler DSM model shown in Exhibit 19-3, where the squares on the diagonal identify sets of coupled activities, the DSM in Exhibit 19-14 uses such blocks to show which activities are executed together (in parallel, sequentially, and/or iteratively) within each phase. Arrows and dashed lines represent the major iterations between sets of activities within each phase.

Activity

Approve product architecture/configuration
Define extended layout team
Determine project quality objectives
Establish the need for prototypes
Establish prototype specifications
Establish DMU, PMU, and prototypes to be developed
Prepare activity/resource plan
Approve layout team leader's activity/resource plan
Verify the feasibility of the LO team's plan
Approve no. of DMU, PMU, and prototypes
Verify that planning phase is complete
Authorize go ahead to next phase
Provide CAD models in PDM
Provide style models
Extract CAD models from PDM
Convert nonstandard CAD models
Construct DMUs from CAD models
Verify DMU completeness
Review issues document from past project
Define volumes for new components
Construct DMU for the verification process
Request missing CAD models
Provide missing CAD models in PDM
Verify DMU using checklist #80195
Verify style compatibility
Prepare alternate solutions
Analyze issues with the layout team
Verify overall DMU with all stakeholders
Update issues document
Modify CAD models
Modify styling
Modify component positioning in DMU
Select two models of style
Freeze DMU (step 1)
Define information required for assembly process
Specify component connectivity constraints
Perform detail design for component connectivity
Verify assembly feasibility
Verify safety objectives
Verify vehicle maintenance feasibility
Establish/communicate modifications to be done
Select one model of style
Freeze DMU (step 2)
Verify that all critical CAD models are present
Prepare reference list of drawings for prototyping
Build prototypes for design validation (DV1)
Run experiments on prototypes
Verify project quality objectives
Authorize go ahead to next phase
Freeze DMU (step 3)

EXHIBIT 19-14 Design structure matrix model of the digital mock-up (DMU) process used to validate layout of the automobile's engine compartment.

Courtesy of FIAT Auto